CENSORS AT WORK

ALSO BY ROBERT DARNTON

Poetry and the Police: Communication Networks in Eighteenth-Century Paris

The Devil in the Holy Water, or the Art of Slander from Louis XIV to Napoleon

The Case for Books: Past, Present, and Future

George Washington's False Teeth: An Unconventional Guide to the Eighteenth Century

The Corpus of Clandestine Literature in France, 1769–1789

The Forbidden Best-Sellers of Prerevolutionary France

Berlin Journal, 1989–1990

The Kiss of Lamourette: Reflections in Cultural History

Revolution in Print: The Press in France, 1775–1800

The Great Cat Massacre and Other Episodes in French Cultural History

The Literary Underground of the Old Regime

The Business of Enlightenment: A Publishing History of the Encyclopédie, 1775–1800

Mesmerism and the End of the Enlightenment in France

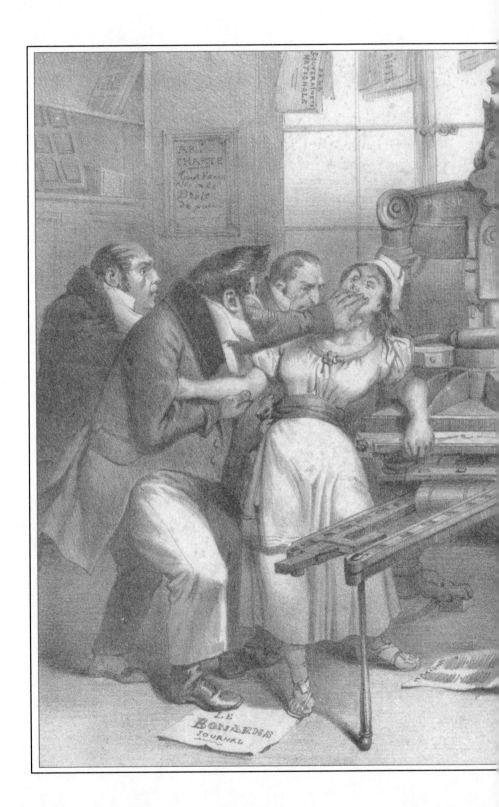

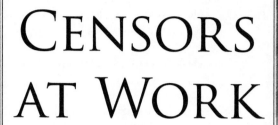

CENSORS
AT WORK

*How States
Shaped Literature*

ROBERT DARNTON

W. W. NORTON & COMPANY
New York   London

Frontispiece by J. J. Grandville and Auguste Desperret, *Descente dans les ateliers de la liberté de la presse*. Paris, 1833. Lithograph. Prints & Photographs Division, Library of Congress, LC-DIG-ppmsca-13649.

For information about permission to reproduce selections from this book, write to Permissions, W. W. Norton & Company, Inc., 500 Fifth Avenue, New York, NY 10110

For information about special discounts for bulk purchases, please contact W. W. Norton Special Sales at specialsales@wwnorton.com or 800-233-4830

Manufacturing by Courier Westford
Book design by Helene Berinsky
Production manager: Louise Parasmo

Library of Congress Cataloging-in-Publication Data

Darnton, Robert.
Censors at work : how states shaped literature / Robert Darnton. — First edition.
pages cm
Includes bibliographical references and index.
ISBN 978-0-393-24229-4
1. Censorship—France—History—18th century. 2. Censorship—India—History—19th century. 3. Censorship—Germany (East)—History—20th century. 4. Literature and state. I. Title.
Z657.D26 2014
363'.31—dc23

2014010997

W. W. Norton & Company, Inc., 500 Fifth Avenue, New York, N.Y. 10110
www.wwnorton.com
W. W. Norton & Company Ltd., Castle House, 75/76 Wells Street,
London W1T 3QT

1 2 3 4 5 6 7 8 9 0

CONTENTS

8 CONTENTS

LIST OF ILLUSTRATIONS

CENSORS AT WORK

INTRODUCTION

———•◦•———

W here is north in cyberspace? We have no compass to get our bearings in the uncharted ether beyond the Gutenberg galaxy, and the difficulty is not simply cartographical and technological. It is moral and political. In the early days of the Internet, cyberspace seemed to be free and open. Now it is being fought over, divided up, and closed off behind protective barriers.[1] Free spirits might imagine that electronic communication could take place without running into obstacles, but that would be naïve. Who would want to give up password protection for their email or to refuse filtering that protects children from pornography or to leave their country defenseless in the face of cyberattacks? But the Great Firewall of China and the unrestricted surveillance by the National Security Agency illustrate a tendency for the state to assert its interests at the expense of ordinary individuals. Has modern technology produced a new kind of power, which has led to an imbalance between the role of the state and the rights of its citizens? Perhaps, but we should be wary about assuming that the balance of power in the present has no precedent in the past. In order to gain some perspective on the current situation, we can study the history of attempts by the state to control communication. This book is intended to show how those attempts took place, not always and everywhere but in specific times and places, where they can be investigated in detail. It is an inside history,

13

because it pursues the investigation into back rooms and secret missions, where agents of the state kept watch over words, permitting or forbidding them to appear in print and suppressing them according to reasons of state when they began to circulate as books.

The history of books and of the attempts to keep them under control will not yield conclusions that can be directly applied to policies governing digital communication. It is important for other reasons. By taking us inside the operations of censors, it shows how policy-makers thought, how the state took the measure of threats to its monopoly of power, and how it tried to cope with those threats. The power of print could be as threatening as cyberwarfare. How did agents of the state understand it, and how did their thoughts determine actions? No historian can get inside the heads of the dead—or, for that matter, the living, even if they can be interviewed for studies of contemporary history. But with sufficient documentation, we can detect patterns of thought and action. Only rarely are the archives adequate, because censoring took place in secret, and the secrets usually remained hidden or were destroyed. Given a rich enough run of evidence, however, one can tease out the underlying assumptions and the undercover activities of the officials charged with the policing of print. Then the archives open up leads. One can follow censors as they vetted texts, often line by line, and one can trail the police as they tracked down forbidden books, enforcing boundaries between the legal and the illegal. The boundaries themselves need to be mapped, because they were frequently uncertain and always changing. Where can one draw the line between an account of Krishna's dallying with the milkmaids and unacceptable eroticism in Bengali literature, or between socialist realism and "late-bourgeois" narration in the literature of Communist East Germany? The conceptual maps are interesting in themselves and important because they shaped actual behavior. The repression of books—sanctions of all kinds that fall under the rubric of "post-publication censorship"—shows how the state confronted literature at street level, in incidents that carry the story into the lives of the daring or disreputable characters who operated beyond the fringe of the law.

At this point, the research gives way to the sheer joy of the chase, because the police—or their equivalent, depending on the nature of the government—kept running into strains of humanity that rarely make it into history books. Wandering minstrels, devious peddlers, seditious missionaries, merchant adventurers, authors of every stripe—both the famous and the unknown, including a fake swami and a scandal-mongering chambermaid—and even the police themselves, who sometimes joined ranks with their victims—these are the people who populate the following pages, along with censors of every shape and size. This aspect of the human comedy deserves to be recounted in its own right, I believe, but in telling the stories, as accurately as I can, without exaggeration or deviation from the evidence, I hope to accomplish something more: a history of censorship in a new key, one that is both comparative and ethnographic.

With the exception of masters like Marc Bloch, historians preach in favor of comparative history more often than they practice it.[2] It is a demanding genre, not merely because of the need to command different fields of study in different languages but also owing to the problems inherent in making comparisons. It may be easy to avoid confusing apples with oranges, but how can one study institutions that look similar or have the same names yet function differently? A person called a censor may behave according to the rules of a game that are incompatible with those followed by someone considered to be a censor in another system. The games themselves are different. The very notion of literature carries weight in some societies that can hardly be imagined in others. In Soviet Russia, according to Aleksandr Solzhenitsyn, literature was so powerful that it "accelerated history."[3] To most Americans, it matters less than professional sports. Yet Americans' attitudes have varied greatly over time. Literature weighed heavily on them three hundred years ago, when the Bible (especially the Genevan editions derived in large part from the vigorous translations of William Tyndale) contributed mightily to a way of life. In fact, it may be anachronistic to speak of "literature" among the Puritans, since the term did not come into common use until the eighteenth century. "Religion" or "divinity" might be more suitable, and the same is true of many ancient cultures such as that of India, where literary history cannot be distinguished clearly from religious mythology. Rather than concentrating on terminology, I hope to capture idiom—that is, to understand the underlying tone of a cultural system, its unspoken attitudes and implicit values as they inflected action. Comparisons work best, I believe, at the systemic level. Therefore, I have tried to reconstruct censorship as it operated throughout three authoritarian systems: the Bourbon monarchy in eighteenth-century France, the British Raj in nineteenth-century India, and the Communist dictatorship in twentieth-century East Germany. Each is worthy of study in itself. When taken together and compared, they make it possible to rethink the history of censorship in general.

It might seem best to begin with a question: What is censorship? When I ask my students to give examples, the responses have included the following (aside from obvious cases of oppression under Hitler and Stalin):

Giving grades
Calling a professor "Professor"
Political correctness
Peer review
Reviews of any kind
Editing and publishing
Outlawing assault weapons
Pledging or refusing to pledge allegiance to the flag
Applying for or issuing a driver's license
Surveillance by the National Security Agency
The Motion Picture Association of America's film-rating system
The Children's Internet Protection Act
Speed monitoring by cameras
Obeying the speed limit
Classifying documents to protect national security
Classifying anything
Algorithmic relevance ranking
The use of "she" instead of "he" as a standard pronoun
Wearing or not wearing a necktie
Politeness
Silence

The list could be extended indefinitely, covering legal and nonlegal sanctions, psychological and technological filtering, and all sorts of behavior, whether by state authorities, private institutions, peer groups, or individuals sorting through the inner secrets of the soul. Whatever the validity of the examples, they suggest that a broad definition of censorship could cover almost anything. Censorship may be deemed to exist everywhere—but if everywhere, nowhere; for an all-extensive definition would erase all distinctions and therefore would be meaningless. To identify censorship with constraints of all kinds is to trivialize it.

Rather than starting with a definition and then looking for examples that conform to it, I have proceeded by interrogating censors themselves. They cannot be interviewed (the East German censors discussed in part 3 are a rare exception), but one can recover their voices from the archives and question them by testing and reformulating interpretations while working from one document to another. A few, isolated manuscripts won't suffice. Hundreds are needed, and the run must be rich enough to show how censors handled their ordinary, everyday tasks. The pertinent questions then become: how did they work, and how did they understand their work? If the evidence is adequate, it should be possible to piece together patterns of behavior among the censors and in their surrounding environment—from the sifting of manuscripts by editors to the confiscation of books by the police. The parts played will vary according to the institutions involved, and the institutional configuration will depend on the nature of the sociopolitical order. It would be wrong, therefore, to expect all publications to follow the same path and, when they offended the authorities, to be repressed in the same manner. There is no general model.

But there are general tendencies in the way censorship has been studied over the last hundred years.[4] At the risk of oversimplification, I would cite two: on the one hand, a story of the struggle between freedom of expression and the attempts to repress it by political and religious authorities; on the other, an account of constraints of every kind that inhibit communication. Opposed as they are, I think there is a great deal to be said for each view.

The first has a Manichaean quality. It pits the children of light against the children of darkness, and it speaks to all defenders of democracy who take certain truths to be self-evident.[5] Whatever their logical or epistemological value, those truths function as first principles, not merely in the abstract but in political practice. The First Amendment to the U.S. Constitution provides a starting point for laws and court decisions that have determined the meaning and set the limits of "freedom of speech, or of the press," as the amendment puts it in one, breathtaking sentence.[6] Sophisticates may deride "First Amendment absolutism,"[7] but the freedom invoked in the Bill of Rights belongs to a political culture, one that can even be considered a civil religion,[8] which has evolved over more than two centuries and commands the loyalty of millions of citizens. By adhering to the First Amendment, U.S. citizens keep a grip on a certain kind of reality. They trim their behavior to the rule of law, and when they come into conflict, they take their cases to the courts, which decide what the law is in actual practice.

In arguing for fundamental rights, philosophers use abstractions, but they generally understand that ideas take root in systems of power and communication. John Locke, the philosopher most identified with theories of natural rights, did not invoke freedom of speech when pre-publication censorship ceased to be a rule of law in England. Instead, he welcomed Parliament's refusal to renew the Licensing Act, which provided for censorship, as a victory over the booksellers in the Stationers' Company, whom he despised for their monopolistic practices and shoddy products.[9] Milton also railed against the Stationers' Company in *Areopagitica*, the greatest manifesto in English for freedom of the press—great, but limited (no "popery" or "open superstition" to be permitted).[10] These examples, and others one could cite (Diderot, for instance)[11] do not prove that philosophers failed to advocate the freedom of the press as a matter of principle but rather that they understood it as an ideal to be defended in a real world of economic interests and political lobbies. For them, liberty was not an unworldly norm but a vital principle of political discourse, which they worked into the social reconstruction of reality that took place in seventeenth-century and eighteenth-century Europe. Many of us live in the world that they created, a world of civil rights and shared values. The Internet did not condemn that moral order to obsolescence. Nothing would be more self-defeating than to argue against censorship while dismissing the tradition that leads from the ancients through Milton and Locke to the First Amendment and the Universal Declaration of Human Rights.

This argument may sound suspiciously high-minded. It has more than a whiff of Whiggishness, and it may smell like rank liberalism.[12] I must confess to liberal sympathies myself and to finding *Areopagitica* one of the most moving polemical works that I have ever read. But I also should admit that I sympathize with a second approach to the subject, which undercuts the first. Whether spoken or written, words exert power. In fact, the power of speech operates in ways that are not fundamentally different from ordinary actions in the everyday world. Speech acts, as understood by linguistic philosophers, are intended to produce effects in the surrounding environment; and when they take written form, there is no reason to associate them exclusively with literature. Some literary theorists go so far as to argue that it is meaningless to separate out a category, hallowed and hedged by constitutional restrictions, called freedom of speech. As Stanley Fish proclaimed in a provocative essay, "There is no such thing as freedom of speech—and it's a good thing, too."[13]

It would be possible to cite other tendencies in what is sometimes known as postmodernism[14] to support the same point: in contrast to those who see censorship as a violation of a right, many theorists construe it as an all-pervasive ingredient of social reality. In their view, it operates in individual psyches and collective mentalities, everywhere and at all times. It is so omnipresent that, as in the examples given by my students, it can hardly be distinguished from constraints of any kind. A history of censorship must therefore confront a problem. It may be valid to resist limiting the subject by a restrictive definition, but it could be possible to extend it beyond all limits. We face two conflicting views, one normative, one relative. For my part, I believe they can be reconciled by embracing both and elevating them to another level of analysis, one that I would call anthropological. To make that argument, I will present a "thick description" of how censorship actually operated in three very different political systems.[15]

This kind of history requires immersion in the archives—the historian's equivalent of fieldwork by the anthropologist. My own experience began, many decades ago, in the papers of the Bastille and the great Anisson-Duperron and Chambre syndicale collections of the Bibliothèque nationale de France. By a series of fortunate circumstances, I spent the year 1989–1990 at the Wissenschaftskolleg zu Berlin; and soon after the fall of the Berlin Wall, I got to know some East German censors. In 1993–94, I was able to follow up the information they had provided during another year as a fellow in the Wissenschaftskolleg, and I continued to pursue the subject in several subsequent stints of research in the papers of the East German Communist (SED) Party. Having studied censors at work under two very different systems in the eighteenth and the twentieth centuries, I decided to look for nineteenth-century material from a non-Western part of the world. Thanks to help from Graham Shaw, then in charge of the India Office Library and Records at the British Library, I was able to spend two summers studying the extraordinarily rich archives of the Indian Civil Service.

Finally, after so many expeditions into such fertile sources, I faced the problem of how to work this diverse material into a book. Perhaps in order to communicate the information in all of its richness, I should have written three books. But I wanted to condense the results of the research into a single volume so that readers could make comparisons and study general questions in different contexts. To sort out conceptual and contextual issues as they appear in three countries across three centuries may seem daunting, yet I hope that this book, condensed as it is, will appeal to general readers and will provoke reflection on the problem posed by the convergence of two kinds of power—that of the state, ever-expanding in scope, and that of communication, constantly increasing with changes in technology. The systems of censorship studied in this book show that state intervention in the literary realm went far beyond the blue-penciling of texts. It extended to the shaping of literature itself as a force at work throughout the social order. If states wielded such power in the age of print, what will restrain them from abusing it in the age of the Internet?

PART ONE

Bourbon France:
Privilege and
Repression

The Manichaean view of censorship has special appeal when applied to the age of Enlightenment, for the Enlightenment is easily seen as a battle of light against darkness. It presented itself in that manner, and its champions derived other dichotomies from that basic contrast: reason against obscurantism, liberty against oppression, tolerance against bigotry. They saw parallel forces at work in the social and political realm: on one side, public opinion mobilized by the *philosophes*; on the other, the power of church and state. Of course, histories of the Enlightenment avoid such simplification. They expose contradictions and ambiguities, especially when they relate abstract ideas to institutions and events. But when they come to the subject of censorship, historical interpretations generally oppose the repressive activity of administrative officials to the attempts by writers to promote freedom of expression. France offers the most dramatic examples: the burning of books, the imprisonment of authors, and the outlawing of the most important works of literature—particularly those of Voltaire and Rousseau and the *Encyclopédie*, whose publishing history epitomizes the struggle of knowledge to free itself from the fetters imposed by the state and the church.[1]

There is much to be said for this line of interpretation, especially if it is seen from the perspective of classical liberalism or commitment to the defense of human rights—that is, from a modern viewpoint that itself is derived from the Enlightenment. But whatever its validity as a way of accommodating value judgments to historical objectivity, it lacks grounding in research about how censorship actually operated. What did censors do, how did they understand their tasks, and how did their activities fit into the surrounding social and political order?[2]

TYPOGRAPHY AND LEGALITY

Consider, for example, the title page of an ordinary eighteenth-century book, *Nouveau voyage aux isles de l'Amérique* (Paris, 1722). It goes on and on, more like a dust jacket than a title page of a modern book. In fact, its function was similar to that of dust-jacket copy: it summarized and advertised the contents of the book for anyone who might be interested in reading it. The missing element, at least for the modern reader, is equally striking: the name of the author. It simply does not appear. Not that the author tried to hide his identity: his name shows up in the front matter. But the person who really had to answer for the book, the man who carried the legal and financial responsibility for it, stands out prominently at the bottom of the page, along with his address: "in Paris, the rue Saint Jacques, the shop of Pierre-François Giffart, near the rue des Mathurins, at the image of Saint Theresa." Giffart was a bookseller (*libraire*), and like many booksellers he functioned as a publisher (the modern term for publisher, *éditeur*, had not yet come into common usage), buying manuscripts from authors, arranging for their printing, and selling the finished products from his shop. Since 1275, booksellers had been subjected to the authority of the university and therefore had to keep shop in the Latin Quarter. They especially congregated in the rue Saint Jacques, where their wrought-iron signs (hence "at the image of Saint Theresa") swung through the air on hinges like the branches of a forest. The brotherhood of printers and booksellers, dedicated to Saint John the Evangelist, met in the church of the Mathurin Fathers in the rue des Mathurins near the Sorbonne, whose faculty of theology often pronounced on the orthodoxy of published texts. So this book's address

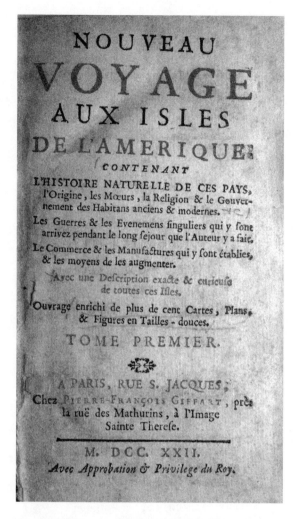

A typical title page of a censored book, Nouveau voyage aux isles de l'Amérique, *1722.*

placed it at the heart of the official trade, and its super-legal status was clear in any case from the formula printed at the bottom: "with approbation and privilege of the king."

Here we encounter the phenomenon of censorship, because approbations were formal sanctions delivered by royal censors. In this case, there are four approbations, all printed at the beginning of the book and written by the censors who had approved the manuscript. One censor, a professor

!-

vû moi-même durant presque huit années la plûpart des choses dont il y est parlé, je les ai trouvé décrites avec une exactitude & avec une netteté qui ne laisse rien à souhaiter. L'Auteur entre dans des détails qui instruiront même ceux du Païs, & par son seul Livre on peut apprendre en Europe ce qu'il y a de plus interessant pour nous à l'Amerique. Il sera difficile d'en commencer la lecture sans éprouver cette douce, quoiqu'avide, curiosité qui nous porte à poursuivre. On n'y trouvera rien qui soit contraire à la Foi & aux bonnes mœurs. Donné à Paris dans nôtre Maison de Saint Honoré ce 17. Aoust 1719.

F. NICOLAS JOUIN, Professeur en Theologie, de l'Ordre des EE. Prêcheurs, & Regent.

APPROBATION DE M. HENRY BESNIER, Docteur Regent en Medecine en l'Université de Paris, & ancien Professeur de Botanique aux Ecoles de la Faculté.

J'AY lû avec une attention singuliere, les Memoires du R P Labat Missionnaire de l'Ordre des EE. Prêcheurs aux Isles Françoises de l'Amerique Rien n'a monavis n'est si utile aux voiageurs, aux Habitans de ce Païs, aux Commerçans, & à ceux qui s'appliquent à l'étude de l'Histoire naturelle. Les remarques judicieuses de l'Auteur sur ce qui concerne cette Partie du Monde, le style simple &

The approbations and privilege printed after the preface to Nouveau voyage aux isles de l'Amérique. Following the text of the privilege (only the first part of it appears here) several notes indicate the legal steps taken for its commercial implementation: 1. It was entered in the official register kept by the Parisian guild of booksellers and printers. 2. The author, F. J.-B. Labat, formally ceded the privilege,

concis de ces Memoires attireront sans dou-
te l'approbation de ceux qui ont connoissan-
ce du Païs , & donneront à d'autres l'envie
d'en connoître la verité en faisant le même
voyage. Rien n'est donc si necessaire au
Public que l'Impression de cet Ouvrage. A
Paris ce 4 Octobre 1719.

BESNIER.

APPROBATION DE M.
l'Abbé RAGUET.

J'AY lû par l'ordre de Monseigneur le
Chancelier *less Memoires des nouveaux
Voyages aux Isles de l'Amerique , par le P. Labat,
de l'Ordre de S Dominique* : & ils m'ont pa-
ru dignes de la curiosité du Public. Fait à
Paris le premier Septembre 1721.

RAGUET.

PRIVILEGE DU ROY.

LOUIS par la grace de Dieu Roi de
France & de Navarre : A nos amez &
feaux Conseillers les Gens tenans nos Cours
de Parlemens , Maitres des Requestes or-
dinaires de nostre Hôtel, Grand Conseil ,
Prevost de Paris , Baillifs , Sénéchaux ,
leurs Lieutenans Civils , & autres nos Ju-
sticiers qu'il appartiendra, SALUT. Nostre
bien amé le P. Jean - Baptiste Labat , Missionnaire de l'Ordre des FF. Prêcheurs ,
Nous ayant fait remontrer qu'il souhaite-

which had been granted to him, to two booksellers, Giffart and Cavelier fils. (As a preceding note indicated, only booksellers or printers were permitted to sell books.) 3. Giffart and Cavelier fils certified that they had divided the privilege into four parts; each kept one part, and together they ceded one part to Cavelier's father and one to Theodore le Gras, who also were booksellers.

at the Sorbonne, remarked in his approbation, "I had pleasure in reading it; it is full of fascinating things." Another, who was a professor of botany and medicine, stressed the book's usefulness for travelers, merchants, and students of natural history; and he especially praised its style. A third censor, a theologian, simply attested that the book was a good read. He could not put it down, he said, because it inspired in the reader "that sweet but avid curiosity that makes us want to continue further." Is this the language you would expect from a censor? To rephrase the question as the query that Erving Goffman reportedly set as the starting point for all sociological investigation: What is going on here?

The beginning of an answer can be found in the privilege itself, which is printed after the approbations. It takes the form of a letter from the king to the officials of his courts, notifying them that the king has granted the author of the book, whose name now appears for the first time, the exclusive right to reproduce it and to have it sold through intermediaries in the booksellers' guild. The privilege is a long and complex text, full of stipulations about the physical qualities of the book. It was to be printed on "good paper and in beautiful type, in conformity with the regulations on the book trade." Those regulations set detailed standards of quality control: the paper was to be made from a certain grade of rags; the type was to be calibrated so that one *m* would be precisely as wide as three *l*'s. It was pure Colbertism—that is, state interference to promote trade by setting standards of quality and reinforcing guilds behind a protective wall of tariffs—originally devised under the direction of Jean-Baptiste Colbert himself. And the privilege concluded as all royal edicts did: "For such is our pleasure." Legally, the book existed by virtue of the king's pleasure; it was a product of the royal "grace." The word *grâce* recurs in all the key edicts on the book trade; and in fact the Direction de la librairie, or royal administration in charge of the book trade, was divided into two parts: the "Librairie contentieuse" for regulating conflicts and the "Librairie gracieuse" for the dispensation of privileges. Finally, after the text of the privilege came a series of paragraphs stating that the privilege had been entered in the register of the booksellers' guild and that it had been divided into portions, which had been sold to four different booksellers.

Now, to the modern eye, all this looks rather strange: we have censors praising the style and readability of the book instead of cutting out its heresies; we have the king conferring his grace upon it; and we have the members of the booksellers' guild dividing up that grace and selling it as if it were a form of property. What indeed was going on?

One way to make sense of this puzzle is to think of the eighteenth-century book as something comparable to certain jars of jam and boxes of biscuits in England that seem so curious to foreigners because they exist "by special appointment to Her Majesty the Queen." The book was a quality product; it had a royal sanction; and in dispensing that sanction, the censors vouched for its general excellence. Censorship was not simply a matter of purging heresies. It was *positive*—a royal endorsement of the book and an official invitation to read it.

The governing term in this system was "privilege" (etymologically, "private law"). Privilege was the organizing principle of the Ancien Régime in general, not only in France but throughout most of Europe. Law did not fall equally on everyone, for everyone assumed that all men (and, even more, all women) were born unequal—and rightly so: hierarchies were ordained by God and built into nature. The idea of equality before the law was unthinkable for most Europeans, with the exception of a few philosophers. Law was a special dispensation accorded to particular individuals or groups by tradition and the grace of the king. Just as wellborn "men of quality" enjoyed special privileges, so did high-quality books. In fact, privilege operated at three levels in the publishing industry: the book itself was privileged (the modern idea of copyright did not yet exist, except in England); the bookseller was privileged (as a member of a guild, he enjoyed the exclusive right to engage in the book trade); and the guild was privileged (as an exclusive corporation it benefited from certain rights, notably exemption from most taxation). In short, the Bourbon monarchy developed an elaborate system for channeling the power of the printed word; and as a product of that system, the book epitomized the entire regime.

THE CENSOR'S POINT OF VIEW

Such were the formal characteristics of the typographical Old Regime. How does the system look if one studies its operation behind the façades of title pages and privileges—that is, from the viewpoint of the censors themselves? Fortunately, a series of manuscripts in the Bibliothèque nationale de France contains a rich vein of information about how censors performed their tasks in the 1750s and 1760s. Hundreds of their letters and reports to the director of the book trade administration (Direction de la librairie), C. G. de Lamoignon de Malesherbes, reveal their ways of working and especially their reasons for accepting or rejecting a request for a privilege.[3]

Because they were confidential communications to Malesherbes, the reports assessed books with a frankness that could not appear in formal approbations. Sometimes, to be sure, they merely provided assurance that a manuscript contained nothing offensive to religion, morality, or the state— the conventional categories that commanded a censor's attention. But many conveyed positive endorsements about style and substance, even when they consisted of only a sentence or two. Thus a typical recommendation for a privilege: "I have read, by order of Monseigneur the Chancellor, the *Lettres de M. de la Rivière*. They seem to me well written and full of reasonable and edifying reflections."[4] When censors felt enthusiastic about a text, they piled on the praise. One of them gave an elaborate account of all the qualities that justified awarding a privilege to a book about the British Isles: impeccable ordering of the subject matter, superb history, precise geography; it was just the thing to satisfy a reader's curiosity.[5] Another censor endorsed a book about ethics primarily for its aesthetic qualities. Although it lacked a certain grandeur of tone, it was simple and solid, enriched by amusing anecdotes, and recounted in a way that would hold the readers' interest while convincing them of the advantages of virtue.[6] A few positive reports go on at such length that they read like book reviews.[7] One censor got carried away with praise for a travel book, then stopped himself and decided to submit a concise recommendation "to avoid infringing on the territory of the journalists."[8] Far from sounding like ideological sentinels, the censors wrote as men of letters, and their reports could be considered as a form of literature.

Their literary concerns stand out especially in the negative reports, where one might expect the heaviest concentration on the vetting of heresies. One censor condemned the "light and bantering tone" of a treatise on cosmology.[9] Another had no theological objections to a biography of the prophet Mohammed but found it superficial and inadequately researched.[10] A third refused to recommend a mathematical textbook, because it did not work through problems in sufficient detail and failed to give the cubes as well as the squares of certain sums.[11] A fourth rejected a legal treatise on the grounds that it used inaccurate terminology, misdated documents, misconstrued basic principles and was full of misspellings.[12] An account of the campaigns of Frederick II offended a fifth censor, not because of any disrespectful discussion of French foreign policy but rather because "it is a compilation without taste and without discernment."[13] And a sixth rejected a defense of religious orthodoxy against the attacks of freethinkers primarily for its sloppiness:

> It is not a book at all. You cannot tell what the author's purpose is until you have finished it. He advances in one direction, then doubles back; his arguments are often weak and superficial; his style, in an attempt to be lively, merely becomes petulant. . . . In the effort to turn a pretty phrase, he frequently looks silly and ridiculous.[14]

Of course, the reports also contain plenty of comments condemning unorthodox ideas. The censors certainly defended church and king. But they worked from the assumption that an approbation was a positive endorsement of a book and that a privilege conveyed the sanction of the crown. They wrote as men of letters themselves, determined to defend "the honor of French literature," as one of them put it.[15] They often adopted a superior tone, pouring scorn on works that failed to measure up to standards that could have been set in the Grand Siècle. One censor sounded as cutting as Nicolas Boileau, the sharpest critic of the seventeenth century, in rejecting an almanac that contained nothing offensive, except its prose: "Its style is miserable."[16] Another turned down a sentimental romance simply because it was "badly written."[17] A third condemned a translation of an English novel for sheer insipidness: "I find only insipid moralizing interspersed with ordinary adventures, vapid bantering, colorless descriptions, and trivial reflections. . . . Such a work is not worthy of appearing with a public mark of approbation."[18]

This style of censorship created a problem: if manuscripts had to be not merely inoffensive but also worthy of a Louisquatorzean stamp of approval, would not most literature fail to qualify? The censor of the above-mentioned novel chose a conventional way around this difficulty:

> Because [this work], despite its faults and mediocrity, contains nothing dangerous or reprehensible and does not, after all, attack religion, morality or the state, I think that there is no risk in tolerating its printing and that it can be published with a tacit permission, although the public will hardly be flattered by a present of this sort.[19]

In other words, the regime created loopholes in the legal system. "Tacit permissions," "tolerances," "simple permissions," "permissions of the police"—the officials in charge of the book trade devised a whole series of categories that could be used to permit books to appear without receiving an official endorsement. Given the nature of the privilege system, they could hardly do otherwise, unless they wanted to declare war on most of contemporary literature. As Malesherbes put it in reflecting on his years as director of the book trade, "A man who reads only books that originally appeared with the explicit sanction of the government, as the law prescribes, would be behind his contemporaries by nearly a century."[20] More than any previous director of the book trade, Malesherbes extended the use of tacit permissions, an agreement to allow discreet sales of a book provided it did not provoke so much scandal that it would have to be withdrawn from the market—usually with the connivance of the police. Unlike privileges, tacit permissions did not convey an exclusive right to publish a work, but they required approval by a censor and entry in a register. No trace of the approval, including the name of the censor, appeared in the book itself, which often had a false address on its title page to suggest that it had been published outside France. In especially problematic cases, censors could recommend "simples tolérances," an informal agreement by the director of the book trade to look the other way when a book was sold under the counter or "under the cloak." "Permissions de police" were dispensed by the lieutenant general of police for short, ephemeral works, and they, too, could be revoked if they caused offense.

For the censor faced with a new manuscript, this graduated spectrum of legality normally meant choosing among three possibilities: he could recommend through the director of the book trade that the chancellor grant a privilege, and the work would appear with an approbation and the censor's name attached to it; he could recommend a tacit permission, and the work would appear without any official endorsement as if it had been imported from abroad; or he could refuse to sanction it, and it would be published illegally or not at all.[21] To make that choice, the censor had to weigh complex and sometimes contradictory factors: the text's orthodoxy relative to conventional standards of religion, politics, and morality; its substance as a contribution to literature or a field of knowledge; its aesthetic and sometimes its commercial value; its potential influence on current affairs; and its effect on the networks of alliances and enmities embedded in *le monde*—that is, the elite of birth, wealth, and talent who dominated public life in France. Consider two examples.

First, a success story. The chevalier de Mouhy, a hack novelist and sometime police spy, had little talent and less fortune, but he had built up capital in the form of "protections"—the eighteenth-century term for the influence-peddling that made *le monde* go round. In 1751 Mouhy cobbled together some belletristic essays under the title *Tablettes dramatiques* and cashed in one of his chips: an introduction to the chevalier de Pons, one of the counselors of the duc de Chartres. De Pons permitted Mouhy to present his manuscript to the duke during an audience at the château de Saint Cloud. After glancing at the text, the duke made a remark to the effect that he hoped to see it published. Mouhy returned to his garret, penned an effusive dedication to the duke, and after some negotiations over the flattery in one of the lines, persuaded de Pons to persuade the duke to accept it. Next, Mouhy set about clearing the manuscript through the censorship, no easy task, as it contained a few irreverent remarks about men of letters and the Académie française. To ease its way, he cashed in a second chip:

the protection of the maréchal de Belle-Isle. The maréchal wrote to M. de la Reignière, the father-in-law of Malesherbes, explaining that he had accorded his protection to Mouhy and would be pleased if de la Reignière would do the same. Mouhy sent de la Reignière a letter of his own, stressing the dedication, the double protection, and the importance of speed in processing the privilege, because for commercial reasons he needed to get the book on the market as soon as possible. De la Reignière complied with a letter to Malesherbes, and Malesherbes obliged by appointing a sympathetic censor, F.-A. Paradis de Moncrif, a playwright, poet, member of the Académie française, and well-connected figure in *le monde*, thanks to his engaging manners and wit. Moncrif knew what was expected of him, because Malesherbes had pointed out, in sending him his marching orders, that the maréchal de Belle-Isle, one of the most powerful men in France, took an interest in the affair.

So far so good, but Moncrif received a very messy copy, written in a barely legible scrawl. It took him a great deal of time and trouble to work through it, initialing the pages as he approved them, according to normal procedure. Mouhy, pleading for speed, persuaded him to turn over a first batch of the approved pages so that the book could be registered for an approbation at Malesherbes's next audience in the Bureau de la librairie. In this way, the printer could start work on the approved part of the text, while Moncrif censored the rest. Nothing could go wrong, because Moncrif could later check the proofs against the initialed pages of the manuscript. Furthermore, Mouhy had given him carte blanche to cut anything objectionable, while reassuring him at the same time that nothing of the sort could possibly be found in the text. Instead of receiving proofs, however, Moncrif was given a copy of the newly printed book, along with the copy-text that the printers had used. The copy-text contained a great many passages that did not exist in the manuscript that Moncrif had approved, including some remarks on page 76 that were certain to offend his colleagues in the Académie française. Moncrif dashed to the bookstores that had received the first copies, tore out the offending page, and required Mouhy to replace it with a cancel before the bulk of the edition could be marketed. In the end, therefore, the censor saved his reputation, and the author got the book he wanted, minus one page, thanks to his ability to brazen his way through the bureaucracy and to pull strings.[22]

The second case had a less happy ending. Guillaume Poncet de la Grave, an attorney and minor man of letters, was a far more substantial personage than the chevalier de Mouhy, but he was far less successful at mobilizing protectors, even though he eventually became a censor himself. In 1753 he completed a *Projet des embellissements de la ville et des faubourgs de Paris*, a book-length proposal for beautifying Paris by redesigning public spaces. Favored with the same censor, Moncrif, who specialized in works about the beaux arts, Poncet also tried to launch his book under the banner of an influential patron by asking permission to dedicate it to the marquis de Marigny, brother of Mme de Pompadour and the key official in charge of royal building projects. He got nowhere. Marigny returned the draft of the dedication with a flat refusal; and when pressed for an explanation, he replied, "To accept the dedication of a work would be to give it a public approbation." Nor would he let Poncet take his case to Mme de Pompadour: "As my sister has very little free time, I do not foresee a moment when I could introduce you to her."[23] The failure of the dedication then became an obstacle to the approbation, because the censor did not want to make enemies in Versailles.[24] Poncet and Moncrif discussed the stalemate at length during a meeting in the château des Tuileries. According to Poncet, Moncrif found the manuscript perfectly worthy of an approbation and confessed that his "duty as a censor" required him to approve the manuscript; but nothing would induce him to cross Marigny.[25] For his part, Marigny had his own ideas about architectural projects and did not want to appear to favor other schemes, especially if they would require an increase in taxation. Versailles, as usual, was short of cash. But why should such considerations stand in the way of a loyal subject's publishing a book that offended neither church nor king nor anything else, except the taste of one well-placed marquis?

Baffled, Poncet went over Moncrif's head by appealing to Malesherbes. "It is hard for an author to be exposed to so much difficulty in France," he wrote. "I never knew how to play the courtier. Too bad for me." But then he lapsed into courtier language himself: "If I did not know your equity, Monsieur, I could strengthen my case by invoking my family ties with Messieurs d'Auriac and Castargnier. Although I do not frequent their company, they know perfectly well who I am; my name is well known to them. . . . Blood never betrays itself among the wellborn."[26] Malesherbes asked Moncrif for his version of the story. The censor confirmed his desire to avoid compromising himself with influential persons and requested to be relieved of the case. He also wrote an indignant letter to Poncet, complaining about being exposed to the disfavor of Malesherbes. Poncet was therefore reduced to supplicating for another censor and a tacit permission. When his book finally appeared without a privilege and approbation a year later, its fate was exactly what could have been predicted from the beginning: it offended no one, and no one took any notice of it.

These two episodes reveal more about the way censorship actually operated on a day-to-day basis than the well-known stories about the repression of Enlightenment works. In fact, authors and censors worked together in a gray area, where the licit shaded off gradually into the illicit. They shared the same assumptions and values—not surprisingly, because they usually came from the same milieux.[27] Most censors were authors themselves, and they included writers who were aligned with the Enlightenment such as Fontenelle, Condillac, Crébillon fils, and Suard. Like the *Encyclopédistes*, they belonged to the world of universities and academies, the clergy, the professional classes, and the royal administration.[28] They did not make a living by censoring books but pursued careers as professors, doctors, lawyers, and holders of various administrative posts. Censoring was a sideline for them, and most of them did it without pay. Of 128 censors in 1764, 33 received a modest emolument of 400 livres a year, one received 600 livres, and the rest got nothing at all.[29] After long and loyal service, they could hope to receive a pension. The state had set aside 15,000 livres for the pensions of retired censors in 1764. But the reward for most censors came in the form of prestige and the possibility of patronage. To be listed as "Censeur du Roi" in the *Almanach royal* was to occupy a prominent place among the servants of the crown, one that could lead to more-lucrative appointments. One censor informed Malesherbes that he had accepted his position with the understanding that his protector would advance his career, but the protector had died and therefore he had no more interest in vetting manuscripts.[30] Insofar as the status attached to the position of "Censeur du Roi" can be gauged by the number of men who occupied it, it did not decline in the course of the century. The number kept growing—from about 10 in 1660 to 60 in 1700, 70 in 1750, 120 in 1760, and nearly 180 in 1789.[31] The growth corresponded to the great increase of book production as measured by the annual requests for official permission to publish a book during the eighteenth century—from about 300 in 1700 to 500 in 1750, and more than 1,000 by 1780.[32] Authors, publishers, and censors all participated in an industry that was expanding. But the censors profited least from it.

Why were so many men of letters, many of them also men of principle, willing to take on such a job? The "job description," as we would put it today, hardly looked inviting: little or no pay, no desk, no office, not so much as a blue pencil provided by the government; yet censoring involved a good deal of tedious labor and the constant risk of offending important people or even of incurring opprobrium. But to put the question in that way is to succumb to anachronism. Except for rare protests, like Figaro's famous outburst in *Le Mariage de Figaro*,[33] most of the outrage directed against censors came from the era after 1789, when the belief had taken hold among ordinary citizens that individuals have a natural right to freedom of expression. How can one make sense of censorship as a system that commanded respect in a world organized according to other principles?

EVERYDAY OPERATIONS

One could begin by considering the relation between censorship and the growth of the state, a process that had acquired enormous momentum in France since the time of Richelieu. By the time of Malesherbes, the old absolutist monarchy was being transformed by a new phenomenon, one that shaped modern society in general, according to Max Weber: bureaucratization. "Bureaucracy" as a term appeared in the 1750s, accompanied by increased reliance on paperwork, printed forms, rational procedures for executing tasks, and hierarchies of salaried employees extending from clerks and copyists to "premiers commis" and "chefs de bureau."[34] Of course, many offices remained venal until the end of the Ancien Régime, and the state handled its financial and legal business in an arbitrary and irrational manner that contributed mightily to its collapse in 1789.[35] As part of the state apparatus—a section within the Chancellerie, or what we would call the Ministry of Justice—the Direction de la librairie hardly resembled a modern bureaucracy. It did not even have offices. Malesherbes did business from his town house in the rue Neuve des Petits Champs near the rue de la Feuillade, a fashionable section of Paris close to the place Vendôme. When he dealt with questions of censorship—and a wide variety of other affairs connected with the book trade—he operated from a room known as a "bureau." But the room served for "audiences," in which he received supplicants and petitioners in the manner of a grand seigneur—as befitted him, for he belonged to the great Lamoignon dynasty within the nobility of the robe: he owned the office of "premier président" in the Cour des Aides, which adjudicated tax issues, and his father held the highest office in the kingdom as Chancelier de France.[36] The censors who worked under Malesherbes had no bureaus of their own. They vetted manuscripts in their private apartments or whatever space they occupied while doing their primary jobs. To describe them with eighteenth-century neologisms like *bureaucrate, buraliste,* or *paperasseur* (paper pusher) is to get them wrong.[37]

Yet the paper trails they left behind indicate a procedural formality and self-consciousness that can be seen as symptoms of a bureaucratic way of doing business—mixed, to be sure, with archaic elements peculiar to an industry dominated by a guild, the Communauté des libraires et des imprimeurs de Paris. Booksellers, who had to be members of the guild, frequently came to Malesherbes's audience, a crowded, lively affair, held every Thursday, in order to submit manuscripts with requests for privileges.[38] Malesherbes assigned each manuscript to a censor by issuing a *billet de censure,* also known as a *renvoi.* This was a printed form, addressed to the censor, which contained a standard phrase:

Monsieur . . . . ,
will be pleased to take the trouble to examine this manuscript with the greatest possible attention and diligence in order to give a rapid judgment of it to M. LE CHANCELIER.

N.° 40   Lettre sur les Peintures d'Herculanum
          aujourdhui Portici

Monsieur de Boze

prendra, s'il lui plaît, la peine d'exa-

miner ce ms

avec le plus d'attention & de diligence

qu'il lui sera possible, pour en donner

incessamment son jugement à M. LE

CHANCELIER.

Ce vingt huit fevrier

1751 de la maison de Malesherbes

Je n'ai rien trouvé que d'honête et de sensé dans ce
petit ouvrage sur les peintures d'Herculanum, et dont
l'impression ne pût être autorisée par un Privilége en
forme, si on le demandoit aulieu d'une permission tacite.
a Paris ce 2.ᵉ mars 1751.

                        DE BOZE

A printed billet de censure dated February 28, 1751, and signed by Malesherbes, directing a censor, de Boze, to examine the manuscript entitled "Lettre sur les peintures d'Herculanum." On the bottom, de Boze wrote a jugement dated March 2, 1751, testifying that the manuscript was worthy of a tacit permission or a privilege. The note at the top indicated that it was to receive a tacit permission, and the number at the top left identified it for registration in the "Feuille des jugements."

Malesherbes's secretary filled in the name of the censor, the title of the manuscript, the date, and, at the top left of the page, the number of the application. This number with the corresponding information, was entered into a register called the *livre sur la librairie*. After receiving the manuscript accompanied by the *billet de censure*, the censor went over the text, initialed each page as he read it (unless he decided to reject the manuscript, which obviated the need for initialing), and noted any changes that he considered necessary. In straightforward cases that met his approval, he often wrote his "judgment," as it was known, at the bottom of the *billet de censure*, which he returned to Malesherbes. Thus a typical positive judgment:

> I have found nothing but decent and reasonable [material] in this little work on the paintings of Herculaneum, whose printing can be authorized by a formal privilege, if it is requested, rather than by a tacit permission.[39]

In more complicated cases, the censor would send his judgment in the form of a letter to Malesherbes. He might also render an oral opinion and discuss the case at length with Malesherbes during a working session for censors, known as the *bureau de jeudi* (Thursday office hours), which also took place in Malesherbes's town house.

Either way, a judgment was a private exchange between Malesherbes and a censor, which sometimes had an informal tone and went on at considerable length. An approbation, by contrast, was an official approval of a request for a privilege, which was usually published alongside the privilege in the printed text of the book. Censors tended to use more careful and succinct language when they wrote approbations. They normally sent them with their judgment to Malesherbes's residence, where his staff (he may have used only a secretary and a clerk or copyist) superintended the next stage of the process.[40] They kept a copy of the approbation for their records and made another copy, known as the *feuille* (sheet), to be sent to the Keeper of the Seals, who eventually infused it with the full force of the law by stamping it with the "grand seal" (*grand sceau*) at his disposal and issuing a privilege like the one quoted at the beginning of this chapter. The Keeper of the Seals returned the stamped approbation (*feuille scellée*) with the privilege to the bureau of the director, where it could be claimed at a Thursday audience by the bookseller or, after 1777, the author (the edicts on the book trade of August 30, 1777, explicitly permitted authors to hold privileges in their own names, as had occasionally happened earlier, and also to sell their printed books). The bookseller had to pay a fee of thirty-six livres, twelve sous—a fairly hefty sum, the equivalent of nearly a month's wages for an unskilled laborer. He would then take the *feuille scellée* and the privilege to the administrative office (Chambre syndicale) of the Parisian booksellers' guild for registration. Once a clerk of the guild had copied the full text of the privilege into a register, the bookseller had acquired an exclusive right to reproduce the text for a certain period of time, usually at least ten years. He could then take the manuscript to be printed, either by a master printer of the guild (in principle, printing was limited to forty masters in Paris) or by himself (if he had been accepted as a master printer in addition to his official capacity as a master bookseller). Once the proofs had been pulled, the censor made his final appearance in the process, because he had to initial each page of the proofs in order to verify that the printed text corresponded to the manuscript that he had also initialed, page by page.

The system involved enough shuffling and shifting of paper to open up possibilities for error and cheating, as in the case of Mouhy's attempt to slip some nasty remarks about his enemies in the Académie française into un-initialed proofs, which he had hidden from his censor's attention. But the standard procedure expressed an attempt to impose rational order on the complex task of vetting texts as they passed from manuscript to print. The filling out of printed forms, the numbering of documents, the tracking of dossiers, the copying and registering and sealing and initialing—can it all be taken as symptomatic of full-fledged bureaucratization? Not in the strict, Weberian sense of the word. The Direction de la librairie can best be understood as a bureaucracy without bureaucrats. It represented an inter-mediate stage in the Weberian process, and as such it typified the Ancien Régime's efforts to transact its business more effectively without abandon-

A page from the "Feuille des jugements" showing the numbers of the billets de censure with jugements, the titles of the books, the names of the censors, and the decisions concerning the nature of the permission (whether a privilege, a permission tacite, or a permission simple) and the length of its duration.

ing the system of privilege and protection that permeated a baroque state attached to a royal court.

Censors had to cope with the strains and contradictions of this proto-modern, baroque bureaucracy as best they could, accepting assignments as they came. Malesherbes usually allotted the work according to the censors' fields of expertise, which appeared with their names under standard rubrics in the *Almanach royal*: theology; jurisprudence; natural history, medicine, and chemistry; surgery; mathematics; belles-lettres, history, and related subjects designated only as "etc."; geography, navigation, and travel; and architecture. The workload varied enormously. A few censors vetted only one or two manuscripts a year, whereas others seemed to be constantly occupied, snatching what time they could from their normal occupations. The pressure took its toll on workhorses like the abbé Buret, an ecclesiastical censor, who felt overwhelmed in July 1762. Having just slogged through a book on philosophy and another on theology, he had to take on a translation of Saint Augustine as well as a tome on church administration thirteen days before he was to go on vacation. He begged for a reprieve so that he could visit his family in the country and look after the affairs of his benefice.[41] The abbé de La Ville complained that he had read so many historical tracts of such mediocrity that when he received a new manuscript he could not tell whether he had already read an earlier version of it. He could only give "quick and superficial attention" to the works that piled up on his desk, he confessed.[42] Theology was even more of a grind, according to the abbé Foucher. After laboriously cutting and correcting a treatise on the soul, he heaved a sigh and exclaimed, "Long live history books and anthologies!"[43]

Most censors seem to have taken their tasks seriously and to have worked hard. While examining a treatise on trade and exchange rates, one of them corrected the spelling and redid much of the arithmetic.[44] Others produced lists of factual mistakes, repaired faulty grammar, noted stylistic flaws, and took special care to signal phrasing that could give offense. They often objected to harshness of tone, defending an ideal of moderation and propriety (*bienséances*).[45] In such cases, they penciled in suggested improvements. One censor demanded that an entire manuscript be recopied with plenty of space between the lines so that he could insert corrections.[46] Censoring with that degree of attention resembled the care with which readers assess manuscripts for publishers today.

Because it involved so much care, hard work, and responsibility, censorship bound author and censor together in a relationship that was often close and sometimes verged on collaboration. The choice of the censor belonged to the director of the book trade, who often consulted authors and accommodated those who sent him special requests. Malesherbes knew all the important writers of his time and sometimes intervened to steer their manuscripts past the dead ends and wrong turns that lay along the route to a privilege or a tacit permission. The most eminent authors expected special treatment, for deference and string-pulling belonged to the mores of *le monde*. Voltaire was always asking for special favors, not only with Malesherbes but with ministers, the lieutenant general of police, influential salon lions, and anyone else who could clear passage for his works—that is, his legal works; he published his illegal tracts outside the law and anonymously or, better yet, under the names of his enemies.[47] In the course of his tortuous relations with Rousseau, Malesherbes virtually masterminded the publication of key works, notably *La Nouvelle Héloïse* and *Emile*. Less famous but equally well connected authors sometimes managed to have their manuscripts approved by people who were not official censors at all, because Malesherbes could issue a *billet de censure* to authorize special cases. When asked to expedite a legal treatise by an influential lawyer named Aubert, he sent a blank *billet de censure* to Aubert himself and asked him to fill in the censor's name.[48] Inside maneuvering of this sort meant that friends and colleagues often censored one another's works. Fontenelle approved the *Oeuvres diverses* of Moncrif, his fellow censor and fellow member of the Académie française.[49] One censor, Secousse, even approved a law anthology that he had edited himself.[50] Sometimes obscure writers received such special treatment, evidently because Malesherbes found their pleading persuasive. A priest who had written a *Plan général d'institution publique pour la jeunesse du ressort du parlement de Bourgogne* asked Malesherbes to assign the manuscript to a friend of his, a censor named Michault. There was no danger of favoritism, he emphasized, because Michault was "a man of integrity, sincere, and too committed to the glory of letters to turn a blind eye to any work unworthy of publication. I have complete confidence in his wisdom, and I will correct anything he censors with all the docility and regard that I owe to him." Malesherbes agreed.[51]

In principle and usually in practice, authors were not supposed to know the identity of their censors. Censors sometimes insisted on anonymity as a condition of doing their job. Moncrif had so many connections among the literary and social elite that he felt unable to function if his identity were to be revealed to the authors of the manuscripts he vetted.[52] Yet leaks sometimes occurred, to the consternation of the censors, including Moncrif.[53] After learning that one of his negative reports might be shown to the author, a particularly sensitive censor insisted that his signature be trimmed off the bottom of the page.[54] Even a positive report could cause difficulty, because when a censor's name was printed with an approbation and a privilege in the text of a book it made him appear to be complicit with the author, and it could expose him to the wrath of the author's enemies. A literary censor begged Malesherbes to give only a *permission tacite* to an orthodox work that was critical of Voltaire, because he feared that he would become the butt of attacks by Voltaire's partisans if his name appeared alongside the approbation.[55] Voltaire and d'Alembert demanded toleration for their own works, but they tried to get Malesherbes to suppress those of their enemies—and Malesherbes refused.[56] As a matter of principle, he favored free debate,[57] but his censors frequently had to cope with partisanship. A typical quarrel involved a censor's approval of a *Cours de chimie* by a doctor named Baron, who criticized some anti-Newtonian arguments of an anonymous tract. Unfortunately, the tract had been written by Jean-Baptiste Sénac, the first doctor to the king, who was a powerful figure in the world of medicine, and in a furious letter to Malesherbes, Sénac demanded that the censor be punished, for he was "as guilty as the author." Malesherbes replied that both the approbation and the book concerned only ideas, not personalities; in fact, the censor had not known that Sénac was the author of the anonymous work. But as soon as he heard of Sénac's reaction, Baron panicked. He wrote a desperate letter to Malesherbes in an attempt to head off sanctions from Versailles. His book dealt with scientific theories, he protested. Wasn't free debate about ideas a basic right enjoyed by everyone in the republic of letters? And, moreover, "How could I be such an enemy to myself as to abuse the protection with which you honor me and to alienate in a lighthearted manner the first doctor to the king?" Nothing ever came of this incident, but it exposed the contradictory elements at the core of the literary system of the Ancien Régime: on the one hand, a respect for the ideal of a free and open republic of letters; on the other, the realities of power and protection. Censors, like authors, had to operate in an area where this contradiction made itself felt in their everyday activities.[58]

While attempting to accommodate the powers that could intervene in their operations and at the same time trying to improve manuscripts, censors frequently developed sympathy for the persons whose texts they vetted. They often corresponded with the authors and even met with them, although the authors were not supposed to know who had censored their work until it had received an approbation. After sending some critical notes to a theologian who had written a treatise on the Incarnation, one censor found himself drawn into an elaborate debate about church doctrine.[59] Another arranged a meeting with an author in order to explain a delicate point: the manuscript was excellent, but it undermined its argument by an excessively polemical tone; the author needed to learn how to respect literary *bienséances*.[60] A third censor approved a history of La Rochelle, although he disapproved of its turgid style. Working like a copyeditor, he went over the manuscript with a pencil, struck out the most offensive passages, and got the author's agreement to rewrite them.[61] In some cases, authors refused to make changes, and their censors stopped working with them—or Malesherbes assigned another censor to the case, sometimes at the suggestion of the original censor.[62] More often, the authors accepted criticism and rewrote passages "with good grace," as a censor put it admiringly.[63] Sympathy led to flexibility on the part of the censors. They bent the rules when faced with a "poor devil" who turned out hack work of bad quality in order to keep the wolf from the door.[64] To be sure, the censors sounded condescending when they dealt with hacks. They adopted a deferential tone when they worked over manuscripts by well-known and well-protected writers. But either way, they played such an active part in the process of creating a book that they assumed responsibility for it. In a typical memorandum to Malesherbes, a censor expressed regret that he could not devote more time to improving the style of a manuscript, but the author wanted it back in a hurry and therefore would have to take all the blame if it were criticized after its publication.[65]

Of course, collaborations could go sour. After failing to persuade authors to rewrite according to their specifications, censors sometimes refused to have anything more to do with them.[66] Debates over texts degenerated into quarrels. Censors complained about copy, authors about delays.[67] A retired naval officer found it painful to be ordered to cut his poetry and then, after some self-inflicted wounds, to be required to cut still more.[68] And a mathematician who believed he had found a formula for squaring the circle was indignant at the refusal of his manuscript. It contained nothing against religion, the state, or morality; yet the censor had rejected it on the grounds that he did not want to get into trouble with the Academy of Sciences, of which he was a member (the academy had refused to consider any more treatises on that subject).

> Is that then the reward for an enormous labor, the most unpleasant, the most difficult, and at the same time the most necessary that any geometrician has ever undertaken? What a recompense to encourage ardor and emulation among us! Or, to put it correctly, what a source of disgust and discouragement, if we are not all equally allowed to be useful to the world that we inhabit.[69]

Despite the occasional disputes, censorship, of the business-as-usual variety, drove authors and censors together rather than apart. Their relations usually involved varying degrees of collaboration, not relentless doses of repression. Insofar as one can calculate the refusal rate, it was low, often about 10 percent.[70] But, of course, manuscripts that seriously challenged the official values of church and state were not submitted for censoring to the Direction de la librairie. They went to presses located across France's border along a fertile crescent of publishing houses that extended from Amsterdam down to Brussels and Liège, through the Rhineland, into Switzerland, and finally to the papal state at Avignon. This unambiguously illegal literature, supplemented by a huge trade in pirated works, provided great business for the foreign publishers, who sold it in France through a vast system of smuggling and underground distribution.[71] The drain on the French economy was so great that the directors of the book trade, particularly Malesherbes and his successor, Antoine de Sartine, did everything possible to enlarge the limits of legality by favoring tacit permissions, simple permissions, tolerances, and other devices that would favor domestic production. Economics mattered as much as politics or religion in the administration of censorship.[72]

But the administrators did not have a free hand, because they could not make any important decisions in Paris without considering the consequences in Versailles. Whenever a sensitive question arose, Malesherbes went over the heads of his censors and consulted key figures in the ministries and the court. Was a treatise on military fortifications publishable? The manuscript went to the minister of war. A study of foreign trade? The controller general of finances would have to decide. A history of Ireland with special reference to war and diplomacy? The foreign minister needed to approve the manuscript before it could be assigned to a censor. A book about the need to create a new hospital in Paris? A censor had given it preliminary approval, but the crucial decision on its fate had to come from the minister in charge of the "Department of Paris."[73] Dedications were equally delicate, because a public personage who accepted the dedication of a book implicitly endorsed it and became identified with it. Writers were always flinging themselves on grandees in the hopes that a dedication would lead to patronage. They usually did not get past a great man's antechamber or his secretary, and they sometimes attempted end runs by publishing an unauthorized dedication and presenting the potential patron with a specially bound copy. Malesherbes had to prevent such forbidden behavior. He did not permit a dedication unless the author could produce a letter testifying to its acceptance, and he always had a censor vet its text.[74]

The argument at this point may seem to be slipping toward an extreme. Censors provided positive endorsements of books. They concentrated on substantive and aesthetic issues rather than on threats to the church, state, and morality. They often sympathized with authors, met with them, and even collaborated on the printed texts. Instead of repressing literature, they made it happen. Did they not do any ideological police work of the sort that is usually identified with censorship?

Problem Cases

It is possible to make the positive aspects of censorship stand out by selecting the evidence that makes it look good. In the foregoing description of the censors' activities, I have assessed the evidence as impartially as I can; but by concentrating on the ordinary, everyday aspect of their work, I have neglected the spectacular episodes that have attracted the attention of most historians, and I have not discussed cases where censors explicitly dealt with ideological issues. The midcentury years were a time of great ferment. In fact, Malesherbes's term as director of the book trade, 1750–63, coincided closely with the period when the most important works of the Enlightenment were published, from the *Encyclopédie* (its prospectus first appeared in 1750; the last ten volumes of its text were published together in 1765) to Rousseau's *Emile* and *Du Contrat social* (both published in 1762). Malesherbes was a friend of the *philosophes*, and his directorship has often been interpreted as a turning point in the history of the Enlightenment and of freedom of expression in general. How does it appear, if seen from the perspective of daily labor among the censors who worked under him?

A close reading of all the reports, correspondence, and memorandums of the censors from 1750 to 1763 shows little concern about the works of the *philosophes*. Philosophy in general did not cause much worry. In a report on a book that favored Leibnizian metaphysics, a censor sounded dismissive about the importance of such a subject: "Many of the philosophers among us don't agree about the truth of these principles and claim that the consequences to be drawn from them have a dangerous influence on religion. But as that is merely a philosophical dispute, I don't think there is an adequate reason to prevent the circulation of works that can give rise to it."[75] On a few occasions the censors expressed disquiet about creeping deism of a Voltairean kind.[76] But Voltaire's name rarely appeared in the memos that circulated through the Direction de la librairie. That should not be surprising, because, as already explained, no manuscript that openly challenged the orthodox values of the Ancien Régime would be submitted for approbation and a royal privilege or even for a tacit permission. Such works went to Marc-Michel Rey in Amsterdam, Gabriel Cramer in Geneva, and other publishers who operated outside the realm of French law. The books that reached the censors' desks and that gave them the most difficulty had to do primarily with religion—nuances of theology within the Catholic Church, Protestant doctrines, and above all Jansenism, the austere, Augustinian strain of religion derived from the works of Cornelius Jansen and condemned as heretical by several papal bulls.[77] The authors and publishers of these works sent them to be censored in the belief that they were compatible with orthodox Catholicism. The censors had to decide whether that was the case.

Many of the censors who made those decisions were professors of theology at the Sorbonne. They were fairly flexible concerning Protestant works of a nonpolemical kind, such as books of prayers, which could be edifying, even though Protestants addressed God as *tu* instead of the *vous* favored by Catholics.[78] The censors also granted tacit permissions to nonreligious works by Protestant authors, despite some misgivings about remarks on sensitive subjects such as the nature of marriage.[79] But they refused to tolerate any book that had the slightest whiff of Jansenism or that discussed explosive topics, like efficacious grace, which were raised by the Jansenist controversies.[80] They even refused to approve anti-Jansenist manuscripts—in one case, a thoroughly orthodox work by the bishop of Sisteron—because, as one of them put it, it did no good "to heat up tempers."[81] The censors encountered plenty of defenses of orthodoxy, yet they hesitated to permit them if they weren't convincing enough. One censor rejected a pious attempt to refute deism on the grounds that it was too feeble: "To produce a weak defense of religion is inadvertently to expose it."[82] Religious books did not merely have to be free of heresy; they had to conform to especially high standards of reasoning and style. Otherwise they undermined their own cause and could not be published.[83]

The same line of reasoning applied to political works. The censors did not worry about attacks on the king, which would not be submitted to them for approval in the first place. Instead, they fretted over works that did not praise him effectively enough. A libretto to an opera could be published, according to one censor, but only if the author cut its prologue, which contained an inadequate eulogy of Louis XV.[84] "Politics" for the censors, as for many Frenchmen in the eighteenth century, did not refer to power struggles within the government, which could not be discussed openly, but rather to foreign affairs. Jean-Pierre Tercier, the first secretary in the foreign office, made sure that manuscripts did not deviate from the current line in foreign policy.[85] A disrespectful remark about Prussia could be tolerated during the Seven Years' War (1756–63), when Frederick II fought against France, but not during the War of the Austrian Succession (1740–48), when he was an ally.[86] Similarly, some pro-Jacobite remarks in the first volumes of a history of Ireland seemed admissible to a censor at a time when France supported the claim to the British throne by the Young Pretender (Charles Edward Stuart, later known as Bonnie Prince Charlie), but not when the later volumes were submitted for approval. By then, after the War of the Austrian Succession, France had abandoned the Jacobite cause and Irish history looked different. The case had to be decided by the foreign minister.[87] The minister of war refused to permit the publication of any military treatises, even technical tracts on ballistics, during the Seven Years' War.[88] During the crisis over his attempt to introduce a new and more equitable "twentieth" tax in 1749, the controller general of finances tried to prevent the publication of all books about taxation.[89] The Parlement of Paris constantly opposed tax reform and contested the absolute authority of the king, particularly in connection with the Jansenist quarrels. But the censors rarely dealt with parlementary polemics, probably because works on controversial issues would not have been submitted for their approval.[90] Anything that concerned current events had to be cleared with higher authorities, but censors rarely received topical works.

Instead, they vetted large numbers of historical texts, which raised ideological questions of a different kind. In such cases, they could be remarkably permissive, as in this report on a history of England written by a French monk:

> One could say that it is a history of England intended for Englishmen from the maddest faction of the Whigs. . . . The rage for criticizing priests and monks is carried to such a point that one could imagine one is reading Voltaire. Our author often uses his tone and expressions. He also announces at the beginning that the English nation has the power to choose a king according to its fancy, and he does so in order to demonstrate that James II was legitimately dethroned. . . . Although I have erased the most revolting passages, . . . the text remains covered nonetheless with an English veneer, which makes it impossible to give the author a privilege for printing his book. Still, if Monsieur de Malesherbes wanted to grant him a tacit permission and if one presented it as a work printed in London, the readers would easily be taken in and would surely never guess that it had been written by a French Benedictine monk.[91]

The final category that bore watching, according to Malesherbes and other commentators on the book trade, was literature that offended common standards of morality—the kind that is commonly called pornography today. That term did not exist in the eighteenth century, when erotic literature flourished without causing a great deal of concern—unless it took monks, nuns, and royal mistresses as its dramatis personae. Such books had enough shock value to sell well in the underground trade, but they were never submitted for censorship. A few bawdy novels came to the censors' attention and were generally tolerated.[92] The only case of a grossly indecent work that I have encountered in the censors' reports was *Mystères de l'hymen, ou la bergère de velours cramoisy* (Mysteries of the hymen, or the winged chair of crimson velvet), which a censor dismissed as a disgusting aberration.[93]

After studying hundreds of reports and memorandums by censors, one seems to be staring into the face of an unsuspected problem: if the censors did not concentrate primarily on sniffing out irreligion and sedition, where, aside from special cases like Jansenism and foreign affairs, did they smell danger? Not where we would expect to find it—that is, in the camp of the *philosophes*. Instead, they worried about the court. More precisely, they dreaded entanglement in the webs of protection and clientage through which power was transmitted under the Ancien Régime. Although the literary market was booming by 1750 and a new kind of power was shifting to the marketplace, the royal censors still inhabited a world created by Renaissance princes, where a false step could bring disaster and sanctions remained in the hands of the great (*les grands*).

Danger in this respect did not inhere in ideas but rather in persons—anyone with influence who might be offended by an irreverent or inadvertent remark. One censor struck out a reference in a history book to a misdeed by a member of the powerful Noailles family in the sixteenth century—not that it never happened, but "the house [of Noailles] might complain that it was recalled."[94] Another turned down a perfectly accurate genealogical work on the grounds that it might contain omissions that could offend some great families.[95] A third censor refused to approve an account of French relations with the Ottoman Porte, because it contained "details that concern families who command respect"; and he named names: one nobleman who went mad while serving as ambassador in Constantinople and another who failed to get the ambassadorship because of hostility to his bizarre mother-in-law at court.[96] Everywhere censors trembled at the thought of failing to spot some veiled reference to somebody important. Special research had to be done in Lyon to clear a book of essays that might give offense to local notables.[97] Malesherbes, who belonged to a great family himself, constantly cleared manuscripts with well-placed sources, who could pick up allusions that might escape censors located at humbler levels of society. Grandees expected this service. The duc d'Orléans, for example, thanked Malesherbes through an intermediary for making sure that "nothing concerning his father should be printed before he [the current duke] should be informed."[98]

The genre that most struck terror in the soul of a censor was the roman à clef. Censors often did not know one when they saw one, because they lacked sufficient knowledge of *le monde*. The unworldly abbé Guiroy, for example, asked Malesherbes to name another censor for a novel that did not merely satirize authors—that was admissible—but might aim at higher targets. "I fear allusions. They occur frequently, and I don't dare take on the responsibility for them. If I could figure them out, I might perhaps not worry; but I can't tell who is being referred to."[99] The same danger haunted another clueless censor, who would not clear a manuscript, although he found it superb in every other respect: "It may be an allegory disguised with delicacy and finesse under sacred names, which could be used for malicious applications (*applications malignes*) at court. For those reasons, I think it dangerous to permit its publication in this kingdom, even with a tacit permission."[100] Malesherbes sympathized with the predicament of the men who worked under him. They were not, after all, persons of much standing ("des gens assez considérables") and could not be expected to pick up allusions that would be obvious to anyone from a more exalted sphere. Moreover, they were timid. They would rather reject a manuscript than expose themselves to displeasure if they accepted it.[101] Rejections often expressed a fear of "applications," a term that appears frequently in the papers of the censors and also of the police.[102] It referred to coded references, usually insults and compromising information, in books, songs, epigrams, and bons mots. "Applications" passed unperceived among ordinary readers, but they could inflict serious damage among the great. They represented a form of power that required surveillance in a society where reputation, name, and "face" (*bella figura*) expressed political clout and potential vulnerability, just as they had done in the Italian courts three hundred years earlier.

SCANDAL AND ENLIGHTENMENT

If it is possible to pick up echoes from the Renaissance in the censors' papers, are there audible hints about the Revolution just around the corner? Far from it: one advantage of studying censorship up close between

1750 and 1763 is the opportunity to escape from the view that everything during the last years of the Ancien Régime was leading to the explosion of 1789. But teleology aside, it is important to acknowledge that there were plenty of disruptive forces at work in the world of books. One has to do with the Enlightenment. Although the *philosophes* sent their most audacious works to be published outside France, occasionally they attempted to publish books within the kingdom by submitting them to censorship, and on rare occasions the censors approved them. At that point, they could cause a scandal. Not only could the censor get in trouble, but, more important, the state apparatus could be threatened by outside powers determined to assert ideological control in their own name—that is, by exercising post-publication censorship. Books could cause offense in many quarters—the University of Paris (especially the faculty of theology at the Sorbonne), the parlements (sovereign law courts, which could intervene in times of civic disorder), the General Assembly of the Clergy (it often condemned books in the meetings it held once every five years), and among other ecclesiastical powers, especially French bishops and the Vatican. All these institutions exerted claims to exercise censorship, and the state resisted all of them, determined to maintain its monopoly over the power to control the printed word.

That monopoly was relatively recent. During the Middle Ages, the crown had left the oversight of the book trade to the University of Paris, whose main concern was to maintain the accuracy of copies turned out by scriptoria. After the outbreak of the Reformation, the Sorbonne continued to vet texts, but it could not contain the flood of Protestant works. The crown attempted to solve the problem in 1535 by decreeing that anyone who printed anything would be hanged. That did not work. For the next 150 years, the state built up its repressive apparatus while restricting that of the church. The ordonnance of Moulins (1566) required that books be furnished with a royal privilege before publication, and the Code Michaud (1629) established a mechanism for censoring by royal censors under the authority of the Chancellery. By the end of the seventeenth century, the state had consolidated its power over the publishing industry, and the university no longer played much of a part in the process, but the bishops and parlements continued to condemn books after their publication by issuing *mandements* and *arrêtés* (bishop's letters and parlementary decrees). To be sure, those declarations did not have much effect—unless they occurred during times of crisis.[103]

The greatest crisis took place in connection with the publication of *De l'Esprit* by Claude-Adrien Helvétius in 1758.[104] No book had ever attracted more censure from more would-be censors—an edict from the Parlement of Paris, a resolution from the General Assembly of the Clergy, a *mandement* from the archbishop of Paris, similar outbursts from other bishops, a rebuke from the Sorbonne, a brief from the pope, and prescription by the King's Council. *De l'Esprit* certainly contained enough material—materialist metaphysics, utilitarian ethics, unorthodox politics—to warrant condemnation by anyone committed to orthodox principles. But the scramble to condemn it expressed more than righteous indignation. Each attack on the book was an invasion of the state's authority and an attempt to appropriate aspects of it. Scandalous works had appeared before, of course, but they circulated in the underground channels of the trade. *De l'Esprit* sold openly with a royal privilege and approbation.

The censor was Jean-Pierre Tercier, a top official in the ministry of foreign affairs. Absorbed in the diplomatic maelstrom connected with the Seven Years' War, Tercier had no time for abstract philosophy and little ability to understand it. He normally handled works related to history and international relations. To compound his confusion, he was given the manuscript in separate batches and out of order, making it difficult to follow a consecutive argument. And he was urged to rush through it by Mme Helvétius, a great beauty who turned her charm on him at a dinner party and begged him to finish before she and her husband had to leave for their country estate. In the end, Tercier gave the work a full-fledged approbation, which appeared in print alongside a royal privilege. An atheistic work with a royal stamp of approval! The scandal could be taken as something far more serious than bureaucratic bungling: it suggested that censorship was too important to be left to the royal censors and that outside authorities should have some control over what went on inside the Direction de la librairie.

The Parlement of Paris made the most serious effort to take advantage of the situation. Its attorney general demanded that Tercier retract his approbation, even though the jurisdiction over approbations belonged to Malesherbes, acting in the name of the chancellor and the king. Malesherbes countered this threat by arranging for the privilege of the book to be annulled by an edict of the King's Council. Helvétius was forced to resign an office that he held at court, and Tercier, who had also run afoul of Mme de Pompadour, was dismissed from his position in the ministry of foreign affairs. But the Parlement struck back by forcing Helvétius to disavow his book in a series of humiliating episodes, and it went on to condemn a whole set of Enlightenment works along with *De l'Esprit: La Religion naturelle, poème* (*Natural religion, a poem*), by Voltaire, *Pensées philosophiques* (*Philosophical thoughts*), by Diderot, *La Philosophie du bon sens* (*Good-sense philosophy*), by J.-B. de Boyer, marquis d'Argens, *Pyrrhonisme du sage* (The wise man's pyrrhonism), by Louis de Beausobre, *Lettres semi-philosophiques du chevalier de *** au comte de **** (Semi-philosophical letters from the chevalier de * * * to the comte de * * *), by J.-B. Pascal, *Lettre au R.-P. Berthier sur le matérialisme* (Letter on materialism by the Reverend Father Berthier), by G.-B. Coyer, and the first seven volumes of the *Encyclopédie*. On February 10, 1759, all these books, except for the *Encyclopédie*, were lacerated and burned by the public hangman at the foot of the great staircase of the Parlement. A ceremonial auto-da-fé on such a scale looked like a declaration of war against the Enlightenment.

It could not have occurred at a worse moment. Wild talk about conspiracies and sedition had circulated in Paris and Versailles ever since the half-mad and halfhearted attempt to assassinate Louis XV by Robert-François Damiens on January 5, 1757.[105] Damiens probably was unhinged by the hysteria over Jansenism, which had boiled over in the midst of a dramatic conflict between the Parlement and the crown. Meanwhile, the economy was faltering under the pressure of the Seven Years' War, which drained the treasury and forced the crown to inflict new taxes on its subjects. The war itself turned into a succession of disasters, culminating in the defeat of Rossbach, Frederick II's rout of the combined French and Austrian armies on November 5, 1757. Far from responding with sang froid to the calamities, the government seemed to panic. On April 16, 1757, the King's Council issued a decree threatening to punish with death anyone who wrote, printed, or sold works that merely tended to stir up general feelings ("émouvoir les esprits").[106]

By this time, the stir created by the *Encyclopédie* had given the enemies of the *philosophes* a particularly vulnerable target. Jesuits, Jansenists, and a swarm of polemicists had denounced the impieties and heterodoxies of its first two volumes so vehemently that the King's Council had condemned them in 1752, though without forbidding the publication of the subsequent volumes. In fact, the condemnation had little effect, except to increase sales, which skyrocketed to 4,000 subscriptions. That represented a fortune: 1,120,000 livres at the original subscription price of 280 livres (it eventually came to 980 livres, making the *Encyclopédie* one of the most expensive and probably the most profitable book in the history of French publishing before the nineteenth century).[107] Malesherbes was especially sensitive to the economic aspects of the book industry.[108] He favored the use of tacit permissions in order to prevent capital from seeping across France's borders to foreign publishers. Thanks to his protection, the publication of the *Encyclopédie* continued unabated through volume 7, which appeared in November 1757. Eight months later the storm broke over *De l'Esprit*. Helvétius had not contributed to the *Encyclopédie*, but in his indictment of Enlightenment literature the Parlement's attorney general linked the two books as evidence of a conspiracy to undermine the church and the throne. The Parlement pursued his line of attack, although it spared the *Encyclopédie* from the book burning of February 10, 1759, by banning all sales of the *Encyclopédie* and appointing a commission to investigate it. Malesherbes successfully blocked this move but only by taking charge of the book's suppression. On March 8, an edict of the King's Council revoked the privilege of the *Encyclopédie*. Four months later a royal decree required its publishers to refund 72 livres to each of the subscribers, and Malesherbes ordered the police to raid Diderot's headquarters in order to confiscate all the papers of the gigantic enterprise. While defending its own authority, the state seemed to have opted for a rigorous variety of post-publication censorship.[109]

Before the police raid, however, Malesherbes warned Diderot to remove his papers to a safe place. Diderot replied that he did not know where he could stash so much material on such short notice. Malesherbes obliged by hiding a great deal of it in his own town house. To the outside world, the *Encyclopédie* had been destroyed, but Diderot continued to edit it secretly for the next six years, working with the rump group of collaborators who had not deserted; and the last ten volumes of text came out together in 1765 under the false imprint of Neuchâtel. By then, France had entered a period of peace, the Jansenist controversies had died down, the crown's quarrels with the parlements had subsided, at least briefly, and Enlightenment works continued to be published, although without a royal privilege.[110]

THE BOOK POLICE

By surviving the double scandal of *De l'Esprit* and the *Encyclopédie*, the Enlightenment succeeded in reaching readers at the most dangerous moment of its existence under the Ancien Régime. But that episode, important as it was, can seem so dramatic that it eclipses the more pervasive, long-term aspects of censorship. The events of 1757–59 should not be taken to typify the activities of censors or to make the history of censorship in eighteenth-century France look like a story of the struggle between the *philosophes* and their enemies. It would be more accurate to understand the work of Malesherbes and his men as part of what could be called literary reality—that is, the workaday world inhabited by writers, publishers, booksellers, and influential personages from the court and capital. That world, as described in Malesherbes's *Mémoires sur la librairie* (1759), seemed to be pretty much under control. Yet like many top administrators of the Ancien Régime, Malesherbes had only a vague notion of what was going on outside Paris and Versailles. He did not even know how many cities had inspectors of the book trade (besides Paris only two, Lyon and Rouen) and how many possessed guild offices capable of enforcing royal ordinances (twenty-seven towns had guilds or corporative communities, whose members enjoyed the exclusive privilege to sell books, but only fifteen of them had *chambres syndicales* charged with the responsibility of inspecting all shipments of books). Although he realized that a booming business in illegal books was taking place in the provinces, he had no idea of its extent.

Malesherbes's successor, Antoine de Sartine, who was a far better administrator, tried to get a picture of the realities of the book trade by enlisting the intendants to survey all the booksellers in the kingdom. The result, an extraordinary census that covered 167 towns and was completed in 1764, revealed an enormous industry operating without much concern for the state's attempt to regulate it. That information fed into new regulations intended to create some order in 1777, but like most royal edicts, they had limited effect. Provincial booksellers, both in great cities like Lyon, Rouen, and Marseille and in small towns—Avenches, Bourg-Saint-Andéol, Châteaudun en Dunois, Forges-les-Eaux, Ganges, Joinville, Loudun, Montargis, Nègrepelisse, Tarbes, Valence—plied their trade outside the Parisian range of vision and largely outside the law.[111] About 3,000 dealers of all varieties sold books in the 1770s, yet the quasi-official *Almanach de la librairie* of 1781 lists only 1,004. Most of them lacked authorization. (To operate legally a bookseller had be a member of a guild or at least to have obtained a certificate called a *brevet de libraire*.) They drew a large proportion of their stock from foreign publishers, either directly or through middlemen, and a great deal of it consisted of pirated and prohibited books. We do not have enough data to calculate the proportions, but whatever the statistical balance between the legal and the illegal sector, there was a large disparity between the literature that occupied the censors and the literature that actually circulated in the channels of the book trade.[112]

The authorities were fully aware of this disparity, despite their imperfect information, because they often confiscated illegal books in the Parisian customs and in the required inspections of shipments passing through the provincial *chambres syndicales*. When alerted by informants, they raided bookshops, impounded illegal material, and interrogated the dealers. Police inspectors with special responsibility for the book trade carried out the raids. The most active of them, Joseph d'Hémery, worked closely with Malesherbes and Sartine and developed extraordinarily rich files about every aspect of the publishing industry. Should all this activity be considered a form of post-publication censorship?[113]

To eighteenth-century Frenchmen, it would have been understood as police work. "Police" at that time was a capacious concept, which covered most aspects of municipal administration, including lighting, hygiene, and the provision of food supplies.[114] The Parisian police enjoyed a reputation for perfecting the most modern and well-organized services. In fact, its administration seemed so advanced that it served as a model for treatises on the police, which can be considered as contributions to the literature of Enlightenment. Voltaire referred to "sociétés policées" as social orders that had reached the highest stage of civilization. Nothing could be more misleading than to associate the police of the Bourbon monarchy with the repressive forces of totalitarian regimes. Enlightened or not, however, the literary police of eighteenth-century France confiscated many works of the *philosophes*, along with many more that never made it into literary history but were the primary targets of repression by the state.

To do justice to all aspects of this kind of police work would require a full-length treatise. But its basic character can be understood from a few case studies, which show how inspectors of the book trade (*inspecteurs de la librairie*) handled the task of policing literature. In the course of their rounds, they inspected the great publishing houses and bookstores of the Latin Quarter, but more often the search for illegal books led them into garrets, back rooms, secret printing shops, and clandestine entrepôts, where "bad books" (*mauvais livres*), as the inspectors called them, were produced and distributed. Those books were so bad, in the eyes of the authorities, that there was no question of censoring them. They had to be captured and destroyed—or in some cases walled up in the Bastille, for they existed entirely outside the law.

AN AUTHOR IN THE SERVANTS' QUARTERS

The "inspection" of literature occasionally brought the police into contact with famous authors, but they spent most of their time trailing obscure scribblers who produced the worst of the "bad books." One case illustrates authorship at its most obscure and the detective work used to root out a publishing enterprise from a particularly dangerous site: Versailles itself.[115]

In August 1745, the police discovered that an especially objectionable book about the king's love life, thinly disguised as a fairy tale under the title *Tanastès*, was circulating under the cloak. They picked up a peddler, who told them that he had drawn his stock from a secret entrepôt in Versailles kept by a bookseller named Dubuisson. Dubuisson was promptly whisked off to the Bastille and interrogated. He had got the manuscript, he said, from a certain Mazelin, a valet of the subgoverness of the dauphin; Mazelin had got it from its author, Marie-Madeleine Bonafon, a chambermaid to the princesse de Montauban; and she had parted with it in return for 200 copies of the edition that Dubuisson had arranged to have printed in Rouen, in the shop of the widow Ferrand.

One detachment of police went back to Versailles for Mazelin and Mlle Bonafon; another set off for Ferrand's shop in Rouen; and meanwhile the inspectors continued to haul in peddlers from the streets in Paris. In the end, they filled the Bastille with twenty-one voluble prisoners, whose interrogations reveal a great deal about underground publishing. The most revealing testimony came from the author, Mlle Bonafon. On August 29, after spending two nights alone in a cell, she was led before Claude-Henri Feydeau de Marville, the lieutenant general of police.

The lieutenant general was one of France's top officials, roughly the equivalent of the minister of the interior today. He did not personally interrogate prisoners in the Bastille, except in important affairs of state. In this case, he evidently smelled something suspicious, because chambermaids did not write political novels; in fact, they did not write at all. Marville therefore prepared the interrogation carefully and conducted it like a cat-and-mouse game. He laid traps; Mlle Bonafon tried to avoid them; and the transcript of the interrogation recorded all their moves, for it was written in the form of a dialogue: question-answer, question-answer, each page initialed by Mlle Bonafon as testimony to its accuracy.[116]

Marville got through the preliminaries quickly: Mlle Bonafon took an oath to tell the truth and identified herself as a native of Versailles, twenty-eight years old, employed for the last five years as chambermaid to the princesse de Montauban. Then he came immediately to the point: Had she written any books?

Yes, she said: *Tanastès*, and the beginning of another one, *Le Baron de xxx*, and also a play, which had never been performed and was now in the keeping of the son of Minet of the Comédie française. (She later said that she had also completed the drafts of two other plays, *Les Dons* and *Le Demi-Savant*, and had composed a good deal of poetry.)

"Asked what it was that gave her a taste for writing? Hadn't she consulted someone who was familiar with the composition of books in order to learn how to go about organizing the ones she intended to write?"

"Answered that she did not consult anyone; that since she reads a great deal, this had given her a desire to write; that she had imagined, moreover, that she could make a little money by writing; that no one had taught her the rules of the theater, but that she had learned them herself by reading plays; that she had in fact consulted Minet a few times for her play, *Le Destin*, but as to the other novel she had mentioned, she had worked on it all by herself; that she had never spoken about *Tanastès* to anyone except sieur Mazelin so that he could find someone who would take charge of getting it printed for her."

It was an extraordinary moment: a female servant telling the head of the police force, one of the most powerful men in the kingdom, that she had written a novel because she wanted to write a novel and that she had done it on her own, without help from anyone. The lieutenant general could not take it in. "Had she written the book out of her own imagination?" he asked. "Hadn't someone supplied her with written material to work over? Who was it that had given [that material] to her?" "Replied that no memoirs had been given to her, that she had composed her book by herself, that in fact she had fashioned it in her imagination." Marville did not stop at these general disclaimers. He demanded precise information about the production and diffusion of the book. (Here I will paraphrase the interrogation, keeping close to the wording in the transcript.)

When had she written it?

    In December–January and in March 1745.

What were the arrangements for its publication?

    Mazelin had delivered the manuscript to Dubuisson, who had promised to give her 200 copies in exchange for it. Dubuisson or someone in his employ must have provided the Latin epigraph, the preface, and the notes, which were not her work.

Where was it printed?

    In Rouen, according to Mazelin.

What had she done with her 200 copies?

    She had burned them.

When?

    After she heard that the police had arrested Dubuisson.

At this point, the questioning entered into dangerous territory, because it began to cut into Bonafon's defense. Although she could not deny her authorship of *Tanastès*, she attempted to represent the book as an innocent romance vaguely inspired by the common gossip of the court. Meanwhile, Marville tried to lure her into admitting that she had known all along that it was a scandalous attack on the king. The fact that she had waited until the last minute to destroy her copies demonstrated her intention to profit from the scandal that she had knowingly exploited. So while Bonafon withdrew behind her version of the affair, Marville circled round it, aiming questions at its weak points.

Didn't Mazelin warn her, when he first read the manuscript, that it could lend itself to "mauvaises applications" or dangerous parallels with current affairs?

    Yes, but she had assured Mazelin that it was merely a story and that many such stories appeared every day without giving rise to "applications."

If Mazelin had warned her of the danger, why did she persist in getting the book published?

She had been wrong, she admitted, but she did not see anything sinister in the "applications." She went ahead with the publication only because ". . . she was so hard pressed for money."

Wasn't there a key to the story? Wasn't one joined to the copies she had received?

No: she had seen a key three weeks ago, a manuscript attached to some copies on sale in Dubuisson's stall in Versailles, but she had nothing to do with it.

That remark exposed a weak flank in Mlle Bonafon's defense, and Marville immediately attacked.

So! Long before she had burned her copies, she knew all about the "applications"; yet she had persisted in her plans to sell the book. Indeed, she would have sold off her entire stock had Dubuisson not been arrested. She was guilty of manufacturing and diffusing "the most indecent work in the world"! Wasn't she herself the author of the key? Or was it Mazelin? The precautions they took to camouflage their operation proved that they knew how wicked it was.

Not at all, she replied. She had resorted to secrecy only because she did not want to be known as an author. It was her desperate need for money that had compelled her to publish the book; and she certainly had not written the key, nor did she believe that Mazelin had supplied it.

Marville broke off the interrogation at this point. He had extracted enough information to prove Mlle Bonafon's complicity in a criminal variety of literature, but he suspected there was more to the story than she would admit; for what business did a servant, a female domestic servant, have to do with the writing of novels? To get to the story behind the story, he would have to interrogate the other prisoners in the Bastille; and he had quite a collection of them.

Eventually the lieutenant general and his assistants worked their way through all twenty-one cases, imprisoning some of the suspects, exiling others, and freeing the occasional peddler and printer's devil. They acquired a complete knowledge of the underground network linking Rouen, Versailles, and Paris. But their main concern remained the mystery of authorship—of the key as well as the novel—so they concentrated on Mlle Bonafon. They called her back for two more interrogations, continuing to lay traps, which she continued to avoid. But they made more progress with her collaborators. When they extracted some compromising information from one suspect, they cross-examined another, holding the information back until they caught him in a lie. Then they hit him with his accomplice's testimony in an attempt to provoke a confession. They also tried to break through the prisoners' defenses by a technique known as "confrontation." They summoned Mlle Bonafon and Mazelin from their separate cells and then read the testimony of each to the other, trying to touch off mutual recriminations. When this got them nowhere, they summoned Dubuisson and did the same. His story about the key to the novel flatly contradicted theirs, but no one would back down; so the investigation remained stalled for several days, until at last the interrogators got Maillard, the concierge of the marquis de Prye, to break down. He admitted that he had operated a secret entrepôt in the marquis's town house in Paris. He had supplied the Parisian peddlers, and he had drawn his own stock from Versailles: forty-five copies came from Mazelin and twenty-five from Mlle Bonafon, who was to receive three livres tournois for every copy sold. (A livre, the most common unit of currency, was roughly worth the equivalent of a day's work by an unskilled laborer around 1750.) The package sent by Bonafon included the key, written out in her hand.

Maillard's confession armed the lieutenant general with the information he needed in his third interrogation of Mlle Bonafon. He kept it concealed at first, while he asked the usual questions about the key and got the usual denials. Then he pounced.

Did Mlle Bonafon know a certain Maillard, concierge of the marquis de Prye?

She had seen him once with Mme de Prye in Versailles.

Had she ever written to Maillard or transmitted copies of *Tanastès* to him?

No.

She was lying. He knew full well that she had sent twenty-five copies to Maillard and had been involved in a shipment of forty-five others, hoping to collect three livres from each sale.

At this point, the last bulwark in Mlle Bonafon's defense collapsed, and she had no recourse but to confess, keeping back as much information as she could.

> Yes, she admitted, it was true: she had tried to make some money from the copies that had remained at her disposal. She had confided them to a servant of the prince de Constantin, who had taken them past the customs without difficulty in the prince's carriage.

Had she sent a key in the package?

> Yes, she could not deny it. Maillard needed the key to sell the book; so she wrote it out in her own hand and gave it to Mazelin for Maillard—but with the proviso that it was for Maillard's information only and not to be distributed with the books.

Marville then produced a piece of paper covered with handwriting. Was this the key?

> Yes, she confessed; it was the very copy that she had sent to Maillard, in her own hand. All she could say in defense of herself was that she never made any money from the book.

Brushing this excuse aside, Marville delivered a lecture.

"Brought it to her attention that since her detention she has developed a system of admitting to some of the facts held against her and denying the others." She was guilty of producing and distributing the

most disrespectful and dangerous kind of literature. She had tried to
enrich herself by slandering the crown. And she could expect to stay
in prison until it pleased the crown to accord her grace.

In fact, Mlle Bonafon remained in the Bastille for fourteen and a half
months. Her health deteriorated so badly that, according to a report from
the Bastille's governor, she seemed likely to die unless she were transferred
to a healthier site. She was therefore shut up in the convent of the Bernar-
dines at Moulins, where she remained, without permission to receive either
visitors or letters, for the next twelve years.

Why select this case from the hundreds that fill the archives of the
Bastille? To a modern reader (this is speculation, as I probably am the only
one who has read the text for the last 250 years), *Tanastès* is likely to seem
insipid. But to eighteenth-century readers armed with the key, it was sen-
sational, because it was the first work to reveal the sex life of Louis XV
and the court intrigues that accompanied it. True, gossip in Versailles had
kept the court informed about the king's affairs, from his stumbling start
with the three daughters of the marquis de Nesle (especially the much-
hated duchesse de Châteauroux, who had accompanied Louis to the front
at Metz during the War of the Austrian Succession) to the elevation of
Mme de Pompadour as "maîtresse en titre"; but *Tanastès* exposed everything in print. With help from the key—Tanastès is Louis XV; Oromal,
the cardinal de Fleury; Amariel, the bishop of Soissons, etc.—any reader
could decode the play of power and sex at the heart of the French monarchy. That was how the police read the book. In a report to the government
about their investigation, they wrote,

> This book is an allegorical fairy story from which it is easy to
> make offensive applications to the king, the queen, Mme de Châte-
> auroux, the duc de Richelieu, the cardinal de Fleury, and other gran-
> dees and ladies of the court. It gives an account of what happened
> during the king's illness at Metz in 1744; the renunciation of Mme de
> Châteauroux; her return to favor and her reestablishment; her illness,
> her death, and the new choice of Mme de Pompadour.[117]

This was literary lèse-majesté.

More remarkable, from the perspective of the state's attempt to control the printed word, the entire operation was conducted from the servants' quarters. The author, her go-between (Mazelin), the smuggler (a servant of the prince de Constantin), and the distributor (Maillard) all served the aristocracy in various capacities. Dubuisson was one of many book dealers who did business in Versailles, keeping forbidden works in secret storerooms and selling them under the counter or peddling them "under the cloak" ("sous le manteau," in common parlance). The palace was honeycombed with outlets of the literary underground. And some of the undercover agents were women. The lieutenant general of police could hardly believe that a chambermaid had written a seditious roman à clef, yet Mlle Bonafon had a whole oeuvre behind her—poems and plays as well as her novel. Moreover, *Tanastès* was produced in a printing shop run by a woman, the widow Ferrand in Rouen. Like many widows in the book trade, she had taken over her husband's business after his death. The literary police turned up enough obscure and unexpected characters to suggest that literature, broadly conceived to include all phases in the production and diffusion of books, extended deeper into the society of the Ancien Régime than ever imagined in the great-men, great-books version of literary history.

A DISTRIBUTION SYSTEM: CAPILLARIES AND ARTERIES

The "inspection" of books often began at a final point in their diffusion and then worked its way upstream to warehouse keepers, wagon drivers, printers, publishers, and authors. In order to follow leads in repressing illegal literature, the police had to know their way around the capillary networks of the trade—the back rooms, peddlers' routes, and outdoor stalls, where the poorest population of the literary world tried to scrape together a living. Penury often led to criminality, because the greatest profits were to be made where the risks were greatest—in the illegal trade. The police often arrested marginal dealers who operated in the riskiest sector, struggling to make supply meet demand, and the archives of the

Bastille abound in stories about these "poor devils" ("pauvres diables") at the bottom of the book trade.

The dossier of a Parisian *bouquiniste* (a small-time bookseller who usually operated from an outdoor stall) contains the richest run of information about this aspect of the distribution system. Louise Manichel, known in the trade as "la fille La Marche," ran a stall located in a passageway that connected the garden of the Palais-Royal with the rue de Richelieu in the heart of Paris. Long before Balzac celebrated it in *Les Illusions perdues*, the Palais-Royal had become a vital outlet for the publishing industry. It embodied another aspect of the privilege system peculiar to the Ancien Régime. Because it belonged to the duc d'Orléans, a member of the royal family, it was a "lieu privilégié" (privileged place) outside the range of the police. The inspectors and their spies could examine the wares on sale in the stalls scattered throughout its gardens, but they could not conduct raids and make arrests without obtaining prior authorization from the palace's governor, who usually delayed things long enough for the culprits to escape. As a result, the Palais-Royal, whose grounds were open to everyone in Paris, provided shelter for all sorts of dubious activities—prostitution, gambling, political gossip, and the sale of illegal books. La fille La Marche offered the choicest items to a public hungry for information about ministerial intrigue, the royal sex life, and all forms of libertinism, the philosophical as well as the erotic.

She had no right to do so. In principle, all peddlers and *bouquinistes* had to receive permission from the police and to register with the Direction de la librairie, but the Palais-Royal covered her and several other tiny retailers with its mantle of privilege. They set up stands (*étalages*) under the arcades surrounding the garden and in all the connecting allies and passageways. As occasions arose, they traded among themselves, undercut one another, and made alliances with their counterparts in other relatively safe locations such as the Louvre and the Palais de Justice. They usually drew their stock from marginal booksellers in Paris, who were supplied by clandestine entrepôts and presses in the provinces or abroad. La Marche knew all the tricks of the trade. She had worked in it since she was a young girl, and she inherited her boutique from her mother, who had run it until she died in 1771. Her father, known to the police as "a bad subject who sold very bad books,"[118] ran a similar microbusiness at another site until his health gave out at the age of seventy-four, and her sister peddled "bad books" until the police shut her up in the prison of Fort l'Eveque sometime in the early 1770s. Whether the members of this family read the books they sold seems unlikely. La Marche was not illiterate, but her letters from the Bastille were written in a primitive scrawl and spelled so badly that one often has to read them aloud and listen to the sounds in order to puzzle out their meaning.

In December 1774, the date of the first item in her dossier, La Marche was thirty-eight. She lived with a widow who worked for her as a servant in a sixth-floor flat at the back of a building over a tobacco shop in the rue Saint Honoré—that is, in cheap lodgings, for economic distinctions tended to be vertical in Parisian real estate: the higher the floor, the poorer the tenant. Pierre-Auguste Goupil, inspector of the book trade, began laying a trap for her after he received a report from a spy who had bought an illegal work from her stand and described the milieu that frequented it:

> All the noblemen who seek out the latest publications, book lovers who have them delivered, or women who want them available on their dressing table have recourse to this woman. She always has something to pique their curiosity: *Lettre à un duc et pair* [Letter to a duke and peer], *Lettre du sieur de Sorhouet au sieur de Maupeou* [Letter from Sire de Sorhouet to Sire de Maupeou], *Mémoires authentiques de la vie de Mme. du Barry* [Authentic memoirs of the life of Mme du Barry] *Les soirées du Roi de Prusse* [The king of Prussia's evenings], etc. She lacks nothing and sells everything.[119]

As the titles indicate, La Marche dealt heavily in political pamphlets and scandalous works, many of them aimed against the ministry of Chancellor René-Nicolas-Charles-Augustin de Maupeou, who had provoked a tidal wave of protest literature from 1771 to 1774 by his reorganization of the judicial system in a way that enforced the arbitrary power of the crown. The government did everything possible to suppress these publications, even after the fall of the Maupeou ministry and the advent of Louis XVI in May 1774. One pamphlet that it particularly wanted to eradicate was *Lettre de M. l'abbé Terray à M. Turgot*, which linked the anti-Maupeou protests to the new ministry of Anne-Robert-Jacques Turgot. The lieutenant general of police, Jean-Charles-Pierre Lenoir, ordered Goupil to find the trail of this pamphlet, and Goupil complied by purchasing two copies of it, through a spy, from La Marche's boutique. He then sent another report on her business:

> The demoiselle La Marche continues to sell the *Lettre de M. l'abbé Terray à M. Turgot* in the Palais-Royal. People flock to her boutique as if they were going to a new play, and that creates a sensational effect. Moreover, this pamphlet touches off talk about the persons who are compromised in it; and although it is rather poorly written, the salt of the wickedness that is spread throughout it makes it sold and read.[120]

While tracking books, the police took note of their effect on the Parisian public. A clever pamphlet and a strategically located boutique could stir up undesirable currents of public opinion, and La Marche knew how to play on the sensibility of her customers. Goupil said that she tried to entice his undercover agent with the following sales talk:

> Lowering her voice, she asked him whether he knew *Vie de Mme. du Barry*. "Of course," he replied. "Why?" "Because I still have several copies of 200 that I got from Flanders two weeks ago." Then she added in a teasing tone, "Have you seen this new work? It's the *Bréviaire des chanoines de Rouen* [Breviary of the canons of Rouen]. It comes from the same place." And right away she pulled out from under her stall the book that I enclose, for which she charged 2 livres 8 sous. As you can see, Monsieur, it is a compilation of indecencies well suited for the corruption of morals.[121]

Goupil recommended that he be authorized to raid La Marche's apartment, where he believed she stored her forbidden books and where they might find clues to her sources of supply. Lenoir's dispatched him to make such a "perquisition," and at ten o'clock in the evening of January 23, 1775, Goupil, accompanied by Pierre Chénon, an official (*commissaire*) from the Châtelet court who often collaborated with the book police, entered La Marche's flat. They made a thorough search but turned up only three copies of the *Lettre de M. Terray*, two copies of a pornographic tract, *Le Volupteux hors de combat* (The voluptuary wiped out), and a primitive account book. The following night at eleven o'clock they returned with a *lettre de cachet* for her arrest and carried her off to the Bastille.

La Marche remained in a cell, cut off from all contact with the outside world until January 27, when Chénon conducted the first of two interrogations. He had cross-examined many peddlers and booksellers of her stripe, and he usually did not push his questions very hard when he first confronted them so that he could confound them in later sessions with evidence produced by subsequent detective work. When asked for information about her suppliers, La Marche replied vaguely about men who turned up at her stall with packages and reappeared a few days later to collect payment. She could not provide names or anything in the way of descriptions beyond "medium height" and "a somewhat downcast look." She sold the same works as all the other *bouquinistes* in the Palais-Royal, she said, and she assumed that they were tolerated by the police; but she knew little about their contents, as she never read them. She had no idea that the *Lettre de M. Terray* was prohibited. Her customers had asked her for it; and when an unknown man appeared with a dozen copies in his pocket, she bought them. He kept coming back and she kept selling them until she had disposed of about a hundred copies. Chénon tried to trap her by pointing to entries in her account book, which referred to 500 copies of a "brochure" but she replied that "brochure" was a general term that she used when she summarized her sales at the end of the day. She could not remember what works were covered by that omnibus expression, and she never entered the titles of books in her accounts. Hadn't she also sold *Vie de Madame la comtesse du Barry*? Chénon asked. Only two copies, she replied. She had purchased them from one of her customers, who happened to have a few extra copies that he did not need. She did not know his name or address and could describe him only as a gentleman, about fifty years old.[122]

Chénon broke off the interrogation at that point. He knew from experience that the defense of prisoners often crumbled, despite an initial attempt to deny everything, once they had spent enough time isolated and abandoned in a damp and dingy cell. La Marche sounded desperate in a letter that she wrote to Lenoir on the day after her interrogation. She was the sole source of income for her family, she said. Her father was ailing, her sister helpless, her servant ill, and her business, on which they all depended, about to be ruined. Her letter, which deserves to be transposed as well as translated, indicates her level of literacy as well as her state of mind:

> La supliente in plor votre juistise vous prit de l'a regardé dun neuille de pitié je suis comme unemer de famille qui abesoins daitre ala taite de ses affair je un per de soisante e quinsans son et-tat nes pas sufisans pour le fair subsité et une seurs qui es dan la paine elle napoint dautre secour que de moy, je . . . ne ces de vercé des larme de sens
>
> [La suppliante implore votre justice [et] vous prie de la regarder d'un œil de pitié. Je suis comme une mère de famille qui a besoin d'être à la tête de ses affaires. J'ai un père de soixante et quinze ans. Son état n'est pas suffisant pour le faire subsister, et [j'ai] une sœur qui est dans la peine. Elle n'a point d'autre secours que moi. Je . . . ne cesse de verser des larmes de sang.]
>
> [The suppliant implores your justice [and] begs you to look upon her with an eye of pity. I am like a mother of a family who needs to be at the head of her affairs. I have a father, seventy-five years old. His occupation does not provide enough for him to subsist, and [I have] a sister who is suffering. She has no resource, except for me. I . . . do not cease to weep tears of blood.][123]

Meanwhile, the police pursued other leads. With the help of spies and subordinates, Goupil discovered that the *Lettre de M. l'abbé Terray à M. Turgot* had been distributed by "la femme Mequignon," a *bouquiniste* in the Cour de mai of the Palais de Justice, who peddled it in private homes and sold small allotments of it to her colleagues in other locations, notably the Palais-Royal. She told one of Goupil's agents, who bought a few copies from her, that she had struck a secret deal with the printer who had produced it. He agreed to let her be its sole distributer in Paris in return for a share of her profits. The secrecy was intended to protect her from her husband as well as the police, she explained, because if he learned about the money she was making, he would demand a cut of his own.[124] In his report to Lenoir, Goupil recommended that they use this information to locate the printer, who was apparently working on a second edition, which would include more fictitious letters designed to compromise the reputations of public personages.

At the same time, the police found the trail of the other work that worried their superiors in Versailles: *Vie de Madame la comtesse du Barry, suivie de ses correspondances épistolaires et de ses intrigues galantes et politiques* (Life of Mme the Countess du Barry, followed by her epistolary exchanges and her amorous and political intrigues). It was sold under the cloak by a father-and-son team: Desauges père and fils, who peddled books from their apartment in the rue de Souarre and operated a small boutique in the Place du Louvre under a gateway at the rue Fromanteau. Both were arrested and kept incommunicado in separate cells of the Bastille. Unfortunately, the transcripts of their interrogations are missing (there is only a reference to a marathon session that Chénon conducted with Desauges père until eight in the evening of February 2),[125] but the archives contain many of the letters that they wrote and received. After working through all the evidence, Chénon had enough information to destroy La Marche's defenses in her second interrogation.

He began with a question about the *Vie de Madame la comtesse du Barry.* Was she determined to reaffirm her earlier assertion about how she had acquired it? Certainly, she replied. She had bought her copies from an unknown gentleman. Wasn't it rather from the peddler Desauges? he countered. At that point, La Marche realized that she could not sustain her story. Yes, she admitted, she had held back his name only because "his suffering would not have alleviated hers." Desauges père had supplied her with a dozen copies for five livres each, and she had sold them for six livres apiece. And the *Lettre de M. l'abbé Terray*? She admitted that she had got it from Mequignon—("sieur Mequignon," so apparently the wife had failed in her attempt to hide her income from the husband). There was nothing more to extract from La Marche, and Chénon sent her back to her cell.

At this point the investigation shifted from the microscopic businesses in Paris to the larger world of the book trade. Among the dozens of letters that the police confiscated during their raid in the Desauges apartment, several indicated that Desauges père, who had been peddling books for thirty-three years, drew much of his stock from a dealer in Versailles named Ravinet and that Ravinet relayed shipments Desauges ordered from provincial wholesalers, particularly Jacques Manoury in Caen, Abraham Lucas in Rouen, and a bookseller named Walle, who directed the business of the Veuve l'Ecorché in Bayeux. Goupil and Chénon set out for Normandy in mid-February 1775.

The Parisian book police conducted raids in the provinces when they had accumulated evidence of large-scale violations of the law or when the government ordered them to repress hostile publications.[126] Such missions required careful preparation: advance reconnoitering by spies, cooperation from intendants and their *subdélégués*, assistance from the local police, and reinforcements, if necessary, from the mounted constabulary (*maréchaussée*), all of it cloaked in secrecy so that the suspects would be taken by surprise. On February 20, Goupil and Chénon, accompanied by a local police officer, arrived in the bookstore of Abraham Lucas on the quai de Caen at the sign of Saint Luc in Rouen. They searched the shop and the living quarters above it but found nothing suspicious. Then they summoned Lucas, warned him that they knew he dealt heavily in forbidden books, and demanded to know where he stored them. A tough, sixty-five-year-old veteran of the trade (he had done time in the Bastille in 1771), he refused to be intimidated. But while he was insisting on his innocence, they noticed a hole in the ceiling of the top floor. Lucas claimed that it led to the attic, which served as a bedroom for a servant. But they decided to see for themselves. After climbing up a ladder, they discovered a chest full of highly illegal works such as the pornographic

Histoire de dom B . . . , portier des Chartreux (The story of dom B . . . , porter of the Carthusians) and the atheistic *Christianisme dévoilé* (Christianity
unveiled). They confiscated all of Lucas's accounts and correspondence,
along with the forbidden books, then arrested him and sent him off to the
Bastille under the guard of the police officer.[127]

Three days later, they burst into the bookstore of Jacques Manoury, "A
la Source des Sciences," Place Saint-Sauveur in Caen. While a brigadier
from the constabulary stood guard, they searched the premises and turned
up a large collection of political, pornographic, and irreligious works,
including *Vie de Madame la comtesse du Barry*. They suspected Manoury
of arranging for their publication, but he denied having any connection
with a printing shop. Although only thirty-four, he, too, had many years
of experience in the underground trade and had spent four months in
the Bastille in 1771 for publishing antigovernment tracts. He begged to be
spared the Bastille this time, because he and his wife were ill. In fact, she
was in imminent danger of dying, as was attested by a local doctor whom
they found administering to her at her bedside. Goupil and Chénon therefore agreed to suspend the order for Manoury's arrest; and after impound-
ing his papers and shipping his books to Paris, they set off for their next
stop, the bookstore run by Walle in Bayeux.[128]

The report on that raid is missing from the archives, but Goupil and
Chénon must have found plenty of incriminating evidence, because they
sent Walle to the Bastille accompanied by an armed guard. A local notable
tried to soften the blow by appealing for clemency in a letter to Lenoir.
He claimed that Walle was nothing more than a clerk ("garçon de boutique"), who had no knowledge of books and sold whatever the wholesalers (mainly, in fact, Manoury) offered him without knowing how to set
prices. Yet he had to support the widow l'Ecorché, who had inherited the
store, and her six children, who would be reduced to indigence if he were
not soon permitted to resume the business.[129] Walle's correspondence with
Desauges, which the police had captured while raiding Desauges's apartment, made him look less innocent.[130] But Goupil and Chénon did not
pause over his case, because they had to hurry back to Caen in order to
interrogate Manoury.

They arrived on February 25 and conducted the interrogation at their inn, the Auberge du Palais Royal. The only surviving documentation of it is a list of the books they had seized in his shop.[131] Although it is badly torn, it contains enough titles to demonstrate that Manoury did a large trade in every variety of illegal literature. Along with standard pornography (*Histoire de dom B . . .*, *Thérèse philosophe*), they included much of the recent protest literature directed against the Maupeou ministry:

14 [copies] *Thérèse philosophe* (Thérèse the philosopher)

65 *Haquenettes ou étrennes au seigneur de Maupeou* (The Harpies, or New Year's gifts to Sire de Maupeou)

3 *Margot la ravaudeuse* (Margot, seamstress of old clothes)

2 *Réflexions impartiales sur l'Evangile* (Impartial reflections on the Gospel)

1 *Traité des erreurs populaires* (Treatise on common errors)

2 *Lettres philosophiques par M. de Voltaire* (Philosophical letters by M. de Voltaire)

7 *Le Compère Mathieu, ou les bigarrures de l'esprit humain* (Brother Mathieu, or the motley character of the human mind)

4 *Le Colporteur, histoire morale et critique* (The peddler, a moral and critical story)

7 *Grigri, histoire véritable traduite du japonais* (Grigri, a true story translated from the Japanese)

2 *L'Académie des dames, ou les entretiens galants d'Aloysia* (The ladies' academy, or Aloysia's bawdy talk)

10 *Histoire de dom B . . . , portier des Chartreux* (The story of dom B . . . , porter of the Carthusians)

1 *La Gazette de Cythère, ou histoire secrète de Mme la comtesse du Barry* (The gazette of Cythera, or the secret story of Mme the Countess du Barry)

4 *Vie de Madame la comtesse du Barry* (Life of Madame the Countess du Barry)

92 *Oraison funèbre des conseils supérieurs* (Funeral oration of the high courts [i.e., those established by Maupeou])

42 *Haute messe célébrée par l'abbé Perchel, conseiller-clerc du ci-devant soi-disant conseil supérieur de Rouen* (High mass celebrated by abbé Perchel, clerical councillor of the former, so-called high court of Rouen)

118 *Derniers soupirs du soi-disant parlement* (The last breath of the so-called parlement)

Goupil and Chénon did not dispatch Manoury to prison, perhaps because of his illness and the desperate state of his wife. In the end, therefore, only Lucas and Walle joined La Marche and Desauges père and fils in the Bastille. But the haul of correspondence and account books provided plenty of evidence for the police to reconstruct a business network that extended from London to Geneva.

It would be tedious to describe all the ties that held the network together and all the books that circulated in it. The best way to enjoy a view of the trade at the opposite extreme from the *bouquinistes* of Paris is to consult the papers seized in the shop of Manoury—seven thick bundles that Goupil deposited in the archives of the Bastille.

Jacques Manoury directed one of the largest book businesses in provincial France. He belonged to a dynasty of booksellers established in Caen since the beginning of the century. His father ran a bookstore in the rue Notre Dame in the center of the city and dominated the trade throughout the surrounding area. As the oldest son and likely heir to the business, Jacques learned the trade from his father. He was received as a master in the local guild at the unusually young age of eighteen. During his twenties, while continuing to work in his father's shop, he began to speculate on his own, mainly in the clandestine sector. He first appeared in the records of the police in 1770, when he made a business trip to Paris. They noted that he was staying in an upscale inn (Hôtel du Saint-Esprit, rue de l'Hirondelle, a room on the second floor with a view of the courtyard) and that he had sold two copies of the atheistic *Système de la nature*, which at that time was one of the most sought-after and dangerous works in print, to an undercover agent of inspector Joseph d'Hémery. D'Hémery did not arrest Manoury, but put him down in the files as "a young man, about thirty years old, tall, wearing a sword or hunting knife, hair dressed in the bourse style, grayish frock coat."[132] Manoury was not to be confused with the flotsam and jetsam of the literary underground. He had the air of a gentleman.

A year later, on a mission very similar to that of Goupil in 1775, d'Hémery raided a series of bookstores and printing shops in Caen, Avranches, Saint-Malo, Alençon, and Le Mans. On May 4, 1771, with two local police officers and four members of the constabulary, he descended on the shop of Manoury's father. They inspected every inch of the premises, which consisted of a large sales room, several adjoining rooms on the ground floor, living quarters upstairs, and, on the far side of a courtyard, two storerooms full of books. They found nothing suspect, but they knew from a report by one of their spies that young Manoury had been involved in the publication of Le Procès instruit extraordinairement contre M. de Caradeuc (The extraordinary trial of M. de Caradeuc), a four-volume, anti-government tract related to the political crisis known as the Brittany affair. Louis-René de Caradeuc de la Chalotais, the general attorney of the Parlement de Rennes, had led the Parlement's resistance to various measures, mostly fiscal, of the crown. His imprisonment by lettre de cachet in 1765 touched off a flood of protests by "patriots" against what they construed as royal despotism, and d'Hémery's raids were intended to repress their publications. Armed with a lettre de cachet for Manoury's arrest, they sent him, "very upset and trembling," to spend the night cut off from all contacts in a local prison. (Manoury père was not implicated.) During his interrogation on the following day, he admitted only that he had sold 400 copies of the book. But four days later d'Hémery raided the printing shop of Jean-Zacarie Malassis in Alençon, who confessed that he had run off 1,500 copies on commission for Manoury and a bookseller in Saint-Malo named Hovius. Manoury had picked them up, saying that he intended to ship them to an entrepôt outside Paris and then to market them in the capital. The confession of Malassis, confirmed by further investigation, led to Manoury's detention in the Bastille: four and a half months behind bars and, as he later explained, 20,000 livres in losses.[133]

Only a substantial merchant could withstand such a financial blow. By 1775, Manoury had not only recovered but had established a business of his own on the Place Saint-Sauveur in Caen. A handsomely printed circular described it as follows:

A LA SOURCE DES SCIENCES

J. Manoury, fils aîné, bookseller in Caen, offers a numerous collection of books in all genres, rare and singular, suitable for satisfying book lovers and for supplying great libraries with some of the works they lack.

As he corresponds with the main booksellers in Paris, in France, and in all of Europe, he can always supply not only all the new books announced in journals but even rare works from the modern and the antiquarian trade.[134]

While serving local customers from his shop in Caen, Manoury concentrated on the wholesale trade. His correspondence shows that he supplied retailers in Lille, Rouen, Fougères, Bayeux, Saint-Malo, Rennes, Le Mans, Alençon, Compiègne, and other towns in northwestern France as well as Desauges père in Paris. He also published books, commissioning printers in Rouen, Saint-Malo, Nantes, and an "île anglaise," probably Jersey.[135] With entire editions at his command, he could market books by the hundreds and exchange them, in order to vary his stock, for works produced by other wholesaler-publishers. He corresponded with the most important houses in Amsterdam, The Hague, Geneva, and Neuchâtel.[136] A contact in London offered to provide him with several hundred copies of the antigovernment French tracts being printed there—at a reduced price with a shilling a copy to cover "insurance," in case they were confiscated in France.[137] And a book dealer in Lyon, Gabriel Regnault, held out the promise of equally dangerous and lucrative speculations:

I cannot take your *Trois imposteurs* [Three imposters (an attack on Moses, Jesus, and Mohammed)], as I am having an edition of it printed, nor the *Dom B . . .* , because I have a half interest in an edition that is nearly finished. As for the *Pensées théologiques* [Theological thoughts], I am still overloaded with an old edition. Concerning your [query about] the *Cythères* [i.e., Gazette of Cythera, or the secret story of Mme the Countess du Barry], I don't know whether it refers to some that I procured by exchange from Rouen or to an edition I am about to finish printing, of which I include a title page. If you don't have it, . . . you will be among the first served. . . . *Maupeouana* [i.e., an anthology of works against Maupeou], 2 volumes in-octavo: I am doing an edition, along with *La Fille de joie* [The woman of pleasure], illustrated, and others, which I will offer to you in due time. . . . Once we have established ties, we could certainly do joint publications. . . . I consume a great quantity of these items, and I print only large pressruns, which, however, does not prevent me from doing second editions. . . . You can be sure of my discretion.[138]

In some cases, one can reconstruct each stage in the diffusion process. For example, in May 1774 Regnault commissioned Jacques-Benjamin Téron, a marginal bookseller and printer in Geneva, to produce a three-volume edition of *Journal historique de la révolution opérée dans la constitution de la monarchie françoise par M. de Maupeou* (Historical journal of the revolution in the constitution of the French monarchy produced by M. de Maupeou), one of the most important antigovernment publications during the last years of Louis XV's reign. Regnault (in Lyon) sent 100 copies of it to Manoury (in Caen) in January 1775, taking care to avoid mentioning it by name in a letter that announced the shipment and ended with a P.S.: "Tear this up immediately." (I have found a surprising number of incriminating letters that end with "Burn this" and "Destroy this.") Manoury informed Walle (in Bayeux) that he expected it to arrive in two crates during the first week of February. And on February 24, Walle offered to sell it to one of his clients, a nobleman who lived in a château near Isigny, Normandy, stressing "your taste for literature and especially for patriotism." The correspondence even indicates the increases in price, as the books passed from publisher to wholesaler, retailer, and reader. Regnault sold the *Journal historique* to Manoury for six livres a copy; Regnault sold it to Walle for nine livres; and Walle sold it to his customer for fifteen livres.

There was a great deal of money to be made in the illegal trade, but there were equally great risks—at every level, including that of the largest bookseller-publishers. After running up a debt of 3,000 livres with Manoury—and, no doubt, far more with other suppliers—Regnault disappeared. Clandestine entrepreneurs often went bankrupt. When their speculations outran their resources, they suspended payments and tried to cut deals with their creditors, playing some off against the others—or simply took to the road, abandoning wives and children. Manoury himself went bankrupt at the end of 1778. By arrangements with his creditors, he reestablished his business and apparently continued to market illegal works, his "main line of business"[139] until 1789 or later. But he never regained his reputation among the bankers who paid off the booksellers' bills of exchange. One of them warned the Société typographique de Neuchâtel, a Swiss publisher who had supplied him with many shipments of illegal books, "This man is not at all solid. Beware of exposing yourself to him."[140]

Manoury's greatest problem was squeezing money from retailers like Desauges, who always found an excuse to avoid paying their bills. In January 1775, for example, Desauges sent several orders for the antigovernment tract *Oraison funèbre du conseil supérieur* (Funeral oration of the high court). His customers, he said, "torment [him] like the devil to get it."[141] He successfully smuggled a first batch into Paris from his secret entrepôt in Versailles, but the police captured a second shipment on the outskirts of the city. He asked that Manoury, in his capacity of supplier, share the cost of that loss and send more, along with 100 copies of *Histoire de la vie de Mme la comtesse du Barry*: "Send it as fast as possible. Otherwise, it won't be worth anything, because it's crucial to sell this quickly and without attracting any notice. Add 12 *Portier des Chartreux* [Histoire de dom B . . . , portier des Chartreux], 6 *Nonnes éclairées* [The enlightened nuns, a new edition of *Vénus dans le cloître, ou la religieuse en chemise*] and 2 *Vérités des mystères de la religion* [Truths of the mysteries of religion]."[142] Manoury never received any payment for these books. The police captured most of them, along with Desauges himself and the incriminating cache of letters that they impounded in Manoury's bookstore.

Those letters and a great deal of supplementary evidence demonstrate

that the businessmen at the top of the illegal trade behaved as unscrupu-
lously as the small fry at the bottom. They merely used a different bag of
dirty tricks. They marketed the same book under different titles. They ran
up large debts and then refused to acquit bills of exchange, inventing pre-
texts such as delays in shipments or excessive transport costs. They planted
spies in rival shops and denounced competitors to the police. They bluffed,
lied, cheated, and swindled—some worse than others, some not at all. Voltaire's publisher in Geneva, Gabriel Cramer, and Rousseau's publisher in
Amsterdam, Marc-Michel Rey, were men of taste and integrity. But they
were exceptions. Publishing, at least in the illegal sector, was not a gentleman's business.

Nor was police work. Goupil had to frequent a great many dubious
characters in order to carry out inspections. He captured so many of them
and learned so much about their activities that he and his superiors, especially Lieutenant General Lenoir, acquired a thorough knowledge of the
literary underworld. But so many books circulated outside the law that
they could not confiscate all of them or arrest all of the distributors. They
captured only a few of the middlemen in the chain that connected the
bouquinistes of the Palais-Royal with the entrepreneurs at the sources of
supply. Those whom they sent to the Bastille remained there for only a
few months and then resumed their business, beginning with la fille La
Marche.

Not that she had an easy time of it in her cell. During the long wait
to regain her freedom, she sank deeper and deeper into desperation. After
two months, she wrote,

> Qui son donc mes enmi je né jamais fait de malle ny de paine a qui
> se soit e il faut que je soit a cabalé sou le pois de la doulheure quelles
> donc mon sor je suis comme ci je né extes plus je suis oublié de tout
> le monde
>
> [Qui sont donc mes ennemis? Je n'ai jamais fait de mal ni de peine
> à qui que ce soit, et il faut que je sois accablée sous le poids de la dou-
> leur. Quel est donc mon sort? Je suis comme si je n'existais plus. Je suis
> oubliée de tout le monde.]

[So who are my enemies? I never did any harm or caused any grief to anyone, and [yet] I must be crushed under the weight of suffering. What then is my lot? It is as if I no longer existed. I have been forgotten by everyone in the world.] [143]

She had had one glimmer of hope on the day of her arrest. Before being transported to the Bastille, she had taken Goupil aside and offered to spy for him if he would spare her. She knew all about the illegal activities of the other *bouquinistes*—notably Guyot, Morin, and Lesprit. She would inform him of everything they did and provide him with copies of the latest works so that he would know exactly what was circulating under all the counters of the Palais-Royal. She had performed this service for his predecessor as inspector of the book trade, Joseph d'Hémery. Goupil thought this was an excellent suggestion and proposed it to Lenoir.[144] Although Lenoir turned it down, the idea probably did not die at that point. At the end of March, Lenoir recommended to the duc de La Vrillière, the minister in charge of the Bastille, that La Marche be released: "I believe that she has been sufficiently punished by a detention of nearly two months and that there is no drawback to giving her her liberty."[145] According to a report by the major of the Bastille, she was set free on March 30, 1775: "It is sieur Goupil, police inspector, who brought the order to us . . . and who drove this prisoner home in his carriage. They made peace with one another."[146]

Their reconciliation led to a surprising dénouement. Thanks to information from La Marche and all the other dealers whom he arrested and then cultivated, Goupil acquired such extensive knowledge of the underground book trade that he decided to join it. While pretending to confiscate illegal works, he secretly commissioned their publication. He organized entire editions, impounded a few copies as evidence of his assiduousness in enforcing the law, and marketed the rest by means of peddlers—including, most likely, la fille La Marche. After several successful operations, one of the middlemen in his employ denounced him. Goupil wound up in prison himself and died in the dungeon of Vincennes in 1778.[147]

The police and their prisoners make up a fascinating cast of characters, but the human comedy in which they participated has more than human-interest value. It shows how the state tried to control the printed word. To limit the study of censorship to the censors themselves is to tell but half the story. The other half concerns the repression executed by the police. If one treats police work as a form of censorship, does that stretch the concept too far? To eighteenth-century Frenchmen who proudly put the title *censeur royal* after their name, censorship was restricted to the function of investing books with privileges. Yet many books, perhaps most of them (pirated as well as prohibited works), never circulated within the confines of the legal system. If censorship concerns state sanctions applied to books, the book police were involved in the same kind of activity as the officials working in the Direction de la librairie. "Direction" and "inspection" had distinct meanings in eighteenth-century France, but the history of books should be broad enough to accommodate both of them. It should extend as far as the history of France itself, for one conclusion to be drawn from all the activities of all the people who dealt with books is that their world extended throughout French society, down to peddlers who could barely write and smugglers who could not read. Even authors, as Mlle Bonafon illustrates, sometimes came from the lower layers of society, and women could be found everywhere within the world of books. The case of eighteenth-century France therefore suggests two ways of understanding the history of censorship. One would construe it narrowly, by concentrating on the work of the censors; the other would include it in a broad view of literary history, taking literature as a cultural system embedded in a social order. For my part, I favor the latter and find it useful in studying censorship in other times and places—notably the British Raj in nineteenth-century India, where, in principle, the press was free but the state imposed severe sanctions whenever it felt threatened.

PART TWO

———◆◆◆———

British India:
Liberalism and
Imperialism

At the level of textbooks and courses on world history, liberalism and imperialism appear as abstract forces, sweeping through the nineteenth century on separate trajectories and rarely making contact.[1] They came together, however, in the lives of individuals—not as empty "isms" but as personal experiences, which exposed contradictions underlying systems of power.

The case of James Long, an Anglo-Irish missionary in Bengal, epitomized a contradiction at the heart of the British Raj, for the imperial authorities understood their mission according to liberal principles that they had acquired in the home country. Whether Whig or Tory, Liberal or Conservative, they acknowledged certain rights, such as the right to free expression and freedom of the press. Yet those rights took on an unfamiliar hue in India; and when challenged in court, the agents of the Raj muddled through inconsistencies as best they could—notably when they put Long on trial.

AMATEUR ETHNOGRAPHY

Born in County Cork, Ireland, in 1814, Long combined missionary zeal with a gift for languages and a fascination with foreign cultures. He studied at the Islington College of the Church Missionary Society in London, was ordained as a priest in the Church of England in 1840, arrived later that year in India, and spent the next thirty years as a priest in a village near Calcutta. Along the way, he mastered several Indian languages and became known as an accomplished philologist and folklorist, thanks in part to his scholarly publications, *Bengali Proverbs* (1851) and *Descriptive Catalogue of Vernacular Books and Pamphlets* (1867). His most remarkable work remained unpublished, because it was a confidential report written for the imperial authorities in 1859 about literature—literature and, at least by implication, revolution.

The Sepoy Rebellion of 1857—or, as some Indians prefer to call it, India's First War of Independence—may not qualify as a revolution, but it shook the Raj to its core. Sepoy (Indian soldiers in the British army) overthrew their British officers and with the support of regional leaders, among peasants as well as maharajas and nawabs (rulers of semi-autonomous states), seized control of large areas of northern and central India. After more than a year of bloody conflict, the British restored order; and when they took stock of the damage, they realized that they understood very little about the "natives" they had subjected. In 1858 they dissolved the old East India Company and set about establishing a modern state with a bureaucracy that conducted inquiries about every aspect of Indian society, including books.

Although printing had existed on the subcontinent since 1556, when the Portuguese set up the first press, it remained confined for two and a half centuries to missionary enclaves, imperialist administrations, and a few newspapers. But by 1858 book publishing in many languages had become an important industry, and the new Indian Civil Service (ICS) began to keep track of it. The paper trail in the archives of the ICS begins with occasional "returns" about the output of books. Then it leads through quarterly "catalogues," which registered new publications, and it culminates in annual "reports," which quantified and analyzed book production in each presidency or province. To be sure, state-generated material of this kind has a built-in bias. It often reveals more about the British than about the "natives" they observed.[2] But some of the documents contain remarkable ethnographic observations, and the greatest of them was written in the wake of the Rebellion by James Long.

With the backing of the lieutenant governor and the director of public instruction in Bengal, Long attempted to survey everything printed in Bengali between April 1857 and April 1858. He inspected every Bengali printing shop in Calcutta at least twice during his yearlong investigation. He bought every book from 1857 that he could find in the bookshops scattered through the city's "native quarters." He tabulated prices and press-runs, followed peddlers on their rounds, eavesdropped on oral readings, interviewed authors, and scoured records for information about reading habits in the past. In the end, he turned into an amateur ethnographer and became so infected by his subject that he produced a panoramic view of Bengali literature in general, measured by statistics and colored by sympathetic readings of the books themselves.[3]

Despite his sympathies, which placed him on the side of peasants exploited by British indigo planters, Long wrote as an agent of imperialism, Anglo-Indian style—that is, the liberal variety, which extended from James Mill to John Morley and which celebrated the printed word as a civilizing force. Books, he insisted, could "break down ignorant prejudices" such as the opposition to widow remarriage among "the old school of Hindus."[4] Instead of imposing censorship, as some had proposed, the British should promote the freedom of the press and encourage the development of Indian literature. Had they paid attention to Indian newspapers, he claimed, they might have detected enough symptoms of unrest to have prevented the Rebellion. They needed information in order to maintain their empire, and information came primarily through print.

Long contributed to this cause by amassing data on the production of books. According to his calculations, the total output of works in Bengali before 1820 came to only 30 titles, most of them on Hindu religion and mythology. Only 28 new books came out between 1822 and 1826, and this low level of production, always on the same subjects, continued until mid-century. A turning point came in 1852, when 50 new Bengali books were published, including new genres of "useful works." By 1857, the

year of his investigation, the publishing industry was booming: 46 presses
existed in Calcutta, and they had turned out 322 new works, including 6
newspapers and 12 periodicals, in the last twelve months. Overall book
production for the last half century, according to Long's estimate, came to
about 1,800 titles. The quality of type and paper had improved; printers
had given up their ancient wooden presses; the number of authors had
increased; and an important literary market had emerged, although the
peasants remained mired in illiteracy: "Not 3 per cent of the rural population of Bengal can read intelligently. In Bombay, not 3 per cent can read
at all." By promoting education, the British could relieve the suffering of
the masses: "Government attention has been drawn to ameliorating the
social condition of the ryot [peasant laborer, often a tenant cultivator]—
but mental enlightenment must be an accompaniment to it, to give him
a *manly* feeling to resist zamindar [Indian landlord] and planter [British
indigo growers] oppression—to make him feel he is a man by the quicken-
ing influences of education."[5]

Long did not disguise the Victorian-liberal sentiments that he brought
to his work, and his own tastes tended toward serious literature, written in
a style that conveyed the Sanskrit origins of Bengali, but he gave a sympathetic reading to popular genres, such as almanacs:

> Almanacs circulate where few other Bengali books reach; just
> previous to the beginning of the Bengali year is a busy season with
> the native almanac sellers of Calcutta; book-hawkers in numbers may
> be seen issuing from the printing presses, freighted with the store of
> almanacs which they carry far and wide, some of which they sell at
> the low rate of 80 pages for one anna [one rupee contained sixteen
> annas, and a skilled laborer commonly earned six annas in a day].
> The Bengali almanac is as necessary for the Bengali as his hooka or
> his pan; without it he cannot determine the auspicious days for mar-
> rying (22 in the year), for first feeding an infant with rice (27 days in
> the year), the feeding the mother with rice in the fifth month of ges-
> tation (12 days), for commencing the building of a house, for boring

the ears, putting the chalk into the hands of a boy to teach him to write, when a journey is to be begun, or the calculating the duration and malignity of a fever.[6]

The Tract Society of Calcutta attempted to counter the effect of these booklets by producing Christian almanacs, but their editions found few takers, Long remarked, because they lacked prophecies.

He noted that history books also had slight appeal—the result, he believed, of a conviction among Hindu readers that worldly affairs had little importance in the great scheme of things. Nonetheless, the Bengali public enjoyed sardonic commentaries on current events, particularly in the form of drama. In the hinterland, *jatra* parties (itinerant troupes) toured from village to village, performing plays based on Hindu mythology but seasoned with bawdy episodes, irreverent songs, and asides about British planters and rulers. In Calcutta, works with similar themes—some by pandit playwrights, others improvised in the manner of slapstick or vaudeville—dominated repertories in the vibrant theater district. Calcutta's printers turned out cheap editions of the plays, and peddlers flogged them throughout the province, along with songbooks, another favorite genre, which supplemented the dramas. Although much of this material offended his Victorian sensibility, Long discussed it at length and emphasized its popular appeal:

> The Bengali songs do not inculcate the love of wine or, like the Scotch, the love of war, but are devoted to Venus and the popular deities; they are filthy and polluting. Of these the most known are the Panchalis, which are sung at the festivals and sold in numerous editions and by thousands, some on good paper, well got up [i.e., designed and printed], others on the refuse of old canvas bags. The Panchalis are recitations of stories chiefly from the Hindu Shastras, in meter, with music and singing; they relate to Vishnu and Shiva, intermixed with pieces in the style of Anacreon. . . . The jatras are a species of dramatic action, filthy, in the same style with the exhibi-

tion of Punch and Judy, or of the penny theatres in London, treating
of licentiousness, or of Krishna. A mehtar [lowly house sweeper] with
a broomstick in his hand always cuts a figure in them.[7]

Long attended performances by singers himself, both itinerant bards
and street poets, including one man who could improvise verses in Sanskrit on any subject proposed to him. The songs transmitted a good deal
of comment on political and social issues: "For instance, the appointment of indigo planters as honorary magistrates excited strong feelings
of indignation among many of the ryots in certain districts; a common
remark was, 'Je rakhak se bhakhak'—i.e. the man appointed our protector is become a wolf."[8] Popular prints, run off in the tens of thousands
and pasted on walls, usually confined themselves to religious themes,
such as the exploits of the gods. Long had nothing good to say about
the category "erotic," but noted that it, too, appealed to a broad, popular
public. He found little serious fiction or works comparable to European
novels, although he thought that religious tales were sometimes "written
in such a mode and style as to produce on the readers or hearers the
agreeable effects of fiction."[9] He calculated that more than seven hundred authors had published books in Bengali, and listed them all. None,
he thought, could be considered a great writer, although he admitted to
some admiration for Bharut Chandra, whose *Shishubodh* was "the most
popular book in indigenous schools, but replete with loose morals and
mythology." Chandra's *Videa Sundar*, "a most popular tale, clever but
obscene," had been reprinted recently in an edition of 3,750 and had
sold out in four months.[10] Despite their regrettable bawdiness, the Bengali writers promised to develop a rich literature by adapting Sanskrit
traditions to the interests of a growing reading public. Their numbers
alone indicated that "the Bengali mind has been roused from the tor-
por of ages."[11]

In short, Bengali literature was beginning to flourish, although most
Europeans had no inkling of its existence. To become acquainted with it,
they would have to cross over the line that divided British society from
the "native quarters" of northern Calcutta and venture into the teeming

press rooms and bookshops scattered everywhere, especially along Chit-poor Road, "their Pater Noster Row" in the Battala area. Long explored this territory in detail and also traced the human links that connected the producers in Calcutta to consumers in the hinterland. Except in the rainy season, when they worked in the fields, two hundred peasant ped-dlers regularly stocked up in the printing shops of the capital and fanned out through the countryside, carrying their wares on their heads. By dou-bling the wholesale price, they often made six to eight rupees a month; and their person-to-person salesmanship made them ideal intermediaries in a distribution system aimed at listeners as well as readers: "The natives find the best advertisement for a Bengali book is a living agent, who shows the book itself."[12]

Long paid a great deal of attention to reading as the final stage in the communication process. However biased in his view of "Orientals," he had a good eye for the performative aspects of reading in an overwhelmingly illiterate society:

> With Orientals it is a common practice to be read to, and hence numbers who cannot read themselves listen to those who can. Readers (kathaks) are often hired to recite or chant certain works, and most impressively do some of them execute this—one of them recited lately to myself from memory any passages I selected from the *Ramayana, Raghuvansa, Mahabharata*; the mode of reciting them was most impressive; some of these men earn 500 rupees a month. . . . We know a native who was for years employed by a rich babu to read two hours daily to 40 or 50 females in his house. This has been a practice from time immemorial in Bengal, where "readings" as in all Eastern countries have been so popular, and where intonation, gesture, etc. make a book listened to more telling than when simply read. Women sometimes sit in a circle round a woman who reads a book to them. Allowing them an average of 10 hearers or readers to each book, we calculate that these 600,000 Bengali books [Long's estimate of the total number of copies produced in 1857] have 2,000,000 readers or hearers [presumably a slip for 6,000,000].[13]

MELODRAMA

Long's report stands out as the most thorough account of publishing and the book trade in the papers of the ICS, but it did not lead to a happy ending. In 1861, moved by sympathy for the ryots exploited by the British planters, Long arranged for the publication of an English edition of *Nil Durpan*, a Bengali melodrama about planter oppression, and found himself accused of libel by the indigo planters.

Prosecution for libel had served as the main restraint on the freedom of the press in England after the end of pre-publication censorship in 1695.[14] But despite some notorious convictions—Daniel Defoe in 1703 and Henry Sacheverell in 1710—the press became increasingly outspoken. After a great deal of agitation in the 1760s—Wilkite demands for the liberty of the press and the jury's refusal to convict the publisher of the radical "Junius" papers in 1770[15]—libel ceased to serve as a way of curbing the discussion of social and political questions. The Libel Act of 1792 confirmed this tendency, and by 1850 a large body of case law had imposed limits on libel as a criminal offense. Prosecutors had to produce evidence of damage to the reputation of individuals and could not bring charges based on general political commentary or remarks that might offend vaguely defined groups. In principle, English precedent determined judgments in Indian courts, but cases tried in the subcontinent took place in a very different context, despite the elaborate use of English formalities.[16]

Long's trial in 1861 turned into a courtroom drama, which inflamed passions in Bengal and sent repercussions to the heart of the empire in London. Although Calcutta, the capital of the Raj, was hardly touched by the Rebellion of 1857, it was rocked by the Blue Mutiny of 1859–60, a protest movement of peasants who had been exploited by indigo planters in the hinterland. While speculating on the demand for natural blue dye, which had increased steadily since the 1780s, the planters had forced the ryots to abandon their semifeudal agrarian economy, based on a variety of crops, and a complex system of land rents, for the cultivation of indigo. The planters enticed the peasants to plant indigo by advancing small sums, then cheated on payments to them for the harvests, foreclosed

NIL DARPAN,

OR

THE INDIGO PLANTING MIRROR,

A Drama.

TRANSLATED FROM THE BENGALI

BY

A NATIVE.

CALCUTTA:

C. H. MANUEL, CALCUTTA PRINTING AND PUBLISHING PRESS, No. 10,
WESTON'S LANE, COSSITOLLAH.

1861.

The English translation of Nil Durpan *published without the name of the author
or translator.*

on the debts, and appropriated their land or forced them to continue cul-
tivating indigo under a load of debt, passed on from father to son, which
reduced them to a state of peonage. When faced with insubordination, the
planters sent thugs to beat the peasants, burn their crops, and incarcerate
them in prisons adjoining the factories where the indigo was made into
dye. The Blue Mutiny, an uprising combined with a rent strike, exposed
such extreme abuses that the authorities appointed a commission to investigate them. Its report, issued in August 1860, condemned the tyranny
of the planters and reinforced the agitation of Bengali intellectuals like
Harish Chaudra Mukherjee, editor of the *Hindoo Patriot*.

Unlike the commission's report and the journal articles, *Nil Durpan*
attacked the planters by means of fiction—a play, designed to be performed in Calcutta's theaters and to be read in the form of a pamphlet.
It dramatized the evils of the indigo system so effectively that it became
known as the "Uncle Tom's Cabin of Bengal."[17] The Bengali edition
appeared a few months after the report of the Indigo Commission, and
the English translation, published by Long and distributed with the help
of W. S. Seton-Karr, secretary to the governor of Bengal and former
president of the commission, appeared in 1861. The author of the play,
Dinabandhu Mitra, typified the educated Indians in the lower ranks of
the bureaucracy known as "babus," a term that sometimes had pejorative
connotations, because it could suggest servility and the aping of English
manners.[18] He wrote the text while serving as postmaster in Patna (Bihar)
and had it published anonymously in Dacca. Although he soon became
known as its author, he continued his career unperturbed in the Post
and Telegraph Department until he died of diabetes in 1873, at the age
of forty-four.

In fact, neither the British authorities nor the planters seem to have
paid much attention to the Bengali version of the play. It was the English
translation that aroused the fury of the planters, who claimed that they
had been collectively libeled. They especially objected to the fact that
some copies had circulated through the mail under Seton-Karr's official
frank and that others eventually reached England, where they could provide ammunition to reform-minded backbenchers in Parliament and offi-

cials in the India Office. The *Nil Durpan* affair therefore developed into a conflict within the British community of Bengal, dividing planters with supporters in the legal profession against reformers with allies in the Bengali intelligentsia.

A century and a half after its publication, the English text reads like unalloyed melodrama. It pits villainy against virtue, the former personified by two rapacious planters, the latter by noble peasants. A zamindar family, led by a traditional patriarch and his two progressive sons, attempts to defend their village against the wicked sahibs, who will stop at nothing— torture, murder, rape, the corruption of magistrates, and the burning of crops and houses—to vent their evil appetites. The Bengali agents of the planters—a money lender, a land surveyor, a procuress, a jail keeper—act out the forces that threaten the solidarity of the community. The villagers resist, bound together against their common enemy. They rally around the zamindar, who is the soul of generosity, even though he, too, collects land rents and practices usury. One peasant, the indigent but heroic Torap, demonstrates the limited possibility of violence. He escapes from a factory jail just in time to rescue a pregnant woman from an attempted rape by Mr. Rogue, a particularly nasty planter. While the woman flees to safety, Torap gives Rogue a beating and bites off his nose, but refuses to go further, because he understands that ultimately the peasants must seek justice from the British legal system. The zamindar sons adopt that defense by taking the peasants' case beyond the local magistrate, who is complicit with the planters, to the honest British in a higher court. Before their appeal can succeed, however, tragedy strikes in one episode after another, leaving the stage strewn with corpses. As the curtain falls, the sole survivor of the devastation laments, "The Basu family of Svaropur is destroyed by Indigo, the great destroyer of honour. How very terrible are the arms of Indigo!"[19]

Indigo—not the wicked foreigners, nor the wickedness of the regime they had imposed on India, nor divisions within the old regime, nor its incapacity to defend itself against foreign domination, but a plant and some of the planters who exploited it. Far from conveying a revolutionary message, *Nil Durpan* expressed faith in the ultimate fairness of British rule. The good sahibs would in the end correct the abuses of the bad sahibs, it made clear, citing the report of the Indigo Commission as evidence. In a preface to his text, Mitra assured Indians that they could count on the beneficent rule of Lord Canning, viceroy of India; J. P. Grant, lieutenant governor of Bengal; the Indian Civil Service; and, above all, "the most kindhearted Queen Victoria, the mother of the people."[20] Long expressed similar sentiments in an introduction to the English edition. It had been published, he explained, so that Europeans could understand the indigo system as it was seen by the peasants. It may not be great literature, but it expressed the "native" point of view in the favorite genre of the "natives"—that is, the popular drama, which drew on Sanskrit models to provide a commentary on social issues. In publishing *Nil Durpan*, therefore, Long made available to English readers a perfect example of the vernacular literature that he had studied in his report to the Indian Civil Service.

The planters did not take the *Nil Durpan* affair in that spirit. They took it to court. The trial attracted so much attention that normal affairs reportedly came to a standstill in Calcutta during the sessions, which extended from July 19 to 24, 1861.[21] Two prosecuting attorneys and two defense lawyers developed elaborate arguments before a jury composed of British residents. The prosecutors proclaimed their allegiance to the principle of a free press and agreed that social satire could serve as a legitimate way to expose social abuses, but *Nil Durpan* maligned the entire community of planters. Worse, it set "race against race, the European against the Native."[22] As a result, it endangered all Europeans in India, for the "the late mutinies taught us how unsafe is our position."[23] The main lawyer for the defense replied that the two villains of the play could not represent the planters in general, and in any case the law of libel concerned individuals, not ill-defined groups such as the planters, who had no corporate existence. To condemn *Nil Durpan* would be to declare all satirical and critical literature outside the law—the works of Molière, for example, and *Oliver Twist* and *Uncle Tom's Cabin*. No one considered Dickens a libeler.

When the judge addressed the jury, he kept returning, time and again, to the issue of the liberty of the press. He charged the jurors as Englishmen to consider the history of their country, above all the right of any individual to publish his opinion on any public question and even to attack men in authority. He declared his unwavering commitment to "the liberty of the press and freedom of discussion."[24] Never would he permit his court to set a precedent that might fritter away that great constitutional principle. But the issue before the jury was straightforward: had Long intended to correct social evils or to malign the planters as a class?

The jury decided that Long had committed libel. The judge sentenced him to a fine of 1,000 rupees (which was paid for him by a "native" sympathizer) and a month in prison. In delivering the sentence, he congratulated himself as well as the jury for "a verdict which, I have the satisfaction of feeling, rests upon a constitutional basis and cannot be used hereafter against the liberty of the press."[25]

SURVEILLANCE

The *Nil Durpan* affair was the most dramatic case of censorship—censorship overlaid with protests denying its existence—in the British Raj during the nineteenth century. Other cases existed, several concerning newspapers rather than books and some for publications deemed to be pornographic rather than libelous, but on the whole the British authorities paid little attention to the vernacular press before the Rebellion of 1857. After the Rebellion, as Long's case demonstrated, they did not abandon their adherence to liberal values, nor did they resort to outright repression. Instead, they adopted a system that fits Michel Foucault's concept of control as a combination of knowledge and power—or "surveillance," which could lead to "punishment."[26]

By 1857, the rough-and-ready phase of imperialism had come to an end.[27] Clive's plundering, Wellesley's rapacity, Auckland's aggression, Napier's butchery, and Dalhousie's duplicitous diplomacy had brought most of the subcontinent under British control. In the later phase of imperialism, the British sought to increase their power by expanding their knowledge. They had already acquired considerable mastery of Indian languages—the classical languages, Sanskrit, Persian, and Arabic, and dozens of the vernacular tongues; and district officers had long prided themselves on "knowing the country." But two years of desultory study at Haileybury College in England followed by a few months in Calcutta did not make the agents of the East India Company into "Orientalists." The best of them learned to tap "native informants": holy men, barbers, foresters, bazaar merchants, prostitutes, midwives, astrologers, watchmen, pilgrims—descendants, all, of the *harkaras* and *kasids*, or intelligence gatherers and runners, who had made the Mughal Empire into a vast information system, similar in some respects to the network of spies and informants of the police in eighteenth-century France.[28] But most agents of the Company Raj had hardly begun to know their way around one district before they were transferred to another. The Rebellion caught them completely by surprise.

Although the native soldiers remained loyal throughout most of the subcontinent, the sepoys of the Raj's heartland, the Gangetic territories from Delhi to Calcutta, had shown that they could not be trusted and, equally disturbing, that they had not been understood. Who would have thought that the introduction of a new rifle, the breech-loading Enfield, would have provided the spark for the conflagration?[29] In order to load it, the soldiers reportedly (according to rumor, which may have been as important as actual behavior) had to bite off the tips of the cartridges; and that, to them, was unthinkable, because the cartridges were sealed with the fat of pigs and the grease of cows, making them an abomination to Muslims and Hindus alike. The sepoys thought the sahibs were trying to defile them in order to make them lose caste and convert to Christianity. When their officers talked of military modernization, the soldiers smelled a missionary plot. And their suspicions were confirmed by the Enlistment Act of 1856, which threatened them with the prospect of being shipped across the Bay of Bengal to fight the white man's wars in Burma. By crossing "dark waters" into alien territory, high caste sepoys would become permanently polluted and especially vulnerable to conversion. Forty thousand of them came from the rich province of Oudh, which the British had annexed in the same year, despite the most sacred treaty obligations. But what did the British understand of sacredness? In a fit of "liberal" reforms, they had forbidden suttee (the self-immolation of widows on the funeral pyres of their husbands) and permitted widow remarriage, another bitter pill forced down native throats in 1856, the year of abominations.

When the British inspected the devastation produced by the Rebellion, they began to measure the cultural distance that separated them from the "natives." Many of them withdrew into the world of the cutcherry and the club, reinforced in their racism by reports of black men ambushing women and children and throwing corpses down wells. Strange stories circulated about fakirs and mullahs who had supposedly prepared the Rebellion by passing around red-tinged chapatis (native bread) among the troops or, according to a later version, daubing cow dung on trees. Everything indicated that the "natives" and their conquerors lived in separate mental worlds. But to hold on to their conquests, the British needed to understand the Indians, not merely to defeat them.[30]

After abolishing the East India Company in 1858, the British ruled through an administration that depended on modern modes of information gathering—that is, on an endless flow of words on paper. The ICS, recruited since 1853 by means of competitive examination, produced reports on everything under the subcontinental sun. "Collections" and "returns" poured off the government presses, flooding the official channels of communication with data on harvests, village boundaries, flora and fauna, and native customs. Everything was surveyed, mapped, classified, and counted, including human beings, who appeared in the first Indian census in 1872, divided neatly into castes, subcastes, and a dozen other categories determined by the columns of a printed form. The catalogues of books belonged to this effort to catalogue everything. They constituted a census of Indian literature as the imperial authorities understood it.[31]

By the Press and Registration of Books Act of 1867, the governor-general ordered the ICS to keep a record of every book that appeared in every province of the Raj. The records, known somewhat misleadingly as "catalogues," were compiled four times a year by provincial librarians from memoranda submitted by local officials. Publishers were required to supply the officials with three copies of every book they produced and in return received payment for them at the usual sales price. They also had to provide information on a standard set of topics, which corresponded to columns on the printed forms of the catalogues: the title of the work, its author, language, subject, place of printing, names of printer and publisher, date of publication, number of pages, size, format, pressrun, whether printed or lithographed (lithography was a great stimulus to the production of much vernacular literature), and price. By paying two rupees, the publisher received a copyright; but if he failed to register the book, it would be treated as illegal and he would be punished by a fine of up to 5,000 rupees and/or imprisonment of up to two years.[32]

The act of 1867 was inspired in part by librarians, and it stimulated the growth of libraries, but the catalogues that resulted from it were never available to the general public, despite their innocent-sounding name. They circulated secretly within the channels of the ICS—"A" matter deemed to be "confidential." Taken together, they provided the agents of the Raj with a running account of everything in the subcontinent that appeared in print—or at least everything that printers and publishers submitted for registration. The catalogue entries from 1868 to 1905 cover about 200,000 titles—more by far than the total output in France during the age of Enlightenment. For Bengal alone, the catalogues from those years run to fifteen enormous volumes, each containing 500 pages or more, each page covered with small print. Their scale is staggering: more than a million words, printed with precision in fifteen standard columns. (They were printed so that multiple copies could circulate within the ICS.) They show the ICS talking to itself about the "natives," a discourse on literature by the colonial authorities at the high tide of imperialism.

William Lawler, head librarian of the Bengal Library, the largest in the Raj, serves as a good example of how this discourse first developed. He composed the catalogue covering all the books published in Bengal in 1879, summarizing the narratives of novels, poems, and plays in a way that would make their moral clear for his own readers, the men who ruled over the Bengalis in the ICS. Thus his remarks on the Bengali epic poem *Vana-Vihangini,* or *The Female Bird of the Forest:*

The present work of eight chapters commences with a touching appeal to Mother India, whose sad lot is deplored, and the oppression at the hands of the *Yavans* (or foreigners) pronounced unbearable. The first chapter contains an account of a Brahmin who supported himself and his wife Sundari in a forest by alms, till one day a Nabab [provincial governor] of Bengal, who came on a hunting excursion, chanced to alight there, saw his wife, and during his absence took her away. The second describes the return of the Brahmin husband after the usual day's begging. In the third he finds his wife gone, and is in deep distress thereat. In the fourth chapter, advice is given to the people of Bengal to be more united and act in concert, whereby they will gain strength and recover their lost possessions. The fifth depicts Sundari's distress in the Nabab's house, where she refused to eat and was prepared to kill herself, and how she was eventually released by the wife of the Nabab. In the sixth, the Brahmin husband and wife meet again in the forest and spend their time in much happiness, till in chapter seven they are arrested and taken by the orders of the Nabab. And in chapter eight the husband Sharat is executed, whereupon his wife Sundari dies broken-hearted. From pages 50–55 in chapter three, the poet digresses to portray in forcible language the subjection of the Aryan Bengali race to foreigners, who have placed their feet on the heads of Brahmins, but that the time must come, though it may be distant, when the Aryans will be freed from the yoke.[33]

However faithful he may have been to the original, Lawler retold the tale in a way that would give a district magistrate in the mofussil (hinterland) or a secretary in the India Office in London the sensation of knowing what the "natives" were up to when they published books.

They were up to no good. True, some books celebrated the beneficence of the Raj: law courts, railroads, electricity, cricket, and all the rest. Thus *Daiva-lata*, or *Creeper of Providence*: "The writer . . . praises the English for their just administration and hopes that they will long continue to rule the country and that all India should be grateful for the benefits received from English rule." *Samya*, or *Equality*, even drew on Mill and Carlyle in order to attack the caste system: "A few more works of this kind would make a revolution in the vast quantity of sluggish and silly Bengali literature of the present day." But such laudable works were the exception. The "natives" had an unfortunate tendency to seek amusement in their literature: *Dekhila-hansi-paya*, or *Could Anyone But See the Sight He Would Laugh*, a novella about the mishaps of a dim-witted younger brother, was "one of the altogether silly tales which finds a ready audience amongst the natives, as it tends to excite laughter." As Lawler saw them, the Indians were children, who liked chapbook adventure stories and fairy tales, or printed versions of plays derived from the *Ramayana*, or worse: bawdy accounts of Krishna's dallying with the milkmaids, a perennial favorite adapted from the *Mahabharata*. *Jagannather Rath-arohana-o-Kamini-ranjana*, or *The Pleasure of Females*, took the Krishna theme far beyond the limits of decency, as Lawler understood them. He deplored it as a compendium of "the most openly vulgar and obscene observations ever made, not even having the semblance of an excuse for the public good. It should be at once suppressed." *Rahasya-pratibha*, or *Mysteries Revealed*, a nonfiction account of crime in Calcutta, was equally offensive to Lawler's Victorian sensibility:

> The production is devoid of any merit, the style is colloquial, and the sentiments are obscene. . . . The fact of its publication is a discredit on Bengali literature and the taste of the native reading public. . . . It is devoutly to be wished that some means were available for putting a stop to the threatened publication of more trash like this in a second volume.[34]

The message is clear enough, but it raises problems; for the implicit readers of the catalogue were the masters of India: Why did they not ban the books that Lawler considered so reprehensible? And if they did not intend to repress any "native" literature, why did they follow its production in such exhaustive detail? Foucault's knowledge/power formula may provide part of an answer, but it needs to be nuanced. Some rulers genuinely cared for the welfare of the Indians. Lord William Bentinck, governor-general from 1828 to 1835, did not simply seek to maximize power by abolishing suttee or by admitting Indians to the East India Company. Nor did his adviser, Thomas Babington Macaulay, design an educational system to be conducted in English for an Indian elite merely in order to make the bureaucracy more efficient. They believed in the utilitarian principle of promoting happiness. In fact, the father and the grandfather of liberalism, John Stuart Mill and James Mill, developed that principle into a philosophy while working for the East India Company. J. S. Mill's testimony about the company to the House of Lords in 1852 anticipated his manifesto of liberalism, *On Liberty* (1859). And John Morley, a dedicated Liberal and biographer of Gladstone, tried to translate that philosophy into government policy fifty years later while serving as secretary of state for India.[35]

True, Morley found it impossible to reconcile his commitment to freedom of the press with his need to repress nationalist agitation, and insofar as utilitarianism provided imperialism with an ideology, it strengthened the Raj. In developing "utilities" such as railroads, telegraph lines, and the postal service, the British consolidated their control of the subcontinent. But they also provided irrigation works, police protection, and justice, British style. District magistrates sometimes took the side of peasants against landlords, even though they did not upset indigenous hierarchies. Unlike the rapacious adventurers of the eighteenth century, they subscribed to an ethos of hard work and service. And despite the growth of racism, some symbiosis developed between foreign and indigenous elites. As English education spread and Indians worked their way into administrative bureaucracies and the professions, an Indian intelligentsia took root. The result was not simply the much maligned babu but also the Bengal Renaissance. After the foundation of the Brahmo Samaj (Society of Brahma) in 1828 by Ram Mohun Roy, who began his career as an assistant collector in the East India Company, Indian intellectuals began to work ingredients from their ancient classics into an original variety of modern literature, and they found inspiration in Shakespeare as well as the Upanishads. At a humbler level, babus in the bureaucracies, thousands of them, filled in the

10   BENGAL

CATALOGUE OF BOOKS for the Second

1	2	3	4	5	6	7
Number.	Title (to be translated into English when the title-page is not in that language).	Language in which the book is written.	Name of author, translator, or editor of the book or any part of it.	Subject.	Place of printing and place of publication.	Name or firm of printer, and name or firm of publisher.
						BENGALI BOOKS.—
107	Rádhá Krishna Vilás : or, The Sports of Rádhá and Krishna at Vraja.	Bengali	Jaynáráyana Mukerji.	Poetry ...	Printed and published at the Kávya Prakásha Press, No. 3, Haripál's Lane, Calcutta.	Printed and published by Umeshchandra Bhattácárya.
108	Vana-Vihanginí : or, The Female Bird of the Forest.	ditto ...	Rajanínáth Chatterji.	ditto ...	Printed and published at the Ananda Press, Mymensing.	Printed and published by Chandra Kumár Sarkár.

the oppression at the hands of the *Yavans* (or foreigners) pronounced unbearable. The 1st chapter contains an Bengal, who came on a hunting excursion, chaned to alight there, saw his wife, and during his absence took her away, and is in deep distress thereat. In the 4th chapter advice is given to the people of Bengal to be more united and act the Nabab's house, where she refused to eat and was prepared to kill herself, and how she was eventually released time in much happiness, till in chapter 7 they are arrested and taken by the orders of the Nabab. And in chapter 9th the poet digresses to pourtray in forcible language the subjection of the Aryan Bengali race to foreigners, who the Aryans will be freed from the yoke.

Facing pages of the quarterly catalogue of books published in the presidency of Bengal. The "remarks" in column 16 extend across the page and can be read as a running commentary on "native" literatures by the agents of the British Raj. The catalogues were not intended for the use of readers in the Bengal Library. They circulated in the Indian Civil Service as confidential material and were eventually used in cases brought to try authors and publishers for sedition.

forms and drafted the reports that shaped the Raj's understanding of itself. They helped create British India as a cultural construct, Orientalism and all. That was a complex process, visited on the Indians by the British and executed in large part by the Indians themselves, and there is no better site on which to study its elaboration than column 16 of the Raj's catalogues of books.[36]

Column 16, a catch-all category headed "remarks," was not added to the standard form until August 1871; and the first librarians to use it kept their comments to a minimum, though they did not hesitate to pronounce judgment on the books they registered: "miscellaneous songs, chiefly of a

LIBRARY. 11

Quarter ending 30th June 1879.—(Continued.)

8	9	10	11	12	13	14	15	16	17
Date of issue from the press, or place of publication.	Number of sheets, leaves, or pages.	Size.	First, second, or other edition.	Number of copies of which the edition consists.	Printed or litho-graphed.	Price at which the book is sold to the public.	Name and residence of proprietor of copyright, or any portion of it.	REMARKS.	Number.

NON-EDUCATIONAL—(Continued.)

1879.	Pages.					Rs. A. P.			
April 1st	132	12mo. ...	1st ...		3,000	Printed	0 5 6	Umeshchandra Bhattáchárya, No. 324, Chitpore Road, Calcutta.	Accounts of the sports of Krishna with the *Gopís* or milkmaids, the incarnation of Vishnu by the order of Mahá Vishnu to save the world from sin, par-	107

ticulars of the marriage of Deviki and Rohiní with Vasudeva and the imprisonment of the first and last by Kansa Rájá, and the slaughter of the sons of Deviki by the latter, the births of Valarám and Krishna, and the release of his father and mother by the latter from imprisonment after killing Kansa Rájá.

| „ 21st | 161 | dy. 8vo. | 1st ... | | 400 | ditto ... | 1 0 0 | Rajanínáth Chatterji of Barísál. | The present work of eight chapters commences with a touching appeal to mother India, whose sad lot is deplored, and | 108 |

account of a Bráhmin who supported himself and his wife Sundarí in a forest by alms, till one day a Nabab of The 2nd describes the return of the *Bráhmin* husband after the usual day's begging. In the 3rd he finds his wife gone, in concert, whereby they will gain strength and recover their lost possessions. The 5th depicts Sundarí's distress in by the wife of the Nabab. In the 6th the *Bráhmin* husband and wife meet again in the forest and spend their the husband Sharat is executed, whereupon his wife Sundarí dies broken hearted. From pages 50 to 55 in chapter 3rd have placed their feet on the heads of Bráhmins, but that the time must come, thought it may be distant, when

filthy character"; "a description of the first amorous dalliances of Radha and Krishnu, altogether a filthy book"; "a Hindoo mythological tale. The filthiest poetical effusion imaginable"; "pieces of poetry on different subjects, professedly written for, but not at all suited to boys."[37]

After this initial stage of culture shock, the confrontation of the Victorian with the Bengali imagination in column 16 produced increasingly complicated reactions, and the "remarks" grew apace. Soon they spilled over the neatly ruled lines between the columns, invading the neighboring space, running across the page, filling the whole sheet with a flood of words. By 1875, column 16 began to read like the column of a journal, and the remarks turned into reviews. William Lawler's opinionated comments were typical of the genre. In fact, his opinions did not differ markedly from those of the other librarians, Indians included. The babus displaced the British in 1879, when Chunder Nath Bose succeeded Lawler.[38] From then on, the catalogue was compiled by Indians, aided no doubt by assistants, for no individual could keep up with the literature streaming from the presses in the late nineteenth and early twentieth centuries. But the tone of the remarks remained essentially the same, though the Indian librarians seemed to be less obsessed with sex and more concerned with philological correctness. When they detected signs of restlessness among the "natives," they sounded just as concerned or indignant as their British predecessors. Chunder Nath Bose deplored a Bengali novel, *Surendra-Binodini Natak*: "The story of love is mixed up with another story, the object of which seems to be to excite in the native mind a strong hatred for English rule and the English character. There are passages in which the author's language becomes almost seditious."[39] Should this continuity in the commentaries be taken as a symptom of co-optation, Anglicization, or self-imposed Orientalism? It is difficult to say, given the lack of information about the librarians. But one characteristic stands out: their linguistic virtuosity. Harinath De, a candidate for the post of imperial librarian in Calcutta in 1906, had mastered Latin, Greek, German, French, Italian, Spanish, Sanskrit, Pali, Arabic, Persian, Urdu, Hindi, Bengali, Oriya, Marathi, and Guzerati, along with some Provençal, Portuguese, Romanian, Dutch, Danish, Anglo-Saxon, Old and Middle High German, and a smattering of Hebrew, Turkish, and Chinese. He got the job.[40]

What tendencies emerge from thirty years of these running comments on the daily output of books? First, ethnographic bewilderment. To the British librarians in the 1870s, Bengali literature was a strange assortment of incompatible elements. Thus *Gyananjan*, or *Pigment of Knowledge*: "Miscellaneous verses on time, hope, rich men, the quail and coconuts."[41] The incomprehension went both ways, for the remarks in column 16 also provide glimpses of the Indians observing the British. A popular Bengali compendium of advice and useful knowledge included little essays on the following subjects, according to William Lawler's synthesis: "Toil, sleep, health, fish, salt, indigo, and the pig, which is described as a filthy animal, the flesh whereof is eaten by the lowest class, such as sweepers, *domes*, *mehtars*, and also by Englishmen."[42] In fact, no vernacular literature expressed a state of anthropological purity untouched by the imperialist presence. Indians and Britons had been forming British India for more than a century before the catalogues began to record the British understanding of the Indians' understanding of their common world.

It required a considerable ethnographic effort, nonetheless, for the British to get their bearings in the alien literature. They often came up against pages that remained entirely opaque. Thus *Chinta Lahari*, or *Waves of Meditation*, as read by John Robinson in 1878: "A piece of incoherent and unintelligible writing. A few lines of poetry, a few songs, and some dialogues, all pointless. It is not clear why the author should have taken trouble to write so much nonsense."[43] The remarks take on a less tendentious tone in the later catalogues, no doubt as a result of the Indian librarians' attempts to act as intermediaries, translating and negotiating differences between cultures. But the early catalogues do not generally condemn native folkways. They describe village medicine, magic, domestic life, religious rituals, and even polygamy in a fairly straightforward manner, although they contain enough remarks about Indian "idolatry" to remind the reader where truth is located.[44] When it came to the supernatural, the British showed a preference for beneficent deities like Satya Pir, who was worshipped with offerings of flowers and milk by the Muslims of Eastern Bengal, in contrast to Kali, the terrible Hindu goddess of destruction, who had to be appeased with bloody sacrifices of goats.[45] The mystical and poetical qualities of Hinduism appealed to them. Having studied classical sacred texts, they expressed admiration for the depth of the *Vedas* and the pathos of the *Ramayana*, although they complained about impenetrable obscurities; and when they effused about poetry, they made it sound like English romanticism. Thus "the lament of a widowed lover" in *Nibhrita Nivas Kavya*, or *The Lonely Habitation*: "The description of the earth and other planets as beheld by the spirit of the heroine, beautiful and chaste, in its ascent heavenwards in company with celestial nymphs, is thoroughly poetical. There is considerable similarity between it and certain passages in Shelley's *Queen Mab*."[46]

Popular Bengali literature, by contrast, received nothing but scorn in the catalogues. The librarians dismissed it as cheap stuff, "street literature" flogged by peddlers among the poor of Calcutta and the ignorant villagers of the mofussil (back country). It dealt in urban horrors—lowlife, murders, detectives, prostitutes—and rural fantasies—fairies, magic, adventures, astrology. Judging from the remarks, it was somewhat similar to the penny dreadfuls and chapbooks of contemporary Europe. But its sentimental romances drew on Hindu mythology, and its almanacs combined astrological advice with mantras to be recited while piercing ears or giving a child rice for the first time.[47] Songbooks also circulated widely, mixing traditional ribaldry with comments on current events. And most important of all, printed versions of popular plays, usually small booklets but sometimes volumes of two hundred pages or more, spread the spicy fare of Calcutta's theaters throughout the entire province. All this printed matter was read aloud, in workplaces, bazaars, and the domestic quarters of women; and as Long had observed the readings were performances, some by professionals, who sang or acted out the texts, bringing them alive before a vast audience.

The keepers of the catalogues did not waste space by commenting extensively on this ephemera, but they summarized its contents in a way that would inform the British reader about Oriental exoticism. Thus *Sarbbagyan Gyanmanjari*, or *The Blossoms of All Knowledge*: "Astrology or commonplace fortune telling, including the *Hanuman Charita*, the *Kak Charita* (signs and omens by the noise of crows) and *Spandan Charita*, by the spasmodic action and motion of the veins, eyes, and nerves."[48] Column 16 contained many précis of the plots of plays such as *Rajatgiri Nandini Natak*, or *The Daughter of the Golden Mountain Crest*:

> The son of Joubanashya, Raja of Pingal, fell in love with Khyanaprabha, daughter of the king of Rajatgiri, a fairy, and eventually married her; but an astrologer, who was the enemy of the prince, managed, by his machinations, to have the heroine exiled. Ultimately, however, she is sought after by, and rejoined to, her husband, and the wicked astrologer meets with his deserts by being killed.[49]

Put so baldly, the plot seemed to suggest that the "natives" amused themselves by fairy tales, like children. In the case of drama derived from religious literature, the remarks sounded less condescending. "The plot is taken from the *Ramayana*, and has often been noted in previous catalogues *in extenso*," observed William Lawler in 1879. "The natives seem to have a great predilection for those dramas adapted from the *Ramayana*, which are always acted with much spirit."[50] By 1900, however, the religious element in pulp fiction seemed to be receding before the advance of Western influences, including sentimental melodramas about unrequited love and the evils of drink.[51] Crime stories published in booklets to advertise hair oil made Calcutta look vaguely like dockside London, minus the cold and fog.[52] To the keepers of the catalogue, it was all rather distressing, a symptom of a new plebeian culture grafting itself onto a venerable, ancient civilization. A typical remark deplored a popular drama in 1900 as "a low-class farce. . . . It is a vulgar production and does not call for further notice."[53]

Column 16 does contain some admiring remarks about serious Bengali fiction. Rabindranath Tagore received complimentary notices long before he was awarded the Nobel Prize in 1913.[54] The catalogue hailed *Swarnalata* in 1881 as "perhaps the only novel (as distinguished from a romance or a poetical tale) yet written in Bengali."[55] It noted the influence of Brahmoism (a religious movement based in Bengal to reform traditional Hinduism),[56] the spread of literary reviews,[57] and the appearance of occasional volumes of poetry "inspired by genuine feeling and an appreciation of the beauties of nature."[58] Individual authors stand out, like Ishvarchandra Vidyasagar.[59] But nothing that corresponds to the "Bengal Renaissance" (a term that did not become current until the 1930s) is ever mentioned. Far from indicating any awareness of a general blossoming of modern literature, the catalogues leave an impression of a few good books bobbing about in a rising tide of vulgarity.

The main quality that commanded respect throughout the catalogues was philological prowess. Having received a double dose of education in the classics—Sanskrit and Persian on top of Greek and Latin—the librarians were quick to condemn faulty translations and impure language. They reserved their highest praise for treatises like *Bhasha Tattva*, or *Truths of Language*: "The chapter on the deduction of Bengali case sufffixes and verbal forms from Sanskrit discloses a true philological insight."[60] In reviewing fiction, they gave high marks for correct language and a traditional style.

Thus *Udvaha Chandraloka*, or *The Moonlight of Marriage*: "The book is written in pure, idiomatic Sanskrit, which very few pandits, if any, can write in these days. The metrical introduction . . . will be found to be of great value. The work is in every way worthy of the deep and varied scholarship of its author."[61] A proportionate degree of scorn fell on anything "low" and "vulgar" in style as well as subject matter. The cataloguers favored "Sanskritic" Bengali over "Mohammedan" Bengali, and they were especially severe when they came upon infelicitous writing. A full-scale review of a novel, *Gajimiyar Bastani*, or *Gajimiya's Bundle*, concluded, "The writer, though a Mahommedan, writes Bengali with ease and possesses a wonderful command over the vocabulary of the language. But his style is nevertheless ungrammatical and marked by East Bengalism and an absence of literary grace."[62] The keepers of the catalogues acted as guardians of the flame of culture, the Indian equivalent of the golden age of Greece. They identified civilization with Sanskritization, or what they took to be a cultural strain that led back to an ancient world of classical purity. That, too, belonged to the Raj constructed jointly by the British and the Indians.

SEDITION?

Nothing would seem to be further from political control than an obsession with literary style, but literature under the Raj was political in itself, down to its very syntax.[63] By adopting a Brahmanic view of Indian culture, the British reinforced their basic policy after 1857: leave the indigenous hierarchies in place and rule through the elite. At the same time, they used their surveillance of vernacular literature as a way to watch for signs of danger. When they sifted through poetry, they looked for symptoms of discontent among the "natives" as well as deviation from puranic purity. A reviewer dismissed a collection of thirty-four Bengali poems as "of not much importance"—all except for one:

> There is one poem, however, on the lament of India, wherein the abject and totally dependent state of the natives is brought out. The Briton is pictured as riding about in his conveyance, whilst music

plays to the tune of "Rule Britannia." . . . The natives are described as trembling with fear at the sight of a white man. The loss of independence of the natives and the departure for ever of their good and noble countrymen are deplored.[64]

The cataloguers paid special attention to plays, where they picked up a steady stream of comments on current events, just as James Long had done decades earlier. Spectacular trials like the Baroda case of 1876, which concerned a conflict between an Indian prince and a British "resident" or agent of the Raj, provided playwrights with plenty of material to condemn British justice, personified by a standard cast of villains: tyrannical judges, vicious policemen, and sadistic jailers.[65] By dramatizing miscarriages of justice, the plays made the whole regime look evil; and in some cases, they also attacked social injustices, including the exploitation of peasants by landlords, exactly as in *Nil Durpan*.[66] Behind the landlord loomed the figure of the district magistrate and even the missionary, both of them complicit in the basic task of draining India of its wealth and oppressing its people. A long review of a drama from 1878 concluded,

> The work embraces a variety of topics, such for instance as the utter hypocrisy of many Christian missionaries who, while ostensibly engaged in the work of preaching the Gospel, treat the natives of the country in a most cruel manner and do not shrink even on the slightest provocation to murder them. Their style of preaching, their pronunciation of the Bengali, the abuse they pour upon Hindu gods and goddesses and the wicked and hypocritical character of the native Christian converts are all powerfully satirized. The writer throws much ridicule on the manner in which trials of Europeans accused of murdering natives are conducted in the law courts. How a European beats to death an inoffensive native servant, for instance; how his widow and children are paid a few rupees as compensation for the loss of their guardian; how suborned witnesses are procured. . . . It is an altogether mischievous production, calculated to foster discontent and mislead ignorant people.[67]

It would be possible to string together enough quotations of that sort to suggest that British India was seething with sedition. In fact, however, the great majority of the comments in column 16 made no direct reference to politics; and when they did register signs of restlessness among the "natives," they did not sound particularly worried. Their tone remained matter-of-fact, as if the Indians could be left to let off steam while the British got on with the business of government.[68] Moreover, the Indian publications also expressed a strong countercurrent of support for British rule. Poems celebrated such unlikely subjects as the construction of waterworks:

> The author at first portrays in glowing language the many and lasting benefits conferred on the people of this country by the British government, and then describes such things as watches, coal, gas light, the mint, telegraph, railway, water-works, engine-made paper, the Asiatic Society, etc., all introduced or established by the English. The poetry of the book is pretty good.[69]

The visit of the Prince of Wales and Queen Victoria's assumption of the title Empress of India in 1876 produced bursts of poetical effusion, some of which hailed the British for liberating Indians from "the Mohammedan yoke and oppression," a fairly common theme in Hindu writing.[70] A few tracts contrasted the "Indian character" unfavorably with "the genius of the British."[71] In 1900, one went so far as to urge the Indians to "work more and talk less," avoiding all kinds of agitation in order to win the respect of their rulers.[72] Whether such sentiments were genuine or were a mixture of propaganda and sycophancy cannot be determined from the catalogues, but they occurred often enough to suggest that the British thought they had plenty of support among the literate elite.[73]

Discontent showed through nonetheless, not usually in the form of open opposition to British rule but rather in the themes of humiliation and oppression, which the cataloguers found everywhere by the end of the nineteenth century, even in plays and poems that sang the praises of the Raj. That such contradictions could coexist in the same body of literature may seem odd. Perhaps they are merely an optical illusion, produced by looking at that literature through a double filter: the historian studying the imperialists studying the texts. But contradictions were built into the core of imperialist culture. Seen through the catalogues, Indian literature in the nineteenth century combined self-hatred with hatred of the foreigner and self-assertion with deference to the sahib.

The contradictions derived in part from a cyclical view of history, in which golden ages of expansion gave way to iron ages of decline. The most golden of all took place in the remote past, when the Aryan people built a great civilization on the territory they conquered from 1500 to 450 B.C. The most decadent age began with the Mughal invasion of the sixteenth century and reached its nadir in the present, with the British Raj. Because the gods presided over this process, history shaded off into mythology. Lord Shiva, the god who had favored the Aryans, gave way to Kali, the goddess of destruction, whose ascendance made for misery in the current age of iron. Famine, plague, and poverty left the common people prostrate before the *feringis* (foreigners). Instead of seizing lathis (long, iron-bound clubs) and rallying against the conquerors, the elite adopted their ways. Everywhere, especially in Calcutta, babus were speaking *feringi* language, drinking *feringi* alcohol, and collecting the *feringis*' taxes. Some married without their parents' consent. Some even married widows! A sense of shame and decadence spread throughout the literature, accompanied by protests against foreign domination. "Young Bengal" became a favorite target of popular plays, printed as booklets, which adapted traditional themes to current events. *Sura-sanmilana*, or *The Assembly of the Demi-Gods*, seemed "full of import" to a cataloguer in 1879:

> It represents a meeting or *darbar* held in the presence of the three principal gods embodying the Hindu Trinity, with ten crores or thirty millions of the demi-gods as members to consider in committee the impending famine of 1268 B.C., or 1879 A.D. Lord Lytton [the current viceroy], as Indra, the king of the gods, is to blame for all this, who attends to nothing else but fun and sport and theatrical entertainments, living in the midst of luxury and all that is desirable for

life. He, however, exonerates himself by blaming the depravity of the times, especially among the natives, in this Kali or iron age—the prevalence of lying, lust, drink, etc. Sir Ashley Eden [then governor of Bengal] excuses himself in the person of Varuna, or the Indian Neptune, by saying that he has simply to obey and carry out orders, and has no will of his own in the matter. The alleged culprits are pardoned with a warning to take care that such things do not occur again in future. The names of the Viceroy and His Honor are not openly used, but the facts become evident from the tenor of the play.[74]

To be sure, some works, especially in new genres like the novel, were derived from Western models and celebrated the babu himself as a model of modernity.[75] But the most popular genres, above all drama, made the babu into a symbol of the deplorable effects of Westernization. In 1871, a typical farce turned on the theme "that the civilization of Young Bengal consists in eating meat and getting dead drunk."[76] By 1900, the Anglicized Indian had become a stock figure of traditional farces, used not merely to raise a laugh but to protest against British rule.[77] Poems and songs struck a common chord of indignation.[78] In a typical poem, "the Aryan race is upbraided and asked how the Britons, a nation of shopkeepers, could venture to sit on the Delhi throne?"[79] Everywhere the ancient Aryans served as a rebuke to the degradation of their descendants.[80] To imitate the Aryans was to cast off Western manners and to become more manly, more militant, and (at least in non-Muslim Bengali literature) more Hindu.[81] All these themes, as the librarians patiently culled through them and entered them in the catalogues, expressed a spirit not merely of discontent but of passionate nationalism. At their most vociferous, they sounded like a summons to rise in revolution:

> The Bengali is called a coward and taunted with being so accustomed to the chains of slavery, and so delighted with it, as to forget the very name and meaning of "independence." The poet reminds his countrymen of their noble ancestors and their valorous deeds; describes "independence" as a precious jewel, the very sound of

the name of which gives life to the dead; also that the Americans esteemed it so great a treasure as to have flown to arms with one accord to preserve it.[82]

How serious were these symptoms? To put them in perspective, I have compiled statistics from a broad sampling of the annual reports and have attempted to sketch a general picture of book production at the end of the century.[83] Unfortunately, however, statistical tables based on such sources are inevitably flawed. They sort books into categories like "fiction" and "philosophy," which made sense to the British but did not correspond to Indian conceptions and genres. Moreover, many books may have been published without being submitted to the British authorities for registration. The proportion could have been as high as 25 percent in Bengal, according to the report produced in Calcutta in 1898.[84] The uncatalogued works were mainly ephemeral chapbooks and "bazaar trash" in the view of the cataloguers; but those publications had a wide appeal, and they sometimes conveyed political protest, as in the case of *Nil Durpan*, which could be classified as "bazaar" literature if that category were construed broadly enough.[85]

Nonetheless, arbitrary as they are, the statistics demonstrate the scale of Indian production as well as the British effort to keep track of it. By 1900, Indian presses were churning out well over five thousand new books a year in a wide variety of genres and languages. The rising tide of publications included a few radical tracts, as Lawler and his successors had noted in preparing the reports. It is impossible to estimate their number, but they were not numerous enough to produce many ripples in a vast ocean of literature that looked conventional and calm to the British authorities. In its overwhelming mass, this literature consisted of ancient classics, devotional works, religious poetry, mythological tales, professional manuals, textbooks, almanacs, and cheap, popular fiction.[86]

After 1900, a few anti-imperialist works arrived in the mail from abroad, and others were produced in foreign enclaves like Pondicherry and Serampore. But India did not develop an elaborate underground literature comparable to that of pre-revolutionary France or Communist Eastern

Europe.[87] On the contrary, the government permitted the publication of books that seemed openly seditious to the men who registered them. The remarks in the catalogues and the reports to the lieutenant governors show that the ICS picked up potentially disturbing signals without becoming disturbed. The "natives" might be restive, but the British believed they had things well in hand.

REPRESSION

If examined a century later, after two world wars and countless colonial upheavals, the information looks more ominous than it did at the height of the Raj. It exposed an explosive passion: nationalism. As long as the contradiction between imperialism and liberalism remained latent, that passion could be contained. But when imperialism showed itself to be rule by right of conquest and when the printed word began to penetrate deeply into Indian society, the nationalists aroused a response, books became dangerous, and the Raj resorted to repression. Before 1900, the record seems to bear out the imperialists' conviction that they treated Indian literature liberally: Britannia ruled and the press remained free, free even to lament the country's lack of independence.[88] Afterward, things began to fall apart. The event that opened up the contradiction at the heart of the Raj took place in 1905: the partition of Bengal.

Of course, Bengal was not India. The Indian National Congress first met in Bombay in 1885, and nationalists first turned to terrorism in the Bombay presidency, where Balwantrao Gangadhar Tilak whipped up the passions of Marathi-speaking Hindus with his newspaper, *Kesari*. Groups of nationalist intellectuals also formed around newspapers in Madras (the *Mahajana Sabha*) and in Lahore (*The Punjabee*). But Calcutta, the capital of Indian literary life as well as of the British administration, provided the most fertile soil for agitation. Nationalism took root among its *bhadralok*, a large population of professional people, minor bureaucrats, and rentiers, who felt the pinch at the turn of the century, when the economy slumped and access to careers closed up. By 1905, young men from this milieu had been stirred by the Bengal Renaissance and the Hindu revival. Angry, articulate, overeducated, and underemployed, they warmed to the cult of Shivaji, the Maratha warrior who overthrew the Mughals in the seventeenth century; and they took fire when exposed to novels like *Yugantar*, by Sibnath Sastri, and *Kali, the Mother*, by Sister Nivedita (Margaret E. Noble). They also thrilled to reports of heroic self-sacrifice and nationalist agitation among the Carbonari, the Decembrists, the Italian Red Shirts, the Irish republicans, the Russian anarchists, and the Japanese soldiers, who showed that Asians could defeat Europeans in the Russo-Japanese War of 1904–05. The partition of Bengal, proposed by the viceroy Lord Curzon in 1903 and executed in October 1905, gave them a life-and-death cause in their own backyard.[89]

To the British, the partition made good, solid, bureaucratic sense. Bengal was a vast province of 189,000 square miles with a population of 80 million, more than twice that of Britain, and it could not be administered adequately by a lieutenant governor and a scattering of district officers. But to the Bengalis, the partition was a murderous blow, which cut deep into the flesh of their body politic. They attributed it to a cynical strategy of divide and rule: the new province of Eastern Bengal and Assam would provide the British with a docile Muslim dependency, while the *bhadralok* intellectuals of Calcutta would lose influence relative to the non-Bengali speakers of West Bengal. Speeches, petitions, protest meetings, demonstrations, and loud choruses of the new nationalist anthem *Bande Mataram* ("Hail to Thee, Mother"—i.e., India) fell on deaf ears. Curzon was as unbending as the steel brace that he wore to support his back. And Lord Minto, who succeeded him as viceroy in 1905, showed even less concern for the wishes of the native population, despite the prodding of his superior, John Morley, who took office as secretary of state for India with the Liberal government elected at the end of 1905. Morley favored all sorts of reforms, including the election of Indians to provincial councils; but when he acknowledged the partition of Bengal as a "settled fact," the Bengali intellectuals felt betrayed by the liberal principles that they had imbibed in their English schools.

After the failure of "mendicancy"—the policy of cooperation favored by the moderate wing of the Congress Party—the nationalists took to *swadeshi*, a strategy of boycotting British imports and favoring homemade goods. The boycott of manufactures led to the boycott of institutions—courts, schools, the civil service—and the demand for *swaraj* (self-rule, independence). Groups of militants drew on revivalist Hinduism in order to develop alternative forms of civic life, such as the *ashram* (rural retreat) and the *samiti* (an assembly or association). They founded schools, where they drilled young men in "lathi play," or the use of the traditional sword-staff, and sometimes indulged in wild talk of enforcing the boycott through violence and of resorting to political banditry (*dacoity*, or gang robbery). The agitation became directed against the Muslims as well as the British, because the huge Muslim minority, 30 percent of the population in Calcutta itself, remained untouched by the Hindu revival and unmoved, in most cases, by the boycott. The creation of the All-India Muslim League, with Minto's encouragement, at the end of 1906 confirmed the view that the British were playing a game of divide and rule. Hindu-Muslim riots at Comilla and Mymensingh in the spring of 1907 drove a wedge between the two populations. Under the pretext of restoring order, the British suspended civil liberties and began arresting agitators everywhere from Bengal to the Punjab. But the Hindus themselves split when the Congress Party broke up at its annual meeting in December 1907. And the extremists found themselves increasingly isolated—unable to work with the old, moderate political elite, on the one hand, and incapable of mobilizing the impoverished, illiterate peasant masses, on the other.

Trapped in this impasse, the most radical nationalists tried to blast their way out by means of bombs. The examples of European anarchists, the notion of propaganda of the deed, the appeal of heroic self-sacrifice, and the cult of Kali also reinforced the turn to terrorism. On April 30, 1908, a bomb killed two British women in a railway car at Muzaffarpur. The investigation led to a raid on a terrorist group in Maniktala, a suburb of Calcutta. After one of the group incriminated the others and exposed their entire operation, he was assassinated in the Alipore jail by two more terrorists in August. A subinspector of police and a public prosecutor were murdered in November. In July 1909, a Punjabi extremist assassinated Morley's aide, Sir William Curzon-Wyllie, in London. The terrorists also made attempts on the lives of Minto and one of his aides, Sir Andrew Fraser, but they failed to blow the British administration off course and to spark an uprising of the peasants. The cycle of violence came to an end with an unsuccessful attempt on the life of Minto's successor, Lord Hardinge, in 1912. By then, most of the extremists had been arrested or driven out of the country. The transfer of the capital to Delhi and the reunification of Bengal in 1911, followed by the outbreak of World War I, put an end to this first phase of nationalist agitation. In retrospect, it seems clear that the partition protests and the terrorist campaign never constituted a serious threat to the Raj. But they looked terribly threatening between 1904 and 1912, when the British kept reminding themselves that they were an alien population of a few hundred thousand trying to rule a subcontinent of several hundred million while preaching the virtues of freedom from arbitrary arrest and freedom of the press.

The press had fueled the explosion of nationalism from the very beginning. The leading agitators were men of letters, who drew their inspiration from literature, both Indian and Western, and gathered around newspapers and libraries. Calcutta's most important nationalist circle, the Anushilan Samiti, had a library of four thousand volumes, and its revolutionary weekly, *Yugantar*, which mixed belles-lettres with calls for revolutionary action, took its name from the novel by Sibnath Sastri. Songs, plays, poems, pamphlets, religious tracts, histories, literature of every variety turned up wherever a British agent discovered signs of sedition. The servants of the Raj knew this literature very well, because they had been keeping track of it for forty years in their catalogues and reports. After 1905 the question was: How could they use this information to repress the outbreak of nationalism?

At this point surveillance turned into punishment. It took two forms: repression by the police and prosecution in the courts.

The police action resembled that of authoritarian regimes everywhere. It involved raids on bookshops; interrogation and intimidation of suspects; the arrest of authors, publishers, and printers; the interception of letters and packages in the mail; even the use of secret agents to report on what was said in meetings and what was read in schools. As accounts

of this activity began to churn through the vast digestive tract of the
India Civil Service, it became clear that the literature now deemed to
be seditious was the same as the literature that had appeared for years in
the catalogues. It covered the same spectrum of themes and genres and
included many of the same books, but now the agents of the Raj wanted
to annihilate it, whatever the cost might be in the loss of civil liberties.
"Summary procedures" were necessary, according to the lieutenant governor of the Punjab, for the "natives" were "credulous," "emotional," "inflammable," and liable to explode when provoked by seditious messages.[90] Only
"autocratic government" could keep the "diverse races" of India in check,
according to the lieutenant governor of Burma: all dubious publications
had to be eradicated, but with as little fuss as possible so that no one in
Britain would hear about it.[91] In the Central Provinces, one commissioner
worried about protests from "Sir Henry Cotton and Company and other
misguided politicians in England."[92] But another recommended severe
repression: "The gravity of the situation demands that we take whatever
is absolutely the most effective measure for controlling sedition in the
press without regard to any Western theories or sentiments, which are
not applicable to the condition of this country."[93] Everywhere the men in
the field seemed to regard freedom of expression as a Western luxury that
would make government impossible in India.[94] Lord Minto pressed their
views on Morley, demanding arbitrary power to curb the press.[95] But the
liberty of the press belonged to the most sacred articles in "Honest John"
Morley's Liberal creed; and the disparity between preaching liberalism
and practicing imperialism stood out every week during question time in
Parliament, when backbenchers like Sir Henry Cotton, a well-informed
expert on Indian affairs, exposed the illiberalism of British rule in India
for all the world to see.[96]

    While Minto and Morley dueled in their dispatches, the humbler agents
of the Raj filled the confidential correspondence of the ICS with reports
of repression. In one raid on a nationalist association, the books confiscated by the police included Aristotle's *Politics*, as well as English-language
works such as *The Awakening of Japan* and *The Life and Writing of Joseph
Mazzini*.[97] To print, without comment, accounts of nationalist movements

in Ireland and Italy seemed subversive to officials in Bombay: "Government are teaching the ryot to read, and unless Government see that the ryot is provided with wholesome matter to read, he must inevitably become the prey of the purveyor of literary poison."[98] The Raj officials would not permit the import of a book of excerpts from official documents printed by the government in London, because it made the Indian police look bad.[99] Postal inspectors often seized *The Gaelic American* and anti-imperialist speeches of William Jennings Bryan in the mail. Bryan, translated into Indian languages, seemed especially threatening to the Criminal Investigation Department: "The ignorant Hindu reader imagines that Bryan is qualified to criticize, and that he is English instead of being what he is—an American demagogue and openly hostile to England."[100] The officials hesitated to condemn a book by the fiery Punjabi nationalist Ajit Singh, in which he simply strung together short biographies of great patriots, from Brutus to Robert Bruce, John Hampden, and Samuel Adams.[101] But they planned to prosecute a publisher for reprinting some speeches by Balwantrao Gangadhar Tilak, which had been permitted at the end of the nineteenth century. They also saw sedition in a reprint of a hostile history of the East India Company by William Howitt, which was first published in 1838 and had been available in several public libraries ever since. In a brief for the prosecution, a legal adviser to the government did not dispute the accuracy or the age of the text. Instead, sounding more like a modern reception theorist than an agent of the Raj, he argued that it had taken on new meaning. An unsophisticated reader of the cheap, modern, Urdu edition might believe that the criticism made in 1838 applied to the Raj in 1909. "It is the effect on the general reader that must be considered," he insisted. And as a clincher to his argument, he noted, "The legislature has decreed that the reputation of the present Government of India shall be sacred." The advocate-general of the Government of India concurred: "What some years back would have been innocent matter is today dangerous."[102] The same arguments applied to other books, which had been duly registered in the catalogues without arousing charges of sedition.[103] The literary landscape remained the same as it had been before 1905, but it looked entirely different.

COURTROOM HERMENEUTICS

Having executed this Gestalt switch and filled its jails with arrested authors, the agents of the Raj needed to get them convicted in court. This last step was the most difficult of all, because it threatened to expose the contradiction inherent in liberal imperialism. The British were committed to play by the rules that they had imposed upon the Indians. They believed in those rules—the rule of justice first of all—as the measure of the civilization they had brought to the subcontinent. So they accepted the right of Indians to publish books under the same constraints that applied to Englishmen—that is, freely, subject to the laws of libel and sedition. To be sure, sedition had acquired a peculiar meaning under the Raj. According to Section 124A of the Indian Penal Code of 1860, written in the confusion of the post-Rebellion era, it applied to anyone who "excites or attempts to excite feelings of disaffection to the Government."[104] Disaffection remained undefined until 1897, when a court in Poona condemned Tilak, the most influential nationalist at the turn of the century, to eighteen months of rigorous imprisonment for an article he had published in his newspaper, *Kesari*. Infuriated by the government's failure to take adequate measures during the bubonic plague of 1896, he had cited the Bhagavad Gita as justification for the murder of a Mughal general by Shivaji during a desperate moment in 1659. Some days later, one of Tilak's followers murdered a British official. The judge found Tilak guilty of sedition under Section 124A, setting a precedent for dozens of cases tried during the agitation after the partition of Bengal. Tilak himself was tried and convicted again in 1908, this time with a sentence of transportation for six years to a prison in Mandalay.[105]

By then the government had passed new legislation to strengthen its hand in the courts. The Indian Penal Code Amendment Act of 1898 reaffirmed the catchall character of Section 124A with some additional language, which was vaguer than ever: "The expression 'disaffection' includes disloyalty and all feelings of enmity."[106] The Indian Criminal Law Amendment Act of 1908 did away with trial by jury in certain cases of sedition. The Newspapers Act, also passed in 1908, empowered district magistrates to seize presses of papers they deemed to be seditious. And the Indian Press Act of 1910 required all owners of presses to deposit security and authorized magistrates to confiscate both the money and the presses in order to stop disaffection "both by openly seditious writing and by suggestion and veiled incitement to inculcate hostility to British rule."[107] These measures applied to all publications, books and pamphlets as well as newspapers, and authorized searches of the mail and of bookshops in addition to printing shops. Because the Dramatic Performances Act of 1876 had given district magistrates even broader powers to prevent productions of plays, nearly all the media had become subject to arbitrary action by the authorities.[108] It merely remained for the judges and lawyers to put on convincing performances in the courtrooms.

In retrospect, the verdicts look like foregone conclusions. Judges outraged by terrorist incidents were not likely to be lenient. Most of the authors were convicted and sentenced to "rigorous imprisonment," usually for terms of one to six years, sometimes with an additional punishment of a heavy fine and "transportation" to a sweltering prison in Mandalay. To make the sentences carry weight, however, the judges, lawyers, clerks, and bailiffs had to play their parts effectively. The wigs and robes, the gaveling and taking of oaths, the standing up and sitting down, the legalistic language and formalistic courtesies—"Your Honor," "the Learned Pleader"—demonstrated the legitimacy of British law in an Indian setting. But the Indians had learned to play that game, too. Their pleaders had studied in British schools and could defend their clients by citing British precedents—or, if need be, Shakespeare and Milton. Of course, most citations tended to come from the *Mahabharata* and the *Ramayana*, for that is where the accused writers drew their inspiration. To win their case, the prosecutors had to argue at times on native grounds. But the British had educated themselves in the ways of the "natives" just as the Indians had trained in the schools of the sahibs. Decades of learned commentary in the catalogues demonstrated that the agents of the Raj had developed a vast knowledge of Indian literature. In key cases, the cataloguers themselves testified in court. So the courtroom turned into a hermeneutic battlefield, where each side acted out its interpretation of the other and imperialism appeared, at least for a few moments while the muskets were stored in their racks, as a contest for symbolic dominance through textual exegesis.

Consider the following poem, which was published in a literary review, *Pallichitra*, in 1910 and typifies the material condemned as seditious in the courts.[109] Because its author could not be identified (he was later found and sent to prison for two years), the editor of the volume, Bidhu Bhusan Bose, was put on trial before a district magistrate, R. C. Hamilton, in Khulna, Bengal. After pronouncing Bose guilty of sedition under Section 124A of the Indian penal code, the judge declared that he deserved to be transported for life, so heinous was his crime. In the end, he was sentenced to two years of rigorous imprisonment, and his printer had to serve two months as an accomplice. What, then, was the wickedness in the following words, which are given in the translation from the Bengali provided by the official court translator?

ESHO MA POLLI-RANI

Come Oh Mother Queen of the village, the day is drawing its full length to a close. Let thy children rise up with bounding hearts hearing thy great voice. I have sacrificed my life to take away the crown of victory from the enemy's brow and decorate thee thou Queen of Queens with it in the battle of life.

Led by mistaken ideas and tormented by passion, I did not perceive and could not feel at heart when (thy) golden seat disappeared.

*   *   *

Under the stamp of Asur's feet there are no Parijat flowers in the Nandan Gardens; and in the garb of a beggar, Indrani is sorely suffering in the most recess [sic] of her heart.

The Suras who have conquered death, see all this before them and like cowards shut up their eyes for hatred and shame. Oh, mother, I do not know when for the Swadesh, the gods will rise up in a body, and burning with rage as fierce as the world-destroying fire kill the force of their adversaries, and relying on their own strength and *taking up their own arms, re-establish the throne of the Heavens by offering drinks of blood to the manes.*

Most readers today would probably find the poem utterly opaque. To the district magistrate in 1910, however, it was clear: a case of rank sedition. There was nothing esoteric about it which an "ordinary reader" could not grasp, he claimed, for its meaning was transparent to anyone with an elementary knowledge of Hindu mythology: the queen was Mother India, also referred to as Indrani; the flowery garden was the paradise the British had destroyed; the Asur were devils, that is, the British; and the Suras were gods, that is, the Indians, now reduced to beggary but soon to rise and overthrow their oppressors. The context of current events made the message of the poem horrifyingly clear, as the magistrate explained it:

> The poem was published . . . about the middle of July last; there had previously to its publication been a series of murderous attacks upon English men and women in India, upon British officials especially. The poem would be meaningless unless by the allusions to the slaughtering of the demons (asur) the British race were meant. The object of the writer evidently was to incite his Hindu fellow countrymen to join together to murder the British in India. In view of the terribly pernicious effect such literature as this is found to produce on the younger generation of Bengal, . . . not only is a deterrent sentence necessary, but it is also necessary to remove for some time to come, to prevent him further harming society, one who has been persistently harming society. . . . I do not think there is any reason for treating his offence lightly. I accordingly sentence him to two years rigorous imprisonment.

This interpretation, however, had not gone uncontested. The judge reached it only after a hermeneutic free-for-all between the defense lawyer and the prosecuting attorney. According to the defense, words meant what dictionaries said they meant and what ordinary people understood them to mean. He quoted from dictionaries and called some man-in-the-street type of witnesses in order to drive the point home. One key term, *boyrishir* in Bengali, could hardly refer to the British government, as the prosecution claimed, because its conventional meaning was "from the head of the enemy." Another, *asur*, meant the "forces of darkness." It could not refer to Englishmen, as he demonstrated by showing how it had been used in speeches of the viceroy. As to a third supposedly incriminating term, *rudhir*, it was used in common sayings such as "I will offer my blood," indicating a willingness to make a sacrifice. Anyone familiar with the customs of Hindus knew that they frequently sacrificed animals and that there was nothing offensive in the notion of blood being offered for a worthy cause. At the level of metaphor, the poem used the same figures of speech as in Hamlet's most famous soliloquy. It was a meditation on freedom, based on the opposition between town life and country life, like Goldsmith's "Deserted Village." Indeed, Goldsmith's poem contained a much stronger declamation against tyranny, yet it was commonly read, with no ill effects, by Indian children in British schools. In case the British had forgotten how their own poets celebrated freedom, the defense lawyer treated the court to some stirring passages from Cowper. In comparison with Cowper, he insisted, his client was mildness itself. Of course, the author of the Bengali poem drew on Hindu mythology; but if the court were to forbid all such references, nothing would be left of vernacular literature. To read sedition into such a poem was not merely to get it wrong but to fan the flames of panic instead of calming them.

In rebuttal, the prosecutor raked over the text once more, arguing that the defense's reading of it compounded faulty definitions with incoherent metaphors. *Asur*, for example, could not mean "darkness," "for they are given legs and feet and described as trampling down paradise flowers under foot." The textual exegesis went on and on, until the judge called a halt and offered a reading of his own, line by line, and finally arrived at the bottom line: sedition. The trial had everything that one would expect to encounter in a modern class on poetry: philology, semantic fields, metaphorical patterns, ideological contexts, reader response, and interpretive communities.

Similar debates took place in case after case, for the authorities began to see sedition in all sorts of publications—histories, political pamphlets, religious tracts, plays, and songbooks. What had appeared as the harmless beginnings of a modern literature before 1905 stood condemned as revolutionary agitation by 1910. Literature now looked dangerous, because it was no longer restricted to the literati: it was spreading to the masses—that is, spreading disaffection, and disaffection meant sedition. Considering the impoverished and illiterate state of most Indian peasants, the diagnosis seems exaggerated. But the civil service took it seriously:

> Inflammatory statements . . . are read with avidity and believed without question in bazaars and villages. . . . From the original credulous readers, the report is disseminated among an illiterate population, whose susceptibility to the most extravagant rumors is proverbial, becoming in transit ever more distorted and more violent. . . . The dak [post] arrives, bringing with it the *Sandhya* or *Charu Mihir* or other paper locally popular, and someone among the village leaders reads out passages to a collection of *bhadralog* and others under the shelter of a convenient tree. Even the passing cultivator lays down his plough and joins the expectant group. The poisonous extracts are heard and digested, and then all disperse and go their ways, retailing what they have learnt with heaven knows what embellishments and exaggerations.[110]

Of course, newspapers, as indicated in this report from a district officer, seemed especially threatening, because they combined ideology with news. But books and pamphlets, especially collections of songs and texts of plays, could penetrate even more effectively into the world of the illiterate, because they were acted out in oral performances, which often combined music, mime, and drama. Consider two final examples of court cases.

WANDERING MINSTRELS

On December 11, 1907, R. P. Horsbrugh, a district magistrate in Amraoti, Central Provinces, sentenced Swami Shivanad Guru Yoganand, alias Ganesh Yadeo Deshmukh, to transportation for seven years for distributing and declaiming a seditious songbook, *Swarajya Sapan*, or *Steps to Self-Government*.[111] Deshmukh wrote the songs, had them printed, and peddled them throughout the region, singing as he went. In order to promote sales—so the judge claimed—he changed his name and dressed as a mendicant holy man, a marketing strategy that appealed "to the hearts of the illiterate many in every town and village through which he wandered." By "meter and music," the fake swami whipped up the emotions of "the credulous rustics who would be impressed only too readily by what fell from the lips of a *sanyasi* [Brahmin holy man]." The judge considered this "a very serious crime," sedition of a sort that used to be punished by death:

> It is high time that the public generally realized that sedition in India is no longer a mere vituperative babbling which passes harmlessly over the heads of the mass of the people, as it did perhaps a quarter of a century ago. Education and internal communications have now been so largely developed, and a disaffected press has been so many years at work, that libels against the government . . . have become a political danger, which it is the duty of the criminal courts to check and, if possible, to uproot by stern justice.

As an example of Swami Shivanad's treachery, the judge cited the following verse from one of his songs:

> *O God having an elephant head and a crooked mouth. By turning your kind proboscis give in the hands of the Aryans the banner of devotion to the country.*

It didn't sound like "God Save the King," but what did it mean? A bewildered Morley, after being informed of the case, telegraphed to ask whether the verse merited seven years of transportation to Malaya. He was told that the elephant-headed god, Ganesh, was especially revered in the militant Hindu cult promoted by Tilak. Moreover, the prosecuting attorney had accumulated evidence of insubordination that struck closer to home:

another song asserted, "It is a settled fact that Morley is a bitter Karela."
(A karela is a balsam pear.) And still others played with powerful but
confusing images:

> O impotent! What for bow and arrow? By making their pockets
> empty let them feel a pinch in their stomachs. Show your mettle to
> the English by being resolute. By their oppressions or tyranny we do
> not get sufficient food, nor (do we get) water free. Abuses and curses
> are fruitless in the end. These selfish (Englishmen) eat the butter
> on the sinciput of one's dead brethren. Nobody pays heed to the
> complaints. (That they are) deceitful, of profound contrivance and
> thoroughly cunning is known to the entire world. Ward off or save
> yourselves (from these). By playing Pobara, let your counters go in
> a pair with the help of their own strength (so that) they (the English)
> will decamp. Government will be awe-struck. Language or words
> cannot describe the oppressions and calamities. No fodder has been
> left for cattle.

This text obviously challenged the exegetical capacities of the court.
With help from the official translator, the judge supplied a critical gloss.
The protests about poverty and exploitation included a reference to a
recent increase in irrigation rates. The buttered *sinciput* referred to the
Hindu custom of placing butter on the tops of the heads of corpses in
order to facilitate cremation. And Pobara was a dice game, which evoked
a kind of unity comparable to a perfect throw (a 6 on two dice and a 1 on
the third), while at the same time punning in the original Marathi with
notions of decamping and forming a league.

All this constituted some irreverent play with words, but sedition?
Certainly not, said the swami's lawyer. The translation was all wrong. A
native Marathi speaker would recognize the remark on eating butter as
a reference to the writer's brethren, not to the English; and the punning
about the dice game was nothing more than a verbal conceit. A later
reference to Edward VII was perfectly respectful, as anyone could see by
distinguishing which noun was the subject of the verb. The whole song

expressed a mood of playfulness, not sedition; it merely needed to be read from the viewpoint of a native speaker. But the judge would have none of this argument. He rejected the defense's concept of translation in general and of the song in particular: "Not only would such a translation violate the rules of grammar, but it would disconnect the passage in syntax and in sense from everything which goes before and follows after it." In the end, of course, the prosecution won, and the swami went to jail.

The final case concerns Mukunda Lal Das, the leader of a *jatra* party, or troupe of players, who toured by boat through the Ganges Delta, performing dramas in peasant villages. Their greatest hit in 1908 was *Matri Puja*, a play adapted from a puranic tale about the conflict between the *Daityas* (demons) and the *Devas* (gods). After a successful run of performances in Calcutta, the play had been printed and registered in the catalogue for Bengal. But it was banned in 1908, when the keeper of the catalogue testified in court that it was a "seditious allegory" that attacked the leading figures in the Raj.[112] When Mukunda performed it in the hinterland, he improvised lines to mock local officials and even the king-emperor, George V. He added mime, music, and song; and he also composed his own songbook, which went through several editions and circulated widely along with other songbooks, which took some of their material from his. From Sanskrit texts to modern books and from the Calcutta stage to village vaudeville, *Matri Puja* traveled across a vast stretch of culture. And when Mukunda took it to the masses, the ICS smelled sedition. District officers tried to stop his tour at many points, but he evaded them for nine months until finally, after 168 highly successful performances, he was arrested and brought to trial.

There were actually two trials, which took place before the same magistrate, V. Dawson, in Barisal in January and February 1909. The first concerned the songbook, the second the *jatra* tour. Both were linked with other cases and with a broad investigation of the nationalist movement by the ICS. At the heart of it all was "The White Rat Song," the biggest hit in Mukunda's extensive repertory, which the official translator rendered as follows:

*Babu, will you realise your situation when you die? The white
devil is upon you (literally, upon your shoulders) and is totally
ruining you. Formerly you used to take your food in gold dishes, but
now you are satisfied with steel dishes. A second fool like you is not
to be met with. You have liked pomatum neglecting the indigenous
otto, and it is why they call you "brutes," "nonsense," and "foolish"
(literally, do they willingly call you brutes, etc.). Your granary was
full of paddy, but the white rat has destroyed it. Babu, just take off
the specs, and look around you. Do you know, Deputy Babu, now
your head is under the boots of the Feringhees, that they have ruined
your caste and honor and carried away your riches cleverly?* [113]

The defense lawyer contended that the last line should read, "Status and
rewards these days go only to businessmen, therefore go into business."
Its meaning turned on the pronoun "they," which could not possibly refer
to *feringhees* (foreigners), he argued, owing to the peculiarities of Bengali
syntax and, in particular, the use of "the seventh case with the force of
the nominative." Soon the court was embroiled in a debate about dictionaries, grammatical cases, Sanskrit roots, and the relative value of literal
as opposed to figurative translations. But the judge finally put a stop to
it with his verdict: Mukunda had committed sedition, and he would go
to jail.

In rejecting esoteric exegesis, the judge conformed to a variety of legal
hermeneutics set by the Tilak case of 1897, when Justice Strachey had
instructed the jury (cases of sedition normally took place before juries until
1908, when magistrates were empowered to dispatch with them) to avoid
too much sophistication:

In judging of the intention of the accused, you must be guided not
only by your estimate of the effect of the articles upon the minds
of their readers, but also by your common sense, your knowledge of
the world, your understanding of the meaning of words, and your
experience of the way in which a man writes when he is animated
by a particular feeling. Read the articles, and ask yourself, as men of

the world, whether they impress you on the whole as a mere poem and a historical discussion without disloyal purpose, or as attacks on the British Government under the disguise of a poem and historical discussion. It may not be easy to express the difference in words; but the difference in tone and spirit and general drift between a writer who is trying to stir up ill-will and one who is not, is generally unmistakable.[114]

When it was intent on suppressing sedition, the Raj did not permit its courts to become entangled in Sanskrit syntax and Vedic mythology. Good, solid common sense would do—British common sense, though it was hardly common to the Indians. The judges therefore brushed aside "native" arguments about the meaning of words in a series of cases about seditious publications. In a typical case, which took place four months after the condemnation of Mukunda and also involved "The White Rat Song," the magistrate rejected an argument over etymology by a clever defense lawyer and delivered a hermeneutical pronouncement of his own:

> We must not go back to the etymological origin for the meaning of the words. To do this would in all probability pervert the meaning of all the songs. It is only one in a hundred who understands Sanskrit or who thinks of the Sanskrit equivalent when determining the meaning to be given to any particular word of the Bengali language. . . . The Bengali of the [White Rat] song is ridiculously simple and there can be no argument about the meaning which the man in the street would attach to it. . . . I hold it amounts to an imputation that the English rulers have robbed the country of everything and have trodden even the Deputy Babus under foot. This is sedition pure and simple.[115]

But Mukunda's case involved a great deal more than British intuition about Bengali linguistics. The ICS had worked on it for months, accumulating information that showed how the songs meshed with other cultural practices, which extended across a broad spectrum of Indian society. A background report on the case revealed that Mukunda and his players, a troupe or "party" of sixteen men, had been touring for at least two years through the complex river system of the Ganges Delta. They traveled from village to village, followed by district officers with injunctions to forbid the performances. When an officer arrived, they piled into their boat and took their show to a new location across the district line, where they were immune from the officer's authority. The ICS could map their progress across a large area of Eastern Bengal.

Thanks to local spies, the agents of the Raj also had a pretty good idea of what took place in Mukunda's *jatras* or musical dramas. "A favorite performance introduces an anti-swadeshi deputy magistrate and his wife," a district officer reported. In it, Mukunda "referred opprobriously to Lord Curzon and Sir Bampfylde Fuller" (the lieutenant governor of Bengal). The allusions were transparent in themselves, and they also were identified at the trial of the printer who had produced the published version of the *Matri Puja*—that is, the play which Mukunda had transformed into a *jatra*. The play's author, Kunja Behari Ganguli, had fled; so the court had to content itself by fining the printer 200 rupees and listening to a lecture on mythology and allegory by Manmatha Natha Rudra, the Bengal librarian and keeper of the catalogue. He testified that the play was "clearly a seditious allegory on the present political situation of the country."[116] Ostensibly, the plot concerned nothing more than an ancient myth, but Rudra assured the court that it could easily be read as a commentary on current events:

> The play is based on Chandi in the Markandeya Puran. The Daityas (giants inhabiting the nether world, but now generally used in the sense of demons) headed by their leaders, Sumbha and Nisumbha, have taken possession of the kingdom of heaven from the Devas (Gods) by force and are ruling it despotically. The Devas, three hundred and thirty millions in number, though usually divided among themselves and always envious of each other, are at last made by the oppression of their overlords to come to unity and by the help of the goddess Chandi (the mother of the world), who being insulted

by the Daitya king, herself appears in battle, wins a victory over the Daityas and regains the kingdom of heaven.

The political incidents made use of in the play are:

1. The alleged attempt of the government to put down the cry of Bande Matram and what is called worship of the mother country.
2. The refusal of the people of Eastern Bengal to present addresses of welcome to Sir Bampfylde Fuller.
3. The desire of the nobility to please the Government, which is twitted.
4. The outbreak of famine.
5. The boycott of Manchester goods.
6. The prosecution and whipping of students, which is represented as high-handed and unjustifiable persecution.
7. Persistence of students in the present agitation.
8. Visit of His Royal Highness The Prince of Wales to India and his wish expressed on his return to England that the people should be more sympathetically governed. The Daitya king in the play, who is represented as a good-hearted monarch with a sincere wish to rule his subjects well, regrets that he discarded the advice of his son under the arguments advanced by his counsellors, a set of Pisaches (devils) who are making the meek and weak shed tears, in order that they might extend their own mastery.
9. Outrage of women in Eastern Bengal.

The advocate general of Bengal expanded on this interpretation by citing newspaper reviews, which linked the play to current politics. He showed how the names of the Deva leaders were acronyms of prominent nationalist politicians, while the supreme villain of the play, Crurjan, clearly referred to the viceroy, Lord Curzon. Nearly two years later, the British finally got their hands on Ganguli, the author of the play, who received a relatively lenient sentence of one year's imprisonment, because he pleaded guilty. He also said that he had received 400 rupees from Mukunda for the right to perform it.[117]

Mukunda's performances made the text come alive for the relatively unsophisticated audiences of the hinterland. The judge who condemned him acknowledged condescendingly that he had some facility with words: "The accused, though a person of inferior class, has higher literary attainments than are usually found in men of his class. He can at least sign his name in English and is the compiler of a book of songs."[118] And district officers, despite their hostility, testified to his skill at striking a responsive chord among the "natives": "The amount of mischief which he has succeeded in doing may be gauged by the popularity of the performances, which is undoubted." In fact, Mukunda seems to have had considerable talent as a performer and director of *jatra*, which required an ability to improvise, act, sing, and mime. As he reworked it, Ganguli's text turned into a kind of vaudeville. Mukunda made the collaborationist Indian deputy magistrate—the "Deputy Babu" of "The White Rat Song"—into a stooge and threw in scornful references to the British—from the viceroy down to local district officers—as the spirit moved him. While he improvised, the other actors followed his lead, breaking regularly into song. "On one occasion," a district officer reported, "his performance included the personation [*sic*] of His Majesty the King-Emperor, who was abused and insulted in an indecent manner by a member of the company representing the Indian people."

Although the troupe normally performed in peasant villages, it also played before some eminent Indians and adapted its standard fare to special occasions. In Manakhar the players put on a performance in a Brahmin's house before an image of the goddess Kali. In another private home, they sang swadeshi songs before a group of prominent nationalists, including Aswini Kumar Dutt, who "embraced him [Mukunda] with tears running down his cheeks, and the whole assembly shouted 'Bande Mataram.' " Some performances seemed primarily to be concerts, others to serve as entertainment at nationalist rallies. Everywhere Mukunda whipped up audiences with "The White Rat Song"—"his best known and most objectionable," according to the agents of the ICS. He was hailed throughout the region as "the swadeshi jatrawalla."

When he came to the end of his tour, in November 1908, Mukunda retired to his home Bakarganj, where at last the police arrested him. They searched the premises and the boat, turning up a great deal of incriminating evidence: the "libretto" of *Matri Puja*; songbooks; an account book, which showed that he had made a small fortune, 3,000 rupees, from the 168 performances; and correspondence with Aswini Kumar Dutt, which indicated that the *jatras* belonged to a vast campaign launched from Aswini's nationalist stronghold, the Braja Mohan Institution in Barisal.

The Braja Mohan Institution was both a school and a kind of *samiti*, or home base for nationalist agitation. To the ICS, which followed its activities intensely, it was "a revolutionary organization, designed and trained for an eventual rising against the British government."[119] It had 159 branches in Eastern Bengal, and Aswini Kumar Dutt, its proprietor, had connections with the most famous nationalist leaders, notably Tilak. While providing boys with a basic education, it instructed them in "lathi play" (a military drill, involving a traditional club with a metal head) and trained them to spread the message of swadeshi. They accompanied convicted publicists to jail and escorted them home on their release, chanting Bande Mataram. They promoted the boycott of British goods by burning imported cloth. At religious festivals (*melas*), they proselytized pilgrims. During demonstrations, they tied *rakhis* (red threads) on people's arms to symbolize the blood to be shed in the struggle for independence. They persuaded Brahmins to refuse religious rites to local dignitaries who collaborated with the British. And they also tried to force compliance with swadeshi by getting barbers, laundresses, servants, and even prostitutes to refuse their services to those who wavered. Through it all, they sang nationalist songs, especially those by Mukunda.[120]

The reports on these activities by nervous district officers should not be taken literally. They do not prove that India was about to explode in revolution, but they suggest the context of Mukunda's performances and the ways in which his songs resonated in the surrounding culture. The songs themselves came straight out of the Braja Mohan Institution, which provided Mukunda with a base. One of the teachers at the school, Bhaba-ranjan Mazumdar, included "The White Rat Song" with several others in a songbook, *Deser Gan*, which he had printed in Barisal. It went through three editions, the last at a pressrun of 1,000 copies; and he had it peddled by the schoolboys, along with nationalist pamphlets, which he also had printed. The police tracked the publications to their source, and Mazum-dar was sentenced to eighteen months in prison after a trial that included the usual debates about language and puranic mythology.[121] Mukunda pro-duced his own songbook, *Matri Puja Gan*, at the same time and with the same printer. It consisted of fifty-three songs, many of them, "The White Rat" included, from the libretto that he had composed for the *jatra* version of Ganguli's play. The prosecuting attorney made the songbook the cen-terpiece of the first of the two sedition trials involving Mukunda. He had all fifty-three songs translated and concentrated on four of them, in order to prove, by explication de texte, that Mukunda had fomented sedition through the publication of a revolutionary tract. After considerable dis-cussion of Daityas and Devas, the judge pronounced the inevitable verdict: guilty under Section 124A. He sentenced Mukunda to a year in prison, and then added two more years in the subsequent trial, which concerned the *jatra* tour.

Mukunda received twice as long a prison term for his singing as for the publication of his songs—testimony to the importance of oral communica-tion in a society with a low rate of literacy. But the communication process involved a great deal more than adapting printed texts to diffusion by word of mouth. To Mukunda's audience, culture was performed. For his message to take, it had to be acted out and embellished with commentary in gesture and in song. Therefore *jatras*, as he perfected them, carried the message of swadeshi far beyond the range of the printed word. Their effectiveness was acknowledged by the judge, when he declared Mukunda guilty: "There can be no question that the harm done by the accused by penetrations into remote villages with his mischievous propaganda was infinitely greater than the harm done by him in publishing a printed book." To be sure, *jatras* were a specialty of Bengal, but popular theater posed the same threat to the Raj everywhere. At the other extreme of the subcontinent, the secretary to the Government of Bombay warned the Government of India,

> There has been a great increase in the number of plays of a seditious character, which are performed before large audiences at all the larger centers of population. . . . The effect of such plays is even more pernicious than that of the seditious press, for they appeal to persons who are not reached by the newspapers, and the passions are more easily excited by what is represented in action on the stage than by what is merely read.[122]

The printed word was powerful, nonetheless, because it became transmuted into other forms. Hence the history of "The White Rat Song": it spread through the population by means of performances as well as songbooks, and it conveyed a message that combined Sanskrit literature and contemporary politics. Faced with a culture of such complexity, the ICS felt threatened and the courts confused. But the British had a monopoly of power. When they exerted it, they got their man and condemned him in their court.

THE BASIC CONTRADICTION

What ultimately was going on in the courtrooms of the Raj? Censorship, certainly, because the British used the trials as a means to deter and repress. But they could have clapped the authors and publishers in prison without running them through elaborate legal rituals. Instead, they tried to prove their cases—that is, to demonstrate the justice of their rule to the "natives" and, even more important, to themselves. If the Raj could not be identified with the rule of law, it might be seen to rule by force. If its judges did not uphold the freedom of the press, they might be taken as the agents of tyranny. Yet they could not allow the Indians to use words as freely as Englishmen did at home. So they construed "feelings of enmity" as "disaffection" and "disaffection" as "sedition," translating freely from one idiom to another as the need arose. That the Indians sometimes outplayed them at their own game made no difference, for the British had the ultimate answer: force. Not that they impounded and imprisoned on a great scale. For the most part, they remained true to form, clinging to common sense and muddling through contradictions. Liberal imperialism was the greatest contradiction of them all; so the agents of the Raj summoned up as much ceremony as they could, in order to prevent themselves from seeing it.

PART THREE

Communist East Germany: Planning and Persecution

Ninety Clara-Zetkin-Strasse, East Berlin, June 8, 1990—seven months after the fall of the Berlin Wall, four months before the unification of the two Germanies. The entrance on the left, past a porter's office, up two flights of stairs, down a dim corridor, and through an unmarked door: the sector for GDR fiction. I had arrived at the central nodal point for the control of literature in the German Democratic Republic: the censorship office. I could hardly believe it. After years of studying censorship in distant times and places, I was about to meet two real live censors, and they were willing to talk.

NATIVE INFORMANTS

The talk at first was delicate. Hans-Jürgen Wesener and Christina Horn had never met an American. Until a few weeks earlier, they had never set foot in West Berlin, just a hundred yards from their office, on the other side of the Wall. They were loyal members of the East German Communist Party and veterans of the state machinery for making books conform to the Party line. They had agreed to discuss their work, because they had been assured by a mutual friend, an East German publisher in Leipzig, that I was not on a witch hunt. I merely wanted to know how they did their job. As a fellow at the Institute for Advanced Study in Berlin, I had spent the year witnessing the collapse of the GDR and interviewing East Germans who participated in it. By June 1990, I had learned to be diplomatic in asking questions and skeptical in assessing answers; for everyone had been complicit with the regime in one way or another, and no one wanted to be taken for a Stalinist.[1]

I took a seat in the drab, overheated room furnished in the GDR manner: laminated tables, plastic chairs, linoleum flooring, garlands of artificial fruit hanging from the wall, a scattering of objects made from the indefinable but unmistakable substances known to East Germans as "Plaste und Elaste."[2] Herr Wesener poured the coffee. After some small talk, we began to circle around the question of censorship, a sensitive topic, because censorship was not supposed to exist in the GDR. It was forbidden by the constitution, which guaranteed freedom of expression. Frau Horn said that they did not like the word. It sounded too negative. Their office was actually called the "Head Administration for Publishing and the Book Trade" (Hauptverwaltung Verlage und Buchhandel, abbreviated henceforth as HV), and their principal concern, as they defined it, was to make literature happen—that is, to oversee the process by which ideas became books and books reached readers. In the early 1960s, Frau Horn and Herr Wesener had graduated from the Humboldt University with advanced degrees in German literature. They took jobs in the Ministry of Culture and soon afterward were assigned to the HV, where they rose through the ranks in the sectors of GDR and foreign literature.

It took some time for me to get a clear picture of the bureaucracy's organization, because at first I saw only corridors and closed doors, all of them the same—plain brown with nothing but a number on the outside. East German fiction was number 215, forty doors down a mustard-yellow hallway that seemed to go on forever, twisting and winding around a central courtyard. In fact, the bureaucracy was ordered in hierarchical segments: sectors, divisions, administrations, and ministries located under the Council of Ministries at the peak of the government. And the whole structure was subordinated to the Communist Party (formally the Socialist Unity Party of Germany—Sozialistische Einheitspartei Deutschlands, or

THE CONTROL MECHANISM
FOR LITERATURE IN THE GDR

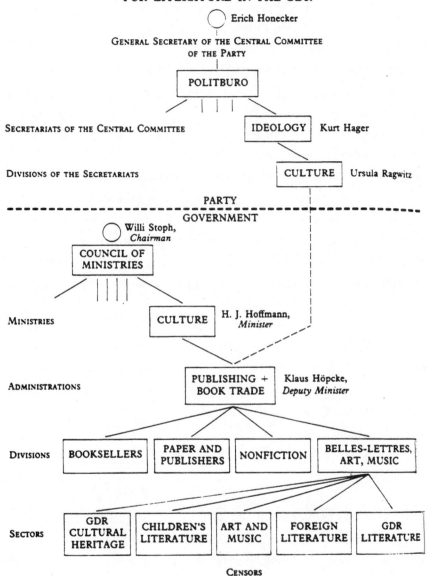

An organizational diagram showing the alignment of the authorities that controlled
East German literature, both in the government and in the Communist (SED) Party.
The censors operated in the unit known as the Hauptverwaltung Verlage und
Buchhandel (Main Administration of Publishers and the Book Trade), or HV for short.

SED—as it had resulted from the merger of the Communist and Social Democratic parties in 1946), which in accordance with the Soviet model was a separate organization with a hierarchy of its own: divisions led to secretariats of the Central Committee and ultimately to the Politburo under Erich Honecker, the supreme power in the GDR.

How all this functioned would be explained to me shortly. When I first arrived, Frau Horn and Herr Wesener seemed eager to demonstrate that they were university people like myself, not faceless bureaucrats and certainly not Stalinists. The top people in the office sometimes came from outside the bureaucracy, they explained. A division chief might have been the director of a publishing house, the editor of a journal, or a leader of the Authors Union. Literature was an interlocking system that spanned many institutions, and the people in literary circles often intersected. They themselves had expected to make lateral transfers into journals or publishing firms, because all were controlled by the Communist Party, and they had always been loyal Party members.

Of course, loyalty had its limits. Both Herr Wesener and Frau Horn had joined the massive demonstration of November 4, 1989, which had precipitated the collapse of the Politburo and the opening of the Wall. They identified with the reformers inside the Party and even with dissident authors like Christoph Hein and Volker Braun, whose works they had helped to censor. They favored "socialism with a human face," the "third way" between the Soviet and the American systems. And they *regretted* the fall of the Wall.

I realized that a great deal of self-justification went into this self-description. No one wanted to appear as an apparatchik during that brief period when East Germany was suspended between two regimes. With the dissolution of the Communist state, censorship had ceased to exist, but the censors continued to report for work, even though the work had disappeared. As functionaries without a function, they sat in their office, pondering their fate and waiting to be swept away by the bureaucracy of a reunited Germany. I could understand the awkwardness of their position and their need to explain it to a stranger who seemed to come from outer space. But why did they defend the Wall?

Herr Wesener surprised me with his answer: the Wall had helped to make the GDR a "Leseland," a country of readers, he explained. It had kept out the corruption of consumer culture. Once breached, it could not withstand the schlock—the sex books, advertising blitzes, and sleazy romances—that was sure to flood the GDR. Schlock came from the West. It was the main product of the literary system on the other side of the Wall, for we, too, had censorship: it was exerted through the pressure of the market.

Having already read various Marxist versions of that argument, I did not contest it. Instead, I asked Herr Wesener to explain his understanding of his job. He agreed that he was a censor, although he did not like the term. What, then, was censorship as he had practiced it? He answered with a single word: "Planning." In a socialist system, he explained, literature was planned like everything else, and to demonstrate the point, he reached into a drawer and handed me a remarkable document entitled "Subject Plan 1990: Literature of the GDR" ("Themenplan 1990. Literatur der DDR").

It was a 78-page overview of all the fiction scheduled to be published in 1990, a literary year that never happened. As Herr Wesener let me keep the copy of the Plan, I later studied it in detail. To my surprise, I found it flat and businesslike in tone. It listed all the projected books alphabetically, according to the last names of their authors. Each entry contained the title of the work, the publisher, proposed pressrun, the genre or series in which it would appear, and a short description of its contents.

After reading the descriptions, I wondered whether East German literature might have contained more schlock than Herr Wesener admitted. The year's output of 202 works (in fiction and belles-lettres, not counting new editions of previously published books) was to include a great many love stories, detective thrillers, historical romances, war novels, westerns, and science fiction. Of course, one cannot assess their literary qualities without reading them; and that is impossible, because most of them were scrapped, along with the censorship, as soon as the year began. But the one-paragraph blurbs accompanying each title in the Plan suggest something like socialist kitsch. Thus *Last der Nähe* (The burden of closeness), by Erika Paschke:

Themenplan 1990
───────────────────────

Literatur der DDR

I. Neue Werke

Irmgard   A b e   Eulenspiegel Verlag
Oben links, wo die Schürze winkt   15 000
                                         Geschichten / cell.Papp.
In diesem neuen Geschichtenbuch der Autorin begegnet der Leser
alten Bekannten wieder wie Herrn und Frau Weise, Walter und allen
jenen, deren Lebensglück durch Mißverständnisse verhindert oder
gefördert wird.

Sonja   A n d e r s   Buchverlag Der Morgen
Zwischen Himmel und Hölle (AT)   15 000
                                         Lebensbericht

Sonja Anders, 32 Jahre alt, verheiratet, Mutter von zwei Kindern,
wird mit schweren Entzugserscheinungen in eine psychiatrische Klinik
eingeliefert. Doch die diagnostizierte Alkohol- und Tablettenab-
hängigkeit ist nur ein Symptom, ist Ausdruck einer Beziehungsstö-
rung zu sich selbst, zu ihrer Mutter, zu anderen Menschen, zum
Leben.

Gunter   A n t r a k   Das Neue Berlin
Zwei Mörder (AT)   100 000
                                         Krimi / DIE-Reihe
Ein Mord ist geschehen. Die Fahndung der K hat schnell Erfolg. Der
Mörder gesteht. Da meldet sich ein alter Mann und behauptet, er sei
der Mörder. Oberleutnant Dirksen und seinem Team scheint es unmög-
lich, nur einem der beiden die Tat zu beweisen. Neben der Ermitt-
lungshandlung werden Hintergründe für Fehlverhalten deutlich gemacht.

Ingeborg   A r l t   Aufbau-Verlag
Um der Liebe willen   15 000

In dem sorgfältig recherchierten zweiten Buch der Autorin, dessen
Handlung im Dreißigjährigen Krieg spielt, ist die Historie nicht
Zierrat, sondern Fundament, um das Wesentliche - wie Menschen mit-
einander umgehen - zu begreifen.

Edmund   A u e   Militärverlag
Reise zum Dalmatinischen Archipel   10 000
                                         Tagebuch-Erz.
Ein Mann reist an die Adriaküste, um das Grab seines Vaters zu suchen.
Unvermutet wird er mit der Vergangenheit konfrontiert, hat Begegnun-
gen mit Menschen, die seinen Vater gekannt haben, erfährt, daß dieser
als Partisan an der Seite jugoslawischer Genossen gekämpft hat.

The Plan for all East German literature that was to be published in 1990.

While Ina Scheidt travels from country to country pursuing her
demanding career as a translator, her mother and her seventeen-year-
old daughter, Marja, become increasingly upset at having to keep the
household going by themselves. One day, Ina brings a man home
with her, and complications among the three are laid bare. The man

recognizes Ina's excessive concern with external values and turns away from her. In this as in her other novellas, the author is concerned with ethical questions about sharing life with others. She sets off notions of human worth and mutual respect against the lack of understanding for others.

This sounds surprisingly soap operatic, and certainly far removed from socialist realism or the stern stuff that one would expect from the "land of workers and peasants." But East Germany was also known as a *Nischengesellschaft*, a society of niches in which people withdrew into private life and sheltered sectors of activity; so novels that moralized about personal relationships may have seemed appropriate to the literary planners, especially if they warned readers against travel—that is, against exposure to the blandishments of the West. While the Plan was being prepared, thousands of East Germans were escaping to West Germany, and the entire GDR spent most of its evenings watching West German television. Perhaps, then, it was no coincidence that several of the projected novels set family dramas within the context of relations between the two German states. Wolfgang Kroeber's *Irgendwo in Europa* (Somewhere in Europe) was to confront "a current problem: why people leave their country?" Kurt Nowak's *Trennungszeichen* (Signs of separation) was to trace a family history on both sides of the German–German border, demonstrating the advantages of life in the East. And *Späte Post* (The Late Mail) by Lothar Guenther, was to show how a young worker made a heroic choice between a draft notice and an invitation to join his father in the West, which arrived in the same mail delivery.

Although it does not contain much strident propaganda, the Plan adheres relentlessly to political correctness, East German style. When lovers kiss and make up, they pay tribute to the deeper quality of personal relationships in a system free from the superficialities bred by consumerism. When Indians fight off invaders in the Dakotas or Amazonia, they strike blows against imperialism. Fighting itself remains resolutely antifascistic, even in science fiction. *Die Bedrohung* (The threat), by Arne Sjoeberg, was to recount the overthrow of a "Führer" who had seized power in the planet

Palmyra by manufacturing a false alarm about an impending catastrophe. And detective stories served as vehicles for exposing the pathology of capitalist societies. Thus *Das Flüstern eines Kleides* (The whispering of a dress) by Wolfgang Kohrt, would explore the whole range of criminality in America in order to lay bare "the emptiness of relations between the sexes, the outrages of daily life, the desire for revenge, the lust for money, speculation on inheritances, and unfulfilled longings."

All these stories had a further subtext, or rather another text altogether, a *Themenplaneinschätzung*, or ideological report on the Plan, which went with the Plan to the Central Committee of the Communist Party for approval by the people at the top of the power system. This document was as remarkable as the Plan itself; so I was especially grateful when Herr Wesener reached into another drawer and gave me a copy, marked "confidential."

The report had been approved by the Central Committee in mid-1988 and covered the Plan for 1989, the last literary year of the East German old regime. In it, one can see the censors making their case for the coming crop of books to the bosses of the Communist Party, and one can hear the unmistakable accent of the state bureaucracy. Socialism is advancing everywhere; everything is pointing onward and upward; production is expanding: 625 titles were scheduled to be published, and the total output would come to 11,508,950 copies, representing a significant advance on the previous Plan (559 titles, totaling 10,444,000 copies).

Nineteen eighty-nine was to be a year of celebration for forty glorious years of socialist rule in East Germany. Therefore, the literature of 1989 would be dedicated, above all, to the past and present of the GDR as they had been defined by Comrade Erich Honecker: "Our party and our people stand in a revolutionary and humanistic tradition of centuries of struggle for social progress, liberty, and the rights and value of mankind." Then, in language loaded with similar pieties of GDR-speak, the report surveyed the main themes of the Plan. For example, it stressed that the year's output of historical novels would express "energetic antifascism," while novels set in the present would conform to the principle of socialist realism and would

Berlin, den 30. Mai 1988

V e r t r a u l i c h

Themenplaneinschätzung 1989

Literatur der DDR

Auf der Grundlage der Orientierungen des XI. Parteitages sowie
in Auswertung der Beratungsergebnisse des X. Schriftstellerkon-
gresses der DDR ist die Zusammenarbeit von Autoren und Verlagen
auf neue literarische Werke gerichtet, die zur Verständigung
über Hauptfragen gegenwärtigen Lebens beitragen, die für die
Stärkung des Sozialismus und die Sicherung des Friedens wirken.

Mit einem Planangebot von 625 Titeln in 11.508.950 Expl.
(255 EA / 4.991.100 Expl.; 370 NA / 6.617.850 Expl.) werden
von den Verlagen alle Möglichkeiten für die Herausgabe von
DDR-Literatur wahrgenommen.

Plan 1988: 559 Titel in 10.444.000 Expl.
203 EA / 4.460.000 Expl.
356 NA / 5.984.000 Expl.

Das Planangebot für 1989 wird bestimmt durch Titel, die anläßlich
des 40. Jahrestages der Gründung der DDR Geschichte und Gegenwart
des ersten sozialistischen deutschen Staates in vielfältigen literarischen Formen widerspiegeln. Daran sind eine Reihe namhafter
Autoren beteiligt. Zugleich ist wie bereits im Vorjahr festzustel-
len, daß immer mehr Autoren der mittleren und jüngeren Schriftstel-
lergeneration das Planangebot bestimmen und einen wesentlichen Bei-
trag zur Literatur der DDR leisten.
Unter thematischen und literarischen Gesichtspunkten werden Erwar-
tungen gesetzt insbesondere in folgende Vorhaben:

*The ideological report on the Plan for 1989, which the censors in the HV produced
to explain the Plan's main tendency for the approval of the Culture Division of the
Party's Central Committee.*

promote the "historical mission of the working class in the struggle for social progress." The authors of the Plan confessed that they had failed to produce an adequate supply of stories about factory workers and trac-tor drivers, but they would compensate for this shortcoming by publish-ing anthologies of older proletarian literature. The report did not mention the slightest indication of dissension. On the contrary, it indicated that authors, publishers, and officials all had their shoulder to the wheel, push-ing literature to new heights at the very moment when the whole system was to come crashing down.

It seems strange to read this testimony about ideological purity and institutional health from the inner workings of a regime that was about to collapse. Was all this paperwork merely an apparatchik fantasy, something that filled the "in" and "out" boxes of the bureaucracy but had little to do with the actual experience of literature among ordinary East Germans?

Herr Wesener and Frau Horn assured me that the Plan really did determine the production and consumption of books in the GDR. Then they described every stage in the system, a long, complicated process, which involved constant negotiations and culminated in the decisions made in their office—with the approval of the Central Committee of the Communist Party. To what extent was their account self-serving? I could not judge, because at that time I had not yet had access to other sources. I therefore did my best to listen, making allowances for the per-spective from which they saw the system—that is, the view from the top, at the HV.

General policy conformed to a Party line set by the quinquennial con-gresses of the SED and Erich Honecker, general secretary of the Party, who worked closely with Kurt Hager, the member of the Politburo responsible for ideology. It passed from the Party leaders down the line of command within the government. Honecker and Hager sometimes intervened per-sonally in literary affairs, but most directives came from "Kultur," as the censors called it—the Cultural Division of the Central Committee of the Party—and arrived in the HV, where the censors were located, through the Ministry of Culture. The HV consisted of four divisions. One admin-istered the economic aspects of literature: the allotment of paper, printing facilities, subsidies, and pricing. Another concerned the general supervision of publishers and booksellers. Censorship, strictly speaking (as we shall see, it took many forms besides blue-penciling texts), occurred in the other two divisions, one for nonfiction and one for fiction. The fiction division was split into five sectors, one of which handled current East German literature. Frau Horn ran it, working with five other specialists (*Mitarbeiter*). Herr Wesener directed a similar team in the sector of foreign literature.

Books originated in different ways. Some may well have begun as a moment of inspiration by an author, but most were arranged by negotiations between authors and publishers. The GDR had seventy-eight publishing houses in the 1980s.[3] In principle, they were independent, self-supporting organizations. In practice, they edited their texts and built their lists in conformity with the Party line, making the most of *Spielraum*—room for maneuver within a flexible system of human relations, which offset the constraints imposed by the institutional structure. The directors and the chief readers of the publishing houses were appointed by the Party and often figured among the nomenklatura, or Party elite. But authors usually developed attachments to particular houses and friendships with certain editors. When an author or his editor came up with an idea for a book, they would work it over together, and send it as a proposal from the publisher to the HV at Clara-Zetkin-Strasse, where an employee would reduce it to a notice on an index card.

Herr Wesener had thousands of the cards in his files. He pulled one out, a printed form on cheap, gray paper with twenty-one printed rubrics: publisher, author, title, proposed pressrun, and so on. One of his underlings had filled in the information and, on the back, had written a short paragraph about the general nature of the book—a translation of a volume of lyrics by the Czech poet Lubomír Feldek, which was proposed for publication in 1990:

> Thanks to his ironic and laconic verses, the author has made a name
> for himself beyond the limits of the Czech language. He is a sensitive
> observer of social processes, which he is able to evaluate from a committed point of view. This would be his first appearance in the GDR.

Once it had accumulated a year's worth of dossiers and index cards, the office began to prepare a Plan. The head of each sector in the HV would bring together representatives of the Authors Union (Schriftstellerverband), publishing houses, bookstores, libraries, universities, and the Ministry of Culture in a committee known in the fiction sector as a Literary Working Group, or LAG (Literaturarbeitsgemeinschaft). The LAG would approve every book proposal, somewhat as an editorial board does for publishing houses in the West, except that it spoke for all segments of the literary industry and had a sharp eye for ideological issues. Back in their office, Frau Horn and Herr Wesener would incorporate the LAG's decisions and its general observations into drafts for the Plan. The Plan itself was an important, secret document (I was later surprised to learn that none of my East German friends had ever known anything about it), which required formal approval by the Party before any of the books could be published. It had to be prepared with care, by means of consultation and mutual criticism among the specialists in all the sectors of the HV. In the end, it was the responsibility of the head of the HV, Klaus Höpcke, who held the title of deputy minister of culture. Höpcke had to defend the Plan before the apparatchiks in Kultur and any potentate of the Party, from Honecker on down, who might be offended by a book.

Kultur, as Herr Wesener and Frau Horn described it, consisted of fifteen hard-bitten ideologues directed by a dragon lady named Ursula Ragwitz. Once a year, Höpcke would take the Plan from each of his five sectors, march over to Kultur, and do battle with Frau Ragwitz. The censors could not tell me how much blood was shed in these encounters. All they knew was that Höpcke would return with decisions, always oral and never with any accompanying explanation: Stefan Heym is out next year; Volker Braun is in, but only with an edition of 10,000 copies; Christa Wolf stays, but merely with a reprint of a work that appeared with the approval of the GDR in West Germany last year.

Herr Wesener and Frau Horn then had to relay the decisions back to the publishers. "This was the hardest part," Herr Wesener explained, "because we could never give any reasons, when there was trouble with a book. All we could say was, 'Das ist so': 'That is what they decided.'"

There were ways of getting around "them," however. When the philistines in Kultur rejected an edition of *Doctor Zhivago*, the staff at Clara-Zetkin-Strasse came back with a report that a complete edition of Pasternak's works was about to be published in West Germany. In order to protect the GDR market from clandestine imports, they persuaded Frau Ragwitz's group to permit *Zhivago* right away. They always left about forty places in the Plan for GDR fiction free, so that they could squeeze in late proposals and reserve some *Spielraum*. If they knew a book would be "hot" ("hot" was a catchword used in the office for controversial works as opposed to those considered to be "quiet"), they left it out of the Plan and slipped it in afterward. Of course, they always had to get clearance from someone in Kultur. But that came more easily on an ad hoc basis than in a formal meeting when the members of Frau Ragwitz's group would try to outdo one another in demonstrating their militancy by turning down books. Also, had I noticed that the Plan contained more entries for reprints (315) than for new titles (202)? That was where they put the "hottest" items—books by East German authors that had appeared in West Germany (usually with the complicity of the authors, despite the attempts of the GDR to prevent all such private arrangements), caused some fuss (but not for the censorship office), and could be published (as inconspicuously as possible and usually in small press runs) in the GDR once things had quieted down.

At this point in the conversation, the censors began to sound as though they had spent most of their time fighting censorship, which they attributed primarily to their opponents in Kultur. They had learned to identify some of the quirks of Frau Ragwitz and her colleagues, they explained. Therefore, they phrased the Plan in a way that would flatter the preferences of certain individuals while avoiding their "allergies," such as any mention of Stalin or pollution. They usually hid difficult books in a mass of unproblematic ones and disguised the difficulties by neutral wording. Although the ideologues in Kultur were wise to such tricks, they could not easily spot unorthodoxies in a document containing hundreds of plot synopses and thematic overviews.

When a particularly difficult proposal came to her office, Frau Horn would draft its entry for the Plan herself, after consulting several veteran co-workers. They would begin with a question, she said: "How much heat can we permit in the Plan?" If a book looked too hot for the current climate of opinion, they would postpone it for a year or two. "Let some grass grow first," they would say to one another. But after putting their heads together, they usually came up with a formula that seemed likely to get past Frau Ragwitz, who in the long run desired nothing more than "quiet" herself. Newcomers could not be entrusted with the delicate task of gauging temperatures. It normally took them two years to learn the ropes, for censorship was difficult and demanding. It required skill, tact, and an understanding of the inner ways of the bureaucracy in both systems—the Party apparatus and the government machinery.

I was not quite ready to see censors as heroes in a culture war, so I asked whether Herr Wesener and Frau Horn ever got involved in the actual vetting of texts. Not much, they assured me. Most censorship took place in the heads of writers, and what the writers failed to cut usually got filtered out by editors in publishing houses. By the time the texts reached the censors in Clara-Zetkin-Strasse, there was little left for them to eliminate. On average, they said, they rejected only a half dozen of the two hundred or so manuscripts in East German fiction that they examined each year. Formally, they never censored anything at all. They merely refused to give books an official authorization to be printed (*Druckgenehmigung*). Herr Wesener handed me a printing authorization, a small printed form with his signature at the bottom. It looked unimpressive, until he explained that it alone could unlock the machinery of the publishing industry. For no printer could accept a work that was not accompanied by a printing authorization, and virtually all the printing houses were owned by the Communist Party.

Of course, a great deal took place before a manuscript reached that point. Once the project for a book had been incorporated in the Plan and the Plan had been approved by the Culture Division of the Party's Central Committee, Frau Horn said that she would notify the publisher, who informed the author, who completed the text—unless it had already been written and only needed some ideological tweaking. The publisher then sent the text to another writer or literary scholar for a critical review and wrote a report of his own. In response to the review, the author might have to make some important changes, which could lead to another round of reports. That done, the reports went off to the HV along with the final draft of the book. Frau Horn went over this material carefully and kept it all on file, because if a difficulty arose, a well-placed Party member might demand to see the surrounding documentation, and there could be trouble for everyone who had been involved in the process. She then began to exercise censorship in the strict sense of the word—a line-by-line vetting of the finished work.

How, I asked, did she go over a novel or a collection of essays? Did she tick off items from a standard questionnaire or work from an established protocol? No, she answered, but she kept her eye out for certain "sensitive points"—for example, unacceptable terms such as "ecology" (a taboo noun; it was associated with the massive, state-produced pollution in the GDR) and "critical" (a taboo adjective; it evoked dissidents, who were to be buried in silence). References to Stalinism were so inimical that Frau Horn would change "opponent of Stalinism" to "contradictor of his time"; and she even replaced "the 1930s" with a safer, vaguer expression: "the first half of the twentieth century." She paid special attention to subjects such as defense, protest movements, church dissidents, and anything related to the Soviet Union. She never allowed statistics about environmental conditions or provocative references to the Berlin Wall. But she no longer worried about topics like crime and alcoholism, which used to be delicate and had to be consigned to books about countries like the United States. A decade earlier, everything concerning the United States was sensitive. They had great difficulty in getting a translation of *The Catcher in the Rye* past Kurt Hager, because he considered Holden Caulfield "a bad role model for our GDR youth." But after Gorbachev's advent in 1985, the Soviet Union became the most problematic subject in their office, and the censors had to be especially wary of anything identified with "SU Lit," as Soviet writing was known in their in-house jargon.

Having cleared this last hurdle, a book received a printing authorization and at last was ready to go into production. Even then, however, things could go wrong. My acquaintances among East German editors had a whole repertory of stories about changes made by overzealous proofreaders and mischievous compositors. The best-known was a supposed typographical error in an anatomy textbook, which proofreaders mysteriously managed not to catch in edition after edition for many years. It concerned a muscle in the buttocks called the "Glutäus maximus," which was printed as the "Glutäus marxismus." Another appeared in a nature poem that had a line about a group of young birds:

> Their heads nest-ward turned
> (Die Köpfe nestwärts gewandt)

By mistake or design, the compositor changed "nest-ward" to "westward," and the proofreader, smelling heresy, covered himself by making it "eastward."

Censorship, as the censors described it, seemed to have endless possibilities for things to go wrong. How did they handle risk? If, as they claimed, they permitted relatively "hot" books, couldn't they get burned? Herr Wesener explained that their procedures had built-in safeguards. When challenged, they could justify their decisions by the reports they received from the publishers; they diluted responsibility by spreading it out among their colleagues; and they were always covered by their boss, Klaus Höpcke. They also covered him. Because his office served as a funnel for all the books produced each year in the GDR, it was vulnerable to pressure and sanctions. If the Central Committee was unhappy with what went on in the office, it did not need to punish him personally, although he was always vulnerable to punishment in the form of a Party reprimand (Verweis), which could damage his career. The Party could cut the resources that it made available to him, above all in allotments of paper. Paper was scarce in East Germany, and Höpcke had to find enough of it to supply the entire book trade, despite the competing claims of newspapers, magazines, and other industries. Because they sympathized with Höpcke's endless struggle for paper, the censors tried to help by keeping things quiet and by diverting the noise away from him. On a few occasions, they even approved difficult texts without informing him, so that he could plead ignorance if he were summoned before the Central Committee. Herr Wesener signed the authorization to print Christoph Hein's outspoken novel, *Der Tangospieler* (The tango player) and kept the decision to himself, in order to provide his boss with what was known in Watergate Washington as deniability.

Höpcke seems to have been a hero to his inferiors. They described him as a hard-boiled, hard-line journalist who took over the HV in 1973 with the worst possible ideas about imposing order on intellectual life. But the more time he spent battling the Party bureaucracy, the more sympathy he developed for independent-minded authors. By the 1980s, he had become an expert at slipping unorthodox books past the Central Committee. Two of them nearly cost him his job. Günter de Bruyn's novel *Neue Herrlichkeit* (New splendidness) caused so much offense at the top of the Party that it had to be withdrawn from bookstores and pulped—only to be reprinted with Höpcke's blessing once things had quieted down. *Hinze-Kunze-Roman*, by Volker Braun, produced an even greater scandal, because it dealt with the relationship between an unsavory member of the Party elite and his chauffeur. After its publication was authorized, Höpcke tried to smooth its way by phoning his friends in the press and warning them to soft-pedal its attack on apparatchik privileges. He even wrote a review of it himself. But it was denounced within the Central Committee as an "intellectual bomb." Höpcke was called on the carpet and given a formal censure. He managed nonetheless to hold on to his position by taking the blame and bending with the wind. And a few years later, at a meeting of the East German PEN organization in March 1989, he supported a resolution condemning the arrest of Václav Havel in Czechoslovakia.

When I left the office at Clara-Zetkin-Strasse, I had no illusions about the bias inherent in what I had heard. Far from sounding apologetic about their work, Frau Horn and Herr Wesener had described it in entirely favorable terms. Censorship as they understood it was positive. In some ways, it was downright heroic—a struggle against heavy odds to maintain a high level of culture while building socialism. Although I could not read the inner workings of their minds, I did not detect any hypocrisy in their self-depiction. They struck me as true believers. How well their faith corresponded to evidence about the actual functioning of the system was another question, one that I could not resolve—unless I had access to the archives.

INSIDE THE ARCHIVES

Fragments of the archives began to appear soon after the two Germanies were formally united on October 3, 1990. In May 1991, an exhibition called "Censorship in the GDR" opened in West Berlin. Although it included only a small selection of papers from the HV, it showed that the activities at Clara-Zetkin-Strasse involved a great deal more than fighting philistinism in the Communist Party. Höpcke's name appeared on many memos that documented the suppression of books and the persecution of East Germany's best-known authors—Christa Wolf, Stefan Heym, Erwin Strittmatter, Erich Loest, Franz Fühmann, Gert Neumann, and Richard Pietrass. His general attitude toward literature shows through a letter that he wrote to the director of the Hinstorff publishing house in 1978 opposing a proposal to do an edition of Kierkegaard: "If Kierkegaard belongs to [our literary] heritage, then so do Nietzsche, Schopenhauer, Klages, Freud. . . . Besides, in deciding what can be published from late-bourgeois philosophy, we want first of all to take into account the situation in the ideological class war. We have had enough of individualistic attitudes to life and lifestyles."[4] The exhibition also contained some disturbing documents related to the censors I had interviewed. For example, they revealed that Christine Horn had led an attack on Gerhard Dahne, an author and fellow censor, who directed the division of belles-lettres in the HV. He had alienated his colleagues by a series of indiscretions. In 1967, he wrote an essay on the West German novelist Heinrich Böll, which the other censors considered so ideologically unacceptable that they suppressed it. In 1975, he published a book that included a passage indicating that censorship existed in the GDR. That was too much for the censors, who censured him by a resolution passed in their Party cell and signed by Frau Horn. And in 1978, he wrote a short story that Höpcke found objectionable. When Höpcke advised him not to publish it, Dahne refused. A year later he was fired. According to a letter by Hans-Joachim Hoffmann, the minister of culture, which was countersigned by Höpcke and addressed to Ursula Ragwitz in Kultur, the dismissal of Dahne represented an attempt to tighten "the political direction of the development of literature." Frau Ragwitz echoed that sentiment in her reply: Dahne would be replaced by a Party member who would "guarantee an effective political direction to the development of literature."[5]

To develop a clearer view of how the system functioned, I needed to get inside the archives myself. In September 1992, when I returned for another year in Berlin, I decided to give it a try. Like many countries, Germany has a thirty-year rule against providing access to documents from the recent past, but there was still a lot of confusion about how to handle the mass of unprocessed material that had accumulated in the drawers and files of an alien and extinct bureaucracy. The archives of the Communist Party, inherited in December 1989 by its successor, the Party of Democratic Socialism, had been left undisturbed in a building at the heart of East Berlin at 1 Torstrasse—formerly named Wilhelm-Pieck-Strasse in honor of the GDR's first president. The building itself bore the marks of German history. Constructed as a department store for a Jewish firm in 1927–29, it had been taken over by the Nazis as headquarters for the Hitlerjugend, appropriated by the Communist Party in 1946 for the offices of its Central Committee, and used from 1959 until 1989 for the Institute for Marxism-Leninism. I walked in, took a seat in a reading room outfitted with the same furniture that I had seen in the censors' office, and started filling in forms. To my amazement, I soon had in front of me dossiers that were only a few years old. Several were memos sent by Kurt Hager to Erich Honecker with Honecker's "E.H." in the margins, signaling their receipt.

Hager and Honecker exchanged notes about everything of any importance. They must have discussed questions related to censorship, I realized, but where did they leave traces of their discussions in the archives? The flow of in-house memos had been so thick that it filled thousands of dossiers, which occupied a great many kilometers of shelf space in the back rooms of the building, and the only available inventory listed little more than "bureaus" of the Central Committee, which stored their files in

chronological order. I chose Hager's bureau and requested dossiers separated by six-month intervals, hoping that something might turn up. After
several days of combing through bureaucratic flotsam and jetsam, I began
to despair of finding anything important. But eventually I came upon a
pink slip, which said that a dossier had been removed for reasons that
would be explained if I inquired with the supervisor of the reading room.
The supervisor could not provide an answer, but he referred me to a person who had managed the archives when they were being generated and
consulted by the Central Committee of the Communist Party. Taking my
courage in my hands—this had been a Stalinist inner sanctum a few years
ago, but what could they do to a visiting American now that the Cold War
really seemed to be ending?—I walked down two flights and around a long,
dark corridor until I arrived at the designated number. I knocked on the
door, braced for a confrontation with a hostile Party henchman. When it
opened, I found to my amazement that I was greeted with a friendly smile
by a young woman, very attractive in the East German manner: blond
hair swept back from her forehead, little or no makeup, simple clothing, a
direct, pleasant manner. She introduced herself as Solveig Nestler, offered
me a seat next to photographs of her two tow-headed children, and asked
what I was looking for. I wanted to study how censorship functioned under
the GDR, I explained, and for some reason I had been refused access to
a particular dossier. It probably contained information about someone's
private life, she said. But if I really wanted to understand the system and
not to uncover personal scandals, she could be of help. She knew where all
the relevant material was located, and she would feed it to me, removing
anything of a compromising, personal nature. For many weeks, therefore, I
got to follow runs of documents that revealed how literature was managed
at the highest levels of the GDR.

Now, I do not pretend to be an expert on the GDR or on modern
German literature. After I made my foray into the archives, some accomplished German scholars located material that I never saw and published
studies that exceeded my ability to do long-term research.[6] But I was able
to pursue a limited range of questions related to my discussion with the
censors. What happened, I wondered, after Klaus Höpcke submitted the

annual Plan to the Culture Division of the Party's Central Committee? What became of other proposals for controlling literature when they passed beyond the HV and into the upper echelons of the Party? How did the Party leaders handle the "hot" dossiers that had made life difficult for Herr Wesener and Frau Horn? And was Ursula Ragwitz really the dragon lady they described?

In her reports about the Plans to Kurt Hager, her superior in the Politburo, Frau Ragwitz noted that Klaus Höpcke sometimes got a rough reception when he defended the work of his colleagues in the HV to her colleagues in Kultur. The latter included eight Party militants, each of whom had special responsibilities and was ready to direct tough questions at Höpcke when he presented the annual Plan. In 1984, for example, Arno Lange, Kultur's watchdog in charge of publishing houses, detected a serious flaw in the Plan for 1985: excessive permissiveness in the treatment of authors by publishers. Negligence by the HV had permitted this tendency to gather force, undercutting the control that the Party exerted through the publishers. Kultur ultimately approved the Plan but only after a lengthy discussion and with a proviso that proposals for books should not often be left to the initiative of the authors; instead, publishers should develop an "offensive strategy," which would strengthen the authors' "ideological potency."[7]

In her report on the Plan for 1982, Ragwitz alerted Hager to a general tendency among publishers to propose manuscripts that were unacceptable on "ideological and artistic grounds." The Reclam Verlag had actually intended to publish some works by Nietzsche and Frederick II, and Kultur had made it clear in a long session with Höpcke that nothing of the kind would be permitted. Fortunately, Ragwitz assured Hager, Kultur had managed to modify the Plan so that it conformed to the Party line laid down by the Tenth Party Congress in 1981. Therefore, the next crop of books in fiction and belles-lettres would stress proletarian themes. Twenty new novels featured worker heroes who threw themselves into the "international class war." Detective stories and "utopian" literature (that is, science fiction), which especially appealed to young readers, would "strip bare the inhumane character of imperialism"; and historical novels would emphasize the

progressive power of the revolutionary tradition. But there was a problem
that Ragwitz had to confront in a follow-up letter addressed to Honecker
himself. At a meeting of the Politburo, Honecker had mentioned his fond-
ness for the Wild West novels of Karl May (1842–1912), which he had read
in his youth. Couldn't the GDR make them into movies? Alas, Ragwitz
reported, the Party had rejected a proposal to reprint May soon after the
war, and the East German Karl May Verlag had emigrated to the West,
taking its rights with it.[8]

Ragwitz's report on the Plan for 1984 mentioned intense discussions
with Höpcke and the long process by which the HV distilled recommendations from publishers, booksellers, and members of the Authors Union
(all represented in the LAG) into the proposals to be vetted by Kultur.
The Plan embodied six ideological themes: (1.) GDR history and the class
struggles of the German proletariat, (2.) the continuing danger of fascism
and its relation to the arms race perpetrated by NATO, (3.) the higher
moral qualities inherent in the development of a socialist order, (4.) the
increased commitment of the working class to the defense of socialism,
(5.) happiness and human worth as values fostered by socialism, and (6.)
arguments against imperialism and the way of life it promoted. Ragwitz
applauded the appearance of new poets with a talent for "political lyrics"
and new authors committed to *Parteilichkeit*, a GDR superlative indicating adherence to the Party line. But she detected symptoms of ideological
weakness: failed attempts to express socialist principles in science fiction
and a variety of socialist realism that made the East German man in the
street look distressingly similar to his West German counterpart. She also
worried about weakness of another kind: not enough paper. The lack of
raw material was causing a decline in production. In 1978, the Plan provided for 3.7 million copies of 170 new works in GDR fiction; in 1984, 2.3
million copies of 123 new works. "Further reduction would not be defensi-
ble on cultural-political grounds."[9]

The warning signals and criticism in the formal reports from Kultur
did not challenge the work of the censors in a fundamental way. They
may have been intended, at least in part, to impress the Party's leaders
with the ideological vigilance of the Ragwitz group, but their sharpness

was blunted by a heavy, rhetorical style, loaded down with bureaucratic jargon.[10] Ragwitz's personal communications with Hager struck a different note. They had known each other for years. Ragwitz had joined the Culture Division of the Central Committee in 1969 and became its leader in 1976. Hager, a member of the Central Committee since 1954 and of the Politburo since 1963, was considered to be the second-most-powerful personage in the GDR after Honecker. As "Chief Ideologist" he had ultimate responsibility for directing cultural life and therefore was in constant contact with Ragwitz. They apparently got on very well, despite their difference in age—or perhaps because of it (Hager was sixty-eight in 1980, Ragwitz was fifty-two).[11]

In a confidential letter, addressed "Dear Kurt" (in official correspondence, everyone appeared with a "Comrade" attached to his or her last name; in personal notes from Hager, Ragwitz was "Dear Ursel") on March 1, 1982, Ragwitz discussed cultural politics in a way that reveals the unofficial operation of the system. At that time, Hager was away on a trip and Ragwitz was about to leave for a health "cure." Because she would not see him for some time, she said that she wanted to bring him up to date on recent developments. A festival of political songs was being organized, and the political lay of the land in the musical sector was good, she assured him, but serious problems had developed in the Deutsches Theater. She assumed he had discussed them with Honecker, and she had asked Hoffmann (Hans Joachim Hoffmann, the minister of culture) to give her his appraisal of the situation. Instead, Hoffmann had written directly to Honecker, who was displeased to receive such a communication and had summoned him to discuss it in a private meeting. When they met, Honecker gave Hoffmann a dressing-down for letting behavior at the Deutsches Theater get out of hand: the troupe had made plans to perform in West Germany and France without getting clearance from the Party, and it had started rehearsing a play that had not yet received approval. This situation had led to some "very serious reproaches about the style of conduct . . . of the culture minister." Ragwitz herself had discussed the problem with Honecker, who said he thought they should purge the leadership of the Deutsches Theater, but they should keep that plan secret so as to avoid trouble with the troupe's sympathizers in the Berliner Ensemble. Meanwhile, Konrad Wolf (an eminent film director and Party stalwart) had fallen seriously ill, so they would have to find a replacement for him as director of the Academy of Arts.[12]

Confidential correspondence of this sort, exchanged behind the backs of powerful figures, indicates that important business was conducted through an informal network of personal ties, which operated alongside the rigid structures of the Party apparatus and the government ministries.[13] The archives don't provide enough evidence to show how profoundly the informal system determined the functioning of the official bodies, but they contain some suggestive documents. For example, after alerting Hager to the unreliable behavior of Hoffmann, Ragwitz took action at the institutional level. At a meeting on March 28, 1984, she and her colleagues resolved to get the upper hand in the conflict between the two "cultures"— their group in Kultur and their counterparts in the Ministry of Culture, where the ideological backsliding was most serious.[14] Having investigated the tendency of literary production to deviate from the Party line, they determined to reassert their "political-ideological influence" by placing more Party militants in strategic positions throughout the system.[15] This ideological offensive did not lead to the purge of Hoffmann, but at a meeting with Hager on April 16, Kultur was empowered to correct the "inadequate understanding of the sharpened class-struggle situation" among all "culture producers," beginning with the editors of literary journals like *Sinn und Form*, who would be summoned to a conference and upbraided for their ideological slackness.[16] The struggle between the two bureaucracies, that of the Party and that of the state, never led to an open conflict, but relations remained strained until the collapse of the GDR.

RELATIONS WITH AUTHORS

Authors were particularly important "culture producers." At the height of Stalinism in the 1950s and 1960s, they could be packed off to prison or condemned to gulag-type labor. But in the 1970s and 1980s the Party relied on milder, carrot-and-stick measures to keep them in line. Permission to travel abroad, or refusal to grant it, was the favorite strategy.

According to a report of a typical, top-level meeting on November 24, 1982, Hager, Hoffmann, and Ragwitz discussed a wide variety of cultural questions: concert tours, the state of the theaters, the need to improve Party discipline in the fine arts, the perpetual problem of the shortage of paper, and less urgent matters like a proposal to erect a statue to Karl Marx in Ethiopia. But the most prominent of the eighteen items on the agenda concerned travel. First came the vexing problem of *R-Flucht* (fleeing from the republic)—that is, how to prevent authors who received permission to travel abroad from remaining there. One measure, favored by Ragwitz, was to prohibit the travelers from being accompanied by their spouses. But no general policy seemed feasible, and therefore they resolved to handle the matter on a case-by-case basis—a tactic whose very irregularity could make it more effective.[17]

In the case of Uwe Kolbe, an angry young poet whom they wanted to entice out of a Bohemian existence in the Prenzlauer Berg section of East Berlin and into the camp of established writers, they decided to permit travel once he had been suitably admonished in a private talk with Höpcke.[18] Lutz Rathenow, a more formidable Prenzlauer Berg dissident, was a more difficult case. He had published his first book, a collection of satirical short stories, in 1980 in West Germany without seeking permission (authors who wanted to publish in the West had to get clearance from the GDR Copyright Office, which exercised its own form of censorship and collected 75 percent of their royalties). As a result, he was arrested and held in custody for a month, thereby producing protests and negative publicity in the West. Two years later when Hager and Höpcke discussed his dossier, they wrote him off as "persona non grata," "an author who continually flings mud at us" and was unworthy of any favorable treatment. They actually wanted to let him out of the GDR in order to keep him out; but Rathenow would not be tempted, because he did not want to be forced into exile, like his hero, Wolf Biermann, the dissident poet-folksinger who was not permitted to return to the GDR when he went on a concert tour in West Germany in 1976.[19]

Other authors yearned to see what life was like on the other side of the Wall, and their desire made them vulnerable to manipulation by the regime. Monika Maron pleaded for permission to travel outside the Communist bloc and received it, although the censors refused to allow publication of her novel *Flugasche* (Flight of ashes).[20] Adolf Endler was permitted to give a series of lectures on lyric poetry at the University of Amsterdam in 1983, but in granting permission, Höpcke recommended that he use the occasion to denounce the recent decision of the U.S. government to set up middle-range rockets in Western Europe. American militarism was not a subject that lent itself to a discussion of lyric poetry, Endler replied, but he would find a way to say in his conclusion that everything he had mentioned in the previous lectures was threatened with obliteration if the Americans had their way.[21]

Höpcke found it more difficult to resolve a parallel case, that of Wolfgang Hilbig, a poet who also attracted invitations from Western Europe in 1983. Not only did Hilbig's poems reflect badly on life in East Germany, but he published them in West Germany, without permission. They were such a success that his admirers in Hanau in the FRG awarded him the Brothers Grimm Prize and invited him to collect it in person. He sent a telegram accepting the invitation—also without seeking the customary permission from the GDR authorities, which left Höpcke in a quandary, because a refusal to allow Hilbig to make the trip would confirm West German views of repression in East Germany. Höpcke's first reaction was to issue a firm *nyet*, all the more so as Hilbig wanted to follow up on the trip to Hanau with one to West Berlin, where he had also been invited. But after discussing the problem on the phone with Hager, Höpcke relented. He summoned Hilbig for a meeting, and lectured him about his disobedience to the GDR's regulations for authors. Nonetheless, he concluded, he would permit Hilbig to accept the prize, provided that he refrain from any criticism of the GDR. In fact, he, too, should condemn the American rockets in his acceptance speech, and a reader from the Reclam publishing house would go over the text, helping him to find words to express the "inhuman striving for world domination by the largest imperial power."[22]

Of course, the regime disposed of many other inducements to keep the authors faithful to the Party line. One was simply to permit them to read the West German press. Volker Braun requested special permission to sub-

scribe to *Die Zeit*, and Höpcke supported him in a memo to Hager by arguing that the subscription would provide Braun with material for a future
novel satirizing capitalism—a book, as it turned out, that he never wrote.[23]
More important advantages came with membership in the official Authors
Union, whose leaders were loyal Party members and whose ranks were
closed to anyone who failed to get the Party's approval. It was extremely
difficult to have a literary career without joining the union, which enjoyed
an annual two-million-mark subsidy from the state and dispensed a great
deal of patronage—commissions to write exhibition catalogues and translations, places in theaters as dramaturges (literary managers), positions in
literary journals, and salaried work for academies and educational institutions. Like everyone else in the GDR, writers could not move from one
city to another without the permission of the state, and they needed help
from Party bosses in order to advance in the long queues of people waiting
to rent an apartment or to purchase a car. Hager's office kept long lists of
writers who sent in requests for visas, cars, better living conditions, and
intervention to get their children into universities.[24]

Just how badly an unorthodox writer could be frozen out of such benefits can be appreciated from the dossier of Rainer Kirsch, a freelance
writer who was expelled from the Party in 1973 for slipping disrespectful
comments about socialism into his play, *Heinrich Schlaghands Höllenfahrt*
(Heinrich Schlaghand's Journey to hell). The play was published in a quasi-
official journal, *Theater der Zeit*—by mistake, according to the journal's
editor, who tried to cover himself with an explanation addressed to the
first secretary of the GDR Playwrights' Union. He had been traveling, the
editor explained, and a subeditor had accepted the text at the last minute
before deadline without examining it adequately. To his horror, the editor
spotted the play's heresies as soon as he read the journal. He would publish a refutation of it, stressing its incompatibility with the Party's cultural
policy, and promised that in the future nothing would appear without his
approval. This defense, such as it was, went with an apologetic letter by
the first secretary to the head of the Culture Division of the Central Committee, Ragwitz's predecessor, Walter Vogt. Kirsch was then drummed out
of the Party.[25]

In the face of this disaster, Kirsch tried to appeal to Hager. He got as far as Hager's assistant, Erika Hinkel, who listened to his self-defense at a meeting in Berlin. Although he accepted the decision of the Party, Kirsch said, his play contained nothing disrespectful of socialism, and he never had any hostile intentions or negative thoughts. On the contrary, he wanted to live in harmony with the Party and the state, and he would demonstrate that commitment in his future writing. All he asked was that he receive permission to move from Halle to Berlin, that he be allotted an apartment (three and a half rooms would do for his family of three), and that he be given a position as a dramaturge in a theater.[26]

The Party ignored this and subsequent appeals, which indicated that Kirsch was sinking into ever-deeper misery in Halle. Relations with local colleagues and officials had degenerated to the point that "life in Halle is nearly unbearable, since I feel almost completely isolated," he wrote in a letter addressed to the *Oberbürgermeister* (mayor) of East Berlin as well as to Frau Hinkel.[27] He lived with his wife and seven-year-old daughter in a cramped, three-room apartment located in an unhealthy inner court-yard. (In 1968 he had separated from his first wife, the poet Sarah Kirsch, who emigrated to West Germany with their son in 1977 after protesting against the expatriation of Wolf Biermann.) His wife, a Russian, had a teaching job, but she suffered terribly from Halle's polluted air. In fact, she had developed chronic bronchitis and laryngitis, which would degenerate into a dangerous case of asthma if she could not escape to a healthier environment. Kirsch therefore renewed his request to move to Berlin, where the journals and publishing houses could provide an opportunity of employment. Ten years later, Kirsch had somehow made it to Berlin, but he was still begging for a sinecure. A teaching position similar to the ones given to three of his fellow writers would be perfect, he wrote in a letter to Hager. Hager turned it over to Ragwitz, who answered with a memo advising emphatically against any patronage. She had consulted Party members in the Authors Union, and they had condemned Kirsch's "political-ideological comportment."[28]

Ragwitz often used phrases of that kind in her memos and letters. She spoke the language of power. Censorship as she exercised it, whether through manipulation or outright repression, belonged to the Communist Party's monopoly of power. Yet it may be inadequate to read the messages exchanged within the nomenklatura merely as attempts to enforce the Party line. Ragwitz had "political-ideological" convictions of her own, and so did her colleagues, as one can see by looking more closely at the dossier of Wolfgang Hilbig.

Unlike most East German writers, even famous dissidents like Christa Wolf and Volker Braun, Hilbig did not fit into the system. He lived as a loner. Far from attempting to rise through the ranks as a member of the Authors Union, he supported himself as a worker in a boiler room.[29] The job left him plenty of time to study literature while writing poetry, and he did not submit his poems to the established literary reviews of the GDR. He published them in West Germany—without seeking permission. After the appearance of his first volume, *Abwesenheit* (Absence) (Fischer Verlag, Frankfurt am Main, 1979), he was punished by a 2,000-mark fine. (His dossier in the Party archives also mentions a brief stint in prison, but apparently that involved an arrest for violent behavior, "Rowdytum," on another occasion.)[30] By 1982, when Fischer published a volume of short stories, *Unterm Neomond* (Under the new moon), he had achieved enough notoriety to be celebrated in the West as a worker-poet who was persecuted in the East, and the GDR tried to repair its reputation as a champion of the working class by permitting an East German edition. But his next book, *Stimme Stimme* (Voice, voice), submitted to the same GDR publisher, Reclam, posed a greater problem for the censors. The Party had decreed that literature should adhere to socialist realism, and at two conferences in the industrial city of Bitterfeld in 1959 and 1964, writers had committed themselves to the "Bitterfelder Weg," a program of collaborating with workers in a common effort to create a distinctively GDR-socialist culture. Unfortunately, the lyrics of the worker-poet Hilbig did not fit that formula. Far from it, Ragwitz explained, in submitting a dossier to Hager on December 14, 1982.

Speaking for Kultur, she recommended against permitting *Stimme Stimme* to be published. True, it had received three favorable reader's reports, and there was no denying Hilbig's talent as a poet. But if they allowed the book to circulate, it would make him into a recognized author; and once his presence was established in the GDR cultural scene, he would exercise a bad influence on the young writers they wanted to recruit in order to perpetuate a healthy, positive, progressive, and socially responsible variety of literature, one rooted in the working class. Hilbig's proletarian background made him all the more dangerous, even though he never attacked socialism or the GDR, because at bottom his work communicated an unacceptable worldview:

> His worldview and artistic positions are distant from our ideology. By taking up reactionary and late-bourgeois traditions . . . Hilbig uses dark colors and pessimistic tones to diffuse a nihilistic and melancholy outlook on the world and on life. . . . Since he gives voice to resignation, loneliness, sadness, suffering, and a yearning for death, Hilbig's commitment to humanism can also be questioned. Even though he often displays his proletarian origins, nothing connects him with the everyday political consciousness of a GDR citizen.[31]

"Late-bourgeois" was GDR jargon for modernism—in Hilbig's case, poetry that could be associated with Rimbaud or Rilke; in other cases, novels that drew inspiration from authors like Proust or Joyce. Ragwitz in Kultur and the censors in the HV did not enforce conformity to the Bitterfelder Weg, which had ceased to set a strict standard for literary style by 1980, but they remained committed to the stylistic conventions known loosely as "socialist realism," and they were suspicious of writing that failed to speak to the conditions of life in "real socialism," as they called it—that is, the concrete world experienced by ordinary people in the GDR.[32] In the 1960s and 1970s, the regime refused to permit literature of this kind. In the 1980s, however, it became less repressive, partly because it worried about scandals that could be exploited by the West German media, whose radio and television broadcasts reached an increasingly wide audience in the GDR. If it refused to allow *Stimme Stimme* to appear in East Germany, the book was certain to appear in the West, accompanied by a great deal of damaging publicity.

In the end, therefore, Hager permitted the publication of *Stimme Stimme*. He had received a letter defending Hilbig from Stephan Hermlin, an influential writer who had had his own difficulties with the censorship. (Hermlin had helped organize the protest against the exile of Wolf Biermann in 1976, but he maintained good relations with the Party leaders.)[33] Hilbig's poems did not breathe optimism, Hermlin conceded, but they did not express the slightest opposition to socialism; and if poets had to pass a test for cheerfulness, little would be left of German literature.[34] Ragwitz ultimately agreed that the book could appear without causing too much damage, but only under certain conditions: Hilbig would have to eliminate certain poems and tone down others; his editors at Reclam would have to vet the final text with great care; the printing would have to be restricted to a small number of copies; and they would have to control its reception by preparing reviews to expose the inadequacy of its "worldview and ideological position."[35] A few months later, as mentioned, Hager agreed to allow Hilbig, carefully guarded by the Reclam publisher, Hans Marquand, to accept a prize in Hanau, West Germany.

From that point onward, Hilbig became the object of a running debate within the bureaucracy about the limits of permissiveness. In 1984, he cooperated with a broadcast from Hesse, West Germany, which made him look like a victim of persecution in the GDR. In 1985, he was awarded a prize by the West Berlin Academy of Arts and asked to be allowed to accept it there. Marquand and Höpcke opposed allowing him out of the country;[36] and while their memos were circulating within the ministry of culture, Hilbig applied for a visa to take up a yearlong fellowship in Darmstadt. This was too much for Hager, who argued against any more concessions in an angry memo to Hans-Joachim Hoffmann, the minister of culture.[37] By then, however, Hilbig had acquired a formidable reputation. Stephan Hermlin and Christa Wolf appealed directly to Honecker, arguing that Hilbig was the greatest talent that had appeared in the GDR during the last twenty years.[38] Hilbig himself wrote to Honecker on August 26, 1985—a proletarian poet addressing a head of state. He put his case respectfully but forcefully. East German writers should be allowed to travel in order to expand their horizons, he said. They should be free to publish in the GDR and abroad. They should be able to express themselves openly without submitting to ideological constraints. And their commitment to socialism should also be free, for "literature without a true and fully developed profession of faith is worthless."[39] There is no record of Honecker's reaction; but three weeks later, in a memo that referred to Hilbig's letter, Hager announced that he had reversed his previous stand and would no longer oppose granting the visa. Hilbig left the GDR at the end of 1985 and did not return.[40]

The Hilbig affair, and all the others that appear in the archives, did not involve any opposition to socialist principles, government policy, or Party leaders. Like all the authors labeled in the West as dissidents, Hilbig tried to work within the system until he reached a breaking point; and even when he published his work in West Germany, he did not reject the fundamental ideals of the GDR. The correspondence about him within the Party elite never questioned his ultimate loyalty to the state. It dealt with seemingly nonseditious matters such as self-feeling (*Selbstgefühl*) and emotional outlook (*Pessimismus*). To an outsider, the style of the memos exchanged among the senior officials, seems surprisingly abstract and inflated. It can be explained in large part by the conventions of bureaucratic rhetoric, for the Party leaders often strung together heavy-duty adjectives such as political-ideological (*politisch-ideologisch*) and late-bourgeois (*spätbürgerlich*) before ponderous nouns like worldview (*Weltanschauung*) and Party-ness (*Parteilichkeit*).[41] But the censors in the Central Committee and the Ministry of Culture took language seriously, and they were deadly serious in discussing the language of the authors they repressed. Words in GDR-speak had particular resonance, even when they sound ludicrous to foreign ears—as in the case of the standard reference to the Berlin Wall as an antifascistic protection wall (*antifaschistischer Schutzwall*).[42] The censors were particularly upset when they discovered that the younger generation of authors used words in the wrong way.

In 1981, a group of young writers submitted a volume of poems and essays for publication by the Academy of Arts. The HV refused to permit it; but instead of submitting to this decision, the authors sent a letter of protest to the minister of culture. They explained that they had put together the Anthology, as they called it (apparently it did not have a full title), at the instigation of a member of the academy, Franz Fühmann, who was a mentor to disaffected writers from the younger generation. It represented the work of thirty-three authors who wanted their voices to be heard and who resented the refusal of the authorities to engage in a dialogue with them. The protest eventually reached Ursula Ragwitz, who recommended in a memo to Hager that they bury it in silence. The authors should be told to take their complaint to the academy, and the academy should be instructed to ignore it. Meanwhile, however, the Party should respond with some measures that would get to the root of the problem, because the Anthology affair was a symptom of discontent that deserved serious attention.[43]

With the help of the secret police, Kultur accumulated a huge amount of information about the Anthology group. Ragwitz summarized their investigation in a 35-page report, which included biographies of the contributors, descriptions of their milieu, and analyses of their poems. From the perspective of Kultur, the poetry was bewildering—a mishmash of unintelligible jargon, bizarre formats, vulgarities, slang, and coded allusions to subjects such as pollution, boredom, rock music, Wittgenstein, and John Lennon. As described in the more familiar idiom of the Party, the Anthology was suspiciously late-bourgeois in style and nihilistic in content.

> A number of the contributions are characterized by pessimism, weariness of life [*Lebensüberdruss*], and despair. . . . A great many of the contributions employ expressive techniques of late-bourgeois literature such as broken syntax, the arrangement of lines to make figurative patterns, and oral and visual punning. Some texts employ jargon, colloquial speech, and vulgarisms, which indicate a different kind of bourgeois influences.

Also, Ragwitz admitted, it had great appeal to young people.[44]

Of course, the enthusiasts could not find this kind of writing in bookstores, because, as Ragwitz insisted in another memo, it would never be permitted.[45] But the angry young poets circulated manuscript copies of their work and gave private readings of it in their favorite territory, the Prenzlauer Berg section of East Berlin. Spies identified places like the Alte Kaffee in Friedrichstrasse and an apartment at Raumerstrasse 23, where students and university dropouts congregated.[46] In one account of a poetry reading, a spy reported that forty-four persons listened raptly in an apartment to the two poets who had edited the Anthology, Uwe Kolbe and Alexander ("Sascha") Anderson. Despite considerable difficulty in making sense of the verse, the audience engaged in a lively discussion about "self realization," "creativity," and "integrity"[47]

The Prenzlauer Berg scene, as it later came to be known, might seem too marginal to warrant so much attention. The poets themselves were marginal characters. Sascha Anderson, for example, appeared in a report as "Anderson, Alexander (28)—(Lyric poetry). Dresden. No fixed job. Unattached author, painter, and songwriter"[48] Moreover, when the archives of the Stasi (secret police) became available after the collapse of the Wall, Anderson turned out to be one of their spies.[49] But the West German media were just as interested as the East German agents in what went on in Prenzlauer Berg, and publicity from the West could cause damage in the East, especially if it emphasized the alienation of the younger generation.

Honecker himself paid great attention to the coverage of GDR literature in the FRG. In April 1981, he received a briefing from Ragwitz about a radio broadcast from the West that spread the word about the disenchantment of the young East German writers and cited as evidence an article in *Neue Deutsche Literatur*, the literary journal of the East German Authors Union. The article was written by Inge von Wangenheim, a respected, sixty-eight-year-old writer with impeccable credentials as a supporter of the regime. She warned that GDR literature might cease to exist by 2000, because writers who were now turning thirty were so disaffected that they would not continue the socialist tradition established by their grandfathers. The broadcast was distorted, Ragwitz assured her chief, and the article should never have appeared. She had scolded the journal's editor for committing a "political error." He replied that the article had received a printing permit from the HV and that Wangenheim planned to include it in a forthcoming collection of her essays. To exclude it at this late stage could cause a scandal, Ragwitz warned Hager. But they could require her to make changes and plant enough critical reviews of the book to blunt its impact.[50] Meanwhile, however, the Western media continued to cause trouble. One broadcast claimed that the only true representatives of GDR literature were authors who escaped the censorship and the "prison syndrome" by emigrating to the FRG.[51] And an article by the West German critic Manfred Jaeger argued that a young generation of angry "wild men" had turned against all official literature and dismissed the writing of a middle-aged generation as uninteresting, except in the case of their mentor, Franz Fühmann, who had inspired the Anthology and whom they revered for remaining true to the critical spirit of Bertolt Brecht.[52] Misguided as they were, the attacks exposed a problem that could not be ignored. What was to be done?

Ragwitz proposed two kinds of measures. First, the regime should take a strong stand in favor of the literary principles laid down as the Party line at the Tenth Party Congress in 1981. After conducting a thorough study of GDR literature in the 1970s, the experts in Kultur had come up with policy recommendations that were adopted at the congress—and their findings confirmed studies done by the Academy of Social Science and the Central Institute for Literary History at the Academy of Sciences. All this research supported the fundamental position taken by the Party: style and subject matter must be understood as crucial elements in the construction of socialism. As the Ninth Party Congress had determined in 1976, literature should concentrate on the "daily life of people under real socialism." Real socialism—the actual existing order of the GDR—called for socialist realism in writing, not the esoteric, individualistic manner of late-bourgeois authors, which was incomprehensible to ordinary people. The man in the street turned to literature for help in understanding his own experience, and help should come through the "development of socialistic consciousness." Recent writing of the late-bourgeois variety did the opposite. By indulging in subjectivism and harping on the disparities between everyday experience and socialist ideals, it had degenerated into a destructive genre of social criticism.[53]

The Party could eradicate that kind of literature by pursuing a cultural offensive aimed in the first instance at the young Anthology writers. The most talented of them should be co-opted by being made candidates for membership in the Authors Union. (Writers could not simply join the union; they had to go through a period of candidacy, normally with a sponsor.) They should be assigned mentors from the union and be given missions that would involve attractive opportunities to travel. Uwe Kolbe could be sent to Angola and Katja Lange to Mongolia. The Anthology contributors who had expressed hostility to the Party should be frozen out of the literary world, but handled with restraint. Although they should not be allowed to publish anything, they should be given jobs that had no connection with literature. And those who were downright "asocial and enemies of the state" should be punished as criminals—that is, presumably be sent to prison or labor in the brown-coal industry, although Ragwitz did not specify what measures she had in mind.[54] While suppressing the literary activities of Prenzlauer Berg, the Ministry of Culture should set up literary centers to encourage young writers and the correct kind of writing in every sector of the country.[55] Editors in publishing houses should be assigned to cultivate talented youth; the HV should develop additional measures; and Kultur should oversee the program, mindful of the need to foster a new generation of "culture providers" and to orient it in the right direction.[56]

AUTHOR-EDITOR NEGOTIATIONS

The memos that circulated at the highest levels of the GDR showed that censorship was not limited to the activities of the censors. It penetrated every aspect of literature, down to the innermost thoughts of the authors and their first contact with editors. Volker Braun defined its character in a note that he scribbled for himself while struggling to get a draft of his *Hinze-Kunze-Roman* past an editor at the Mitteldeutscher Verlag (MDV) in 1983: "The system works all by itself. The system censors."[57] This systemic penetration was deepest at the lowest level, where authors and editors negotiated over the planning and production of manuscripts. Although practices varied, they normally went through the same stages. As described earlier, the idea for a book might germinate in the mind of an author, but it frequently originated among the editors of the GDR's seventy-eight publishing houses or even among the censors and other officials in Berlin. Because the director (*Verlagsleiter*) and chief editor (*Cheflektor*) of the houses were important Party members—powerful apparatchiks or nomenklatura—they exercised great ideological control. Yet lower-placed editors often developed friendly relations with authors, who usually worked with the same house—notably, in the case of contemporary fiction, the Mitteldeutscher Verlag (MDV) in Halle and Leipzig and the Aufbau Verlag in Berlin and Weimar.[58] Instead of writing on their own until they had arrived at a finished manuscript, the authors usually sent the editors early drafts and small segments. The editors responded with suggestions for changes, and a process of negotiation continued until both sides reached agreement about a final draft. At that point, the editor sent the typescript to one or more outside readers, who tended to be trusted advisers, often literary critics and academics. The readers' reports could trigger more rounds of negotiation and changes. When a reworked text had been completed, the publisher prepared a dossier, which included the readers' reports and a publisher's report, usually four or five typewritten pages, by the chief editor, along with information about the author, the format, the amount of paper required, the proposed pressrun, and the price.

The dossier and the text then were sent to the HV office in Clara-Zetkin-Strasse for approval by the professional staff in the manner described by Hans-Jürgen Wesener and Christina Horn. The process of censoring could continue even after the book had been published, because if it provoked a scandal, it could be withdrawn from bookshops and pulped. Certain passages might be excised from later editions, but they also might be added; for the HV sometimes permitted a West German edition by giving clearance through the Copyright Office (Büro für Urheberrechte). To be sure, the Western edition might stir up controversy; but once the dust had settled, its controversial passages could be reprinted discreetly in a new GDR edition.

Censorship took place throughout the entire process—and even beyond it, because authors and publishers remained vulnerable to post-publication sanctions. Yet the most important part of the process is the most difficult to identify, because it happened in the author's head. Self-censorship left few traces in the archives, but East Germans often mentioned it, especially when they felt free to talk after the fall of the Wall. In *Der Zorn des Schafes* (The anger of the sheep, 1990), for example, Erich Loest explained that in 1950, when he began his career as a writer and enjoyed an uncritical faith in the legitimacy of the regime, he had no difficulty in accepting censorship, because he could not imagine treating any subject in any way that would damage the cause of socialism. But after three decades of trimming his prose to the demands of editors, publishers, and the HV, he emigrated to West Germany; and when he resumed writing in the FRG, he realized that an inner voice had been whispering to him all along, at every line he wrote, "Careful, that can cause you trouble!"[59] He called it "that little green man inside the ear."[60] Others used the common expression "scissors in the head."[61] It existed everywhere and made authors complicit with the censorship, even when they tried to resist it. They might exult after persuading an editor to accept one or two contested passages, but in doing so they often managed, with the help of the inner voice, to ignore the fact that they were submitting the entire text to the sanction of the state.[62] This semi-conscious process of complicity sometimes led them to deceive the censor with tricks, but the tricks could also result in self-deception. Joachim Seyppel, a novelist and literary critic who emigrated from the GDR in 1979, wrote that authors occasionally planted a flagrantly provocative passage in a manuscript in order to attract the censor's attention while distracting it from subtler heresies scattered elsewhere in the text. The authors would then pretend to fight fiercely to maintain the passage, lose the feigned fight, and save the remarks that they really wanted to have published. By playing that game, however, they accepted its rules and became complicit with the system. The little green man had won.[63]

The next stage of the process can be understood by consulting the papers of the most important publisher of GDR fiction, the MDV, which I was also able to study in the Party archives during the early 1990s.[64] Most of the information concerned practices in the 1980s and should not be taken to typify censorship during earlier and more repressive periods. For the last decade of the GDR's existence, however, the publisher's archives show how the regime controlled literature at the level of authors and editors. The general character of all its operations can be summarized in a single word: negotiation. The give-and-take, demands and concessions, writing and rewriting began as soon as an idea for a book was adumbrated. In rare cases when an author turned in a supposedly finished manuscript, the editors were astonished—and somewhat offended. After Karl-Heinz Jakobs deposited a "final" draft of his novel *Die Stille* (Silence), the editors complained that he was one of the few authors "who refuse to let the publisher influence the development process of a manuscript and instead submit 'finished' copy."[65]

The negotiating was especially effective in the case of popular genres like crime novels, love stories, and science fiction. An editor persuaded Waltraud Ahrndt to transform the ending of *Flugversuche* (Attempted flights), a boy-meets-girl romance, so that the couple would not live happily ever after. The girl had to reject the boy, because she realized that he had joined the Party only to win her and not from genuine Communist convictions.[66] Horst Czerny modified the plot of his detective story *Reporter des Glanzes* (Society reporter) according to the recommendations of his editor so that it would bring out the negative aspects of life in Bonn, West Germany, where the intrigue took place—namely, "anti-Communism, anti-Sovietism, neo-Nazism, war ideology, threatening lies, and agitation for German reunification." One of the rare crime thrillers set in the GDR, *Der Sog* (The current), by Jan Flieger, had to be rewritten several times, because one of its main characters, a factory manager, was disagreeably stupid. Management in a socialist system could not appear in such a light.[67] The same problem applied to science fiction, which the editors called utopian literature, because descriptions of future societies had to celebrate the inevitable triumph of communism, yet the editors feared that their positive elements could be read as implicit "political-ideological" criticism of the socialist order in the present. Therefore, they persuaded Gerhard Branstner to rework his *Der negative Erfolg* (The negative success) so that his fantasy of the future would express adequate "theoretical considerations from a Marxist way of thinking."[68]

It would be misleading, however, to reduce the editors' function to ideological gatekeeping. They devoted a great deal of attention to the aesthetic qualities of manuscripts, working closely with authors to improve phrasing and strengthen narratives. As far as one can tell from reading their reports, they were intelligent and well-educated critics who had much in common with editors in West Berlin and New York. They sought out talent, worked hard over drafts, chose the most appropriate outside readers, and shepherded texts through a complex production schedule. The main aspect of their dossiers that makes them look different from their counterparts in the West is the absence of any reference to literary demand. I found only one remark about what readers wanted to buy. In discussing *Der Holzwurm und der König* (The wood worm and the king), Helga Duty, the chief editor at MDV, recommended publication, even though that would satisfy the public's unfortunate taste for adult fairy tales.[69]

Instead of trimming their list to the winds from the marketplace, the editors tried to fight off kitsch, and they frequently lost. Duty and her subeditors did everything possible to eliminate the "pseudo-romantic, pathetic, and kitschy quality of the poems collected in *Luftschaukel* (Swing in the air), but the author, Marianna Bruns, was eighty-seven and had been attached to the MDV for many years. She agreed to rework the manuscript—but only up to a point. In the end, the editors did most of the compromising and reluctantly recommended the book for a printing authorization.[70] They refused to be so flexible in dealing with Hans Cibulka, although he was sixty-five and had published with the MDV for thirty years. His volume of poems, *Seid ein Gespräch wir sind* (We are a discussion), was too pessimistic and "undialectic," but above all it mixed metaphors and misused imagery. After lengthy negotiations, they rejected his manuscript, noting "one cannot 'work' with him as with a debutant author."[71]

"Working" with authors could be so intense that it verged on collaboration. Joachim Rähmer was a "debutant" whose first novel, *Bekenntnisse eines Einfältigen* (Confession of a simpleton), had to be completely rewritten. "The work on this novel, especially in the process of drafting, was very demanding," his editor complained.[72] Werner Reinowski caused even more headaches. For ten years after the publication of one of his novels, he kept coming back with proposals for new books, and the MDV kept rejecting them. The editors finally accepted his sketch for a novel entitled *Hoch-Zeit am Honigsee* (Wedding by the honey sea), which had an appropriately proletarian subject but lacked a strong narrative line. After six years of debates and six full-scale drafts, they received a barely acceptable manuscript. It posed no ideological problems. On the contrary, it was too dogmatic. Reinowski neglected the aesthetic aspect of writing so egregiously that he treated literature as nothing more than a means to propagate the Party's social program. In their report, the editors said that they had had enough. They had worked as hard on the book as he did, and they did not want to publish anything more by him.[73]

Most authors proved pliable, and the negotiations with them involved genuine give-and-take. Editors occasionally complied with an author's refusal to accept suggestions, even when a draft seemed insufficiently Marxist.[74] More often they insisted on changes, but diplomatically and with enough concessions to make them palatable. *Wir Flüchtlingskinder* (We children of refugees), an autobiographical novel by Ursula Höntsch-Harendt, dealt with the explosive topic of the expulsion of Sudeten Germans from Silesia after it became Polish territory as required by the Potsdam Agreement of July 26, 1945. The editors required changes that would reinforce the GDR version of events and counteract "revanchist" history from the FRG. In addition to historical allusions, the main character of the novel had to be transformed, and Höntsch-Harendt even had to modify the fictitious version of her father, whom she had portrayed too sympathetically as a social democrat. She also had to cut a rape scene, which reflected badly on the Red Army, and to tone down her demonization of Hitler, which attributed too much of the evil of fascism to the influence of one person. Thanks to their hard work and her cooperation, the editors endorsed a text that corresponded to "historical truth" and would, they believed, help determine the understanding of the younger generation.[75]

In dossier after dossier, one can see how the editors shaped East German fiction, cutting passages, realigning narratives, changing the nature of characters, and correcting allusions to historical and social issues. Whether heavy or light, the editing involved aesthetic as well as ideological considerations, and it was accepted both by authors and by editors as an essential aspect of the game they played when they negotiated over a manuscript. Conflict occurred, but the editors' reports convey an atmosphere of mutual respect rather than struggle and repression. Of course, one must allow for their bias, and they say nothing about the authors who gnashed their teeth and cursed the system for trimming their prose or excluding them altogether. Yet as an account of business as usual, the dossiers suggest a process of constant, workable negotiation. Helga Duty expressed their dominant tone when she noted in the conclusion of her report on Manfred Künne's *Buna: Roman eines Kunststoffes* (Buna: A novel of a synthetic material), an adventure novel about German-American competition to produce synthetic rubber during World War II: "The collaboration between author and publisher was in each phase fruitful and full of trust."[76]

The process of vetting did not stop there, because once a manuscript had been approved by an editor, it had to pass muster with outside readers and finally with the censors in the HV. Editors solicited reports from readers very much as they do in the non-Communist world. They had personal contacts among academics and experts in many fields, and they could steer a dossier to a happy conclusion by their choice of readers. For their part, the readers prepared reports with a good deal of care. They usually produced three to five pages of comments about substance, style, and, if needed, ideological correctness; and they received an honorarium of forty to sixty East German marks for their trouble. Even detective stories got a critical going-over. Editors sent them out to special officers in the police force (*Volkspolizei*) when they needed an assessment about the fine points of gathering clues and performing autopsies.[77]

Political considerations weighed heaviest in reports on works in the social sciences and history. *So war es: Lebensgeschichten zwischen 1900–1980* (Thus it was: Life stories between 1900 and 1980), a sociological study of a light bulb factory by Wolfgang Herzberg, required a great deal of intervention by the editors, because it was based on interviews with workers who expressed "politically unschooled" and "undialectical" recollections of their experience under the Third Reich. After persuading

Herzberg to rewrite several drafts, the editors considered the manuscript ready for publication; but the readers disagreed. One of them objected that the text failed to bring out the monopolistic and capitalistic under-pinning of Hitlerism, and another insisted that quotations from the oral interviews be rephrased so that they would make the proletariat sound more revolutionary. The editors complied, and the author rewrote his text once more before it could be sent with the reports to the HV for final approval.[78]

Once the dossiers arrived in the offices at Clara-Zetkin-Strasse, they underwent censorship of a more professional variety. Unlike the editors and readers, the censors in the HV evaluated a text according to its place within the overall production of books—that is, everything encompassed in the annual Plan—and while taking a broad view of literature, they kept an eye out not merely for unacceptable phrases but also for difficulties that might arise from their opposite numbers in Kultur. Marion Fuckas, an HV official who concentrated on poetry and fiction, illustrates how this kind of vetting took place. She underlined passages in the reports that seemed important to her; and if they corresponded to her own reading of the manuscript, she wrote, "Agreed with the publishers' reports," in a box on the top page of the dossier.[79] *Erinnerung an eine Milchglasscheibe* (Remembrance of a frosted window pane), a volume of poems by Steffen Mensching, serves as an example of how she handled a problematic dos-sier. Her underlining drew attention to Mensching's tendency to develop a "critical accent" when he handled sensitive themes like militarism. But a long report by Silvia and Dieter Schlenstedt, the most trusted outside readers of the MDV, laid that worry to rest. They explained that they had got to know Mensching, who had special appeal to the younger generation, and had persuaded him to withdraw some poems and modify others. He therefore could be promoted as a poet who combined "artistic talent with a basically Marxist aesthetic position," a phrase that Fuckas underlined from Helga Duty's publisher's report. Eberhard Günther, the director of the MDV who had earlier worked as a censor in the HV, confirmed this judg-ment in a letter that stressed Mensching's willingness to make changes in his text. Like the Schlenstedts, Günther had had a talk with him and had persuaded him to substitute two unproblematic poems for "Nachtgedan-ken," which had caused difficulties. Reassured by these items in the dossier, Fuckas gave it her approval, noting that the "distinctive political problem" had been resolved.[80]

She hesitated to endorse a novel by Claus Nowack, *Das Leben Gudrun* (The Life of Gudrun). Although the publisher had recommended it, a read-er's report warned that Nowack's use of late-bourgeois literary technique made it difficult to follow his narrative. Fuckas drew a line next to that pas-sage in the report and expanded on it in a memo of her own. She could not find any "Ariadne's thread" in the narrative that would make it possible for her to grasp what the author was trying to say. Did the late-bourgeois aes-thetics convey an ideological message? she asked. She refrained from pro-nouncing, although she clearly thought it did; but she felt impelled to warn against the growing tendency for authors to write in a way that would cut themselves off from the mass public. The stylistic obscurity in Nowack's novel could not be corrected by cuts and additions, because it pervaded the entire text. But at least it did not offend against Party correctness, and so she would not oppose its publication.[81]

Fuckas handled more conventional manuscripts according to the tried-and-true procedures of the HV. A book about Mozambique and the expe-rience of Africans in Europe had to be purged of suggestions that racism might exist in the GDR. She checked off a list of changes recommended by a reader to be sure that they had been incorporated in the final draft and then sent the text off to the Foreign Ministry for clearance.[82] When a colleague in the HV criticized the weak ending of a novel, Fuckas backed her, overruling the recommendation of Helga Duty, who had emphasized how closely the editors in the MDV had worked with the author through four heavily rewritten drafts. Back went the text to the publisher, which then had to produce a fifth draft before the book received a printing autho-rization.[83] Fuckas also rejected the MDV's recommendation to authorize a memoir about a writer's childhood in Königsberg. Although the text remained true to the Party line in its treatment of "real socialism," it was too sentimental in depicting the author's mother and too indulgent in relating her father's accommodation with the Nazis. The editors insisted that they had worked hard with the author to correct those tendencies, but Fuckas sent the text back, enjoining them to work still harder.[84]

Despite such episodes, the censors in Berlin did not treat the editors in the publishing houses as if they were underlings in a chain of command. The editors sometimes disregarded recommendations that reached them from the HV,[85] and the exchanges took place in an atmosphere of mutual respect and shared professionalism. It was hardly necessary to remind anyone that the Party had a monopoly of power and that its members occupied all the key positions in the publishing houses as well as in the administration. But they exerted power in different ways at different points within the system, and there was room at every point for some degree of negotiation. The negotiating involved a variety of roles and relations— between authors and editors, editors and outside readers, the publisher and the HV, the HV and the Culture Division of the Central Committee, even among individuals occupying peaks at the top of the regime—Höpcke, Hoffmann, Ragwitz, Hager, and Honecker. And most important of all, it took place inside the author's head. Far from being limited to the professionals in the HV, therefore, censorship pervaded the entire system. It was accepted by everyone—authors and editors in addition to bureaucrats and apparatchiks—as an essential aspect of the process for transforming a manuscript into a book.

HARD KNOCKS

Yet the notion of negotiation hardly does justice to the process. To concentrate on the ordinary, business-as-usual side of censorship runs the risk of making everything seem too gentle. The regime ruled by violence, as it demonstrated in repressing the Berlin uprising of June 17, 1953, and as anyone could see from the 500,000 Soviet troops stationed throughout the country until the collapse of the GDR. Less visible but more pervasive were the activities of the secret police (Stasi). Authors and editors knew they were being watched and recorded, but they had no idea about the extent of the surveillance until the Stasi archives became available after the opening of the Wall. Lutz Rathenow discovered that his Stasi files

contained 15,000 pages.[86] Erich Loest's ran to thirty-one dossiers, each
of about 300 pages, merely for the years 1975–81. He first noticed that
someone had tinkered with his telephone in 1976. After he read through
his files in 1990, he learned that the Stasi had recorded all his phone conversations, had mapped out every corner of his apartment, and had developed such elaborate dossiers on all of his friends and relatives that the files
could be read as a multivolume biography of him, more extensive than
anything he could have reconstructed from his own memory and papers.[87]
As dossiers continued to come to light, East Germans were appalled to
learn that information had constituted the backbone of power in the
police state, thanks to boundless collaboration—friends who informed
on friends, husbands and wives who betrayed each other, even dissidents
who reported on literary activities, among them Christa Wolf, who had
briefly cooperated with the Stasi as an "IM" (*Inoffizieller Mitarbeiter*, or
informer) under the code name Margarete.[88]

Although the density of the information gathering increased during
the last decade of the regime, repression tapered off. The GDR was considered a bastion of Stalinism long after 1956, when Nikita Khrushchev
initiated the uneven process of de-Stalinization at the Twentieth Party
Congress in the Soviet Union. But the severity of the sanctions against
intellectuals varied according to the temperature of the time. The worst
period occurred after the Soviet repression of the uprisings in Berlin in
1953 and Poland and Hungary in 1956. Its effect on publishing can be
appreciated by the memoirs of Walter Janka, who was purged as director of
the Aufbau-Verlag in 1956 and revealed the full story of his persecution,
with help from the Stasi files, after the fall of the Wall.

It would be difficult to imagine a more tried-and-true Communist than
Janka.[89] From a working-class background, he led a Communist youth
group until the Gestapo arrested him in 1933, when he was nineteen years
old. After eighteen months in prison, he was exiled to Czechoslovakia;
returned to Germany as an underground activist; joined the anti-Franco
forces in the Spanish Civil War; rose to be a commander of the Karl Marx
Division; distinguished himself in many battles and was wounded three
times; and at the end of the war was imprisoned with his troops for three

years. In 1941, he escaped from prison and made his way to Mexico via Marseille, Casablanca, and Havana. He spent the war years in Mexico City as director (and typesetter) of a small publishing house, which produced works by German exiles such as his friend Anna Seghers and Heinrich Mann, two of the most prominent novelists. Back in Berlin in 1947, Janka worked full-time for the Party until he was appointed director of the Aufbau-Verlag, which he built into the most important East German publisher of fiction and belles-lettres during the postwar period. By the time of the Hungarian uprising, he occupied a key position where politics and culture converged in the GDR. He was therefore well placed to intervene, when he received a phone call from Anna Seghers, who said that all communication with Budapest had been cut off and that Georg Lukács, the philosopher and literary critic who was one of Aufbau's most important authors, seemed to be in danger—presumably because he was a victim of the "counterrevolutionary" forces who had overthrown the Communist regime. Seghers put Janka in touch with her friend and fellow author Johannes R. Becher, who was then the minister of culture, and Becher made arrangements for Janka to undertake a secret mission, with a car and driver furnished by the ministry, in order to negotiate the release of Lukács from whatever confinement that might have been inflicted on him.

As Janka recounted it in his memoir, *Schwierigkeiten mit der Wahrheit* (Difficulties with the truth), the rescue mission was called off at the last minute by Becher, who had been told by the Party chief, Walter Ulbricht, that the Soviets would sort things out. In fact, Lukács had not been captured by the Hungarian revolutionaries. He had joined them and served as a minister in Imre Nagy's anti-Soviet government until the Soviets suppressed it. Although Nagy and others were secretly tried and executed, Lukács was eventually permitted to recant and to resume his philosophical work. Meanwhile, the Stasi carried Janka, handcuffed, off to prison. He was ordered to stand in front of a gigantic portrait of Stalin and then, after the handcuffs were removed, to strip and to submit to a body search, including all of his orifices. He was allowed to get dressed and marched off to a fetid, windowless, underground cell, where he remained separated from the rest of the world for eight months. He was interrogated, insulted, and intimidated, but not tortured. His crime, he learned, was a conspiracy, which he supposedly had hatched with a group of intellectuals inspired by Lukács, to overthrow the Party and install capitalism. When he was finally put on trial, he saw Anna Seghers, Brecht's widow, Helene Weigel, and other prominent literary figures who were friends of his sitting in the front row. They sat there silently, staring straight ahead. The regime had required them to witness Janka's abasement as a way of signaling the start of a new cycle of Stalinization and of calling the intellectuals to heel. Janka had wanted to summon Johannes Becher to testify in his defense, for Becher had not only planned the abortive mission to rescue Lukács but had even proposed liberalizing intellectual life in the GDR by dismantling the censorship office. But Becher was not available. He had taken a 180-degree turn, following the Party line, and the procedure in the courtroom conformed to the classic, Stalinist type of show trial. Janka was not shot, but he was sentenced to five years of solitary confinement (no contact with the outside world, except for visits from his wife, which were limited to two hours per year) in Bautzen, the prison that the Communists had taken over from the Nazi concentration camp.[90]

Janka recounted his arrest and trial without a hint of self-pity or dramatization. In fact, he noted that earlier periods of Stalinism in the GDR had been worse. Intellectuals and political figures had been abducted, tortured, and condemned in secret trials. Some had disappeared in Siberia. Some had gone mad and committed suicide.[91] Even though it did not equal other episodes in brutality, however, Janka's trial and imprisonment initiated a new wave of repression, which was intended to exterminate any ideological infection that might reach the GDR from Hungary and Poland or that might spread from intellectuals inside East Germany. Janka's connection with Lukács served as a pretext for a campaign to stamp out a supposed counterrevolutionary conspiracy that had formed in the offices of the Aufbau-Verlag and Sonntag, a cultural weekly run by editors connected with Aufbau. Their staffs were purged; many editors were imprisoned; and they were replaced by apparatchiks who made sure that nothing was published that deviated from the Party line. The Stasi spread terror among intellectuals by arresting students, teachers, journalists, authors, and assorted "persons-who-think-differently" (*Andersdenkender*)—eighty-seven in all during 1957.[92] After a slight thaw, therefore, Stalinism returned in full force in the GDR in 1957. It functioned as the sharp edge of censorship, especially after the erection of the Berlin Wall in 1961, and it continued to inhibit publishing for the next two decades.

The career of Erich Loest, an author who specialized in various genres of light literature, illustrates the recurrence of repression after the 1950s. Like Janka, Loest recounted his experience in an autobiographical memoir supplemented by a volume of documents from the Stasi archives.[93] He belonged to a younger generation of writers at the Johannes R. Becher Literary Institute in the University of Leipzig, where they absorbed the broad-minded Marxism advocated by the philosopher Ernst Bloch and the literary scholar Hans Mayer—two professors under close surveillance by the Stasi. (Bloch emigrated to West Germany in the wake of the Janka affair, and Mayer remained until 1963, when he, too, went into exile.) Loest stood out among their students, from the perspective of the Stasi, because he took part in uninhibited discussions about de-Stalinization. In November 1957, he was tried and sentenced to seven and a half years of strict imprisonment—also in Bautzen. After his release, he assumed that he could no longer play any part in the closed world of GDR literature. But one day he ran into his editor at the MDV, who suggested that he write detective stories, provided that he used a pseudonym and set the action in capitalist countries, where he could work in allusions to social evils.

Loest churned out so many thrillers that he soon was able to support himself as an independent author. He kept a low profile, living modestly in Leipzig, and avoided contact with the Authors Union, from which he had been expelled. Despite his precautions, he occasionally ran into trouble with the censorship. An entire edition of a spy novel had to be pulped, because it contained a reference to a secret agent of the Soviet Union; and he had to make big cuts in a "krimi" set in Greece, because the censors thought that descriptive passages could be taken as veiled allusions to problems in the GDR. But by 1970 Loest had established himself as a successful author, and his friends urged him to write more serious books.

The MDV thought differently. Its director, Heinz Sachs, who had encouraged Loest both before and after his imprisonment, had dared to publish two controversial works, *Nachdenken über Christa T* (The Quest for Christa T), by Christa Wolf, and *Buridans Esel* (Buridan's Ass) by Günther de Bruyn; and he did so in 1968, when the Prague Spring and the Soviet invasion of Czechoslovakia touched off new fears about unrest in the GDR. Although the authors rode out the scandal, Sachs was forced to publish a confession about his ideological inadequacy in *Neues Deutschland*, the official newspaper of the SED, and then was fired. Loest said that he became a schoolteacher, succumbed to alcoholism, and died in obscurity, a broken man. The new director of the MDV, Eberhard Günther, and its chief editor, Helga Duty, were apparatchiks who toed the Party line, according to Loest's account of his relations with them. They flatly refused to publish his *Schattenboxen* (Shadowboxing), a novel set in the GDR whose hero failed to resume a normal life after serving a prison term in Bautzen. Another publisher, Neues Leben, found the manuscript acceptable—except for one problem: the censors in the HV would not permit the use of the word Bautzen, which evoked an unhappy parallel between Nazi and GDR tyranny. Loest agreed to let his editor expunge it; and when the book appeared, he found that the editor, a sympathetic young woman who later decamped for West Berlin, had neglected, no doubt on purpose, to delete "Bautzen" in two passages of the text.

In 1974, Loest began negotiating with the MDV about another novel, *Es geht seinen Gang* (It goes its way), which dealt with an unacknowledged social problem of the GDR—namely, the difficulty of qualified young technicians to get ahead in their careers. Günther liked the idea well enough to offer a preliminary contract, but Duty and a subeditor found successive drafts objectionable, and so did the outside readers whom they chose for reports. By 1976, Loest was in a relatively strong bargaining position, because his publishers had sold 185,000 copies of his books, which had gone through many editions. But he wanted badly to travel to the West and therefore was willing to be flexible. At last, in April 1977, he and Günther sat down at a table and bargained over a final draft. Günther, who had been a censor in the HV, found twenty-six passages politically unacceptable. The "hottest chapter," which contained provocative remarks about a peace demonstration in which a police dog sank its fangs into the hero's buttocks, had to be drastically cut, Günther insisted; otherwise, he would refuse to send the manuscript to the HV. Loest protested but then took a ballpoint pen and struck out each of the offending sentences as Günther pointed to them. They continued in this way for four hours, Günther insisting and Loest resisting:

> Then it was a matter of a word here, a line there, and the lack of clarity in a certain concept. After the ninth objection, I said, "Come on, Eberhard, let me win a few. It's necessary for my self-respect." "Not the next one," he answered. "But the one after that." After three hours, the tension slackened, and I asked whether we couldn't pause for a friendly drop of something. "First, just a few small things more," he said. Eventually Günther no longer knew what his objection had been to certain turns of phrases. "That, there—not so important. That, there—Well, let it stay. That, there . . ." and I admitted, "Eberhard, in this case, you are right."
>
> Then we sat back, moved at the thought of what lay behind us. . . . We felt respect for one another, like boxers who had slugged it out to the last round.[94]

Suitably edulcorated, *Es Geht seinen Gang* appeared in 1978, both in the GDR and, with the permission of the Copyright Office, in the FRG. It was a big success. As a reward for his cooperation, Loest was allowed to give talks in West Germany, where he was greeted by admiring audiences and publishers eager for copy. Then things cooled. The *Frankfurter Allgemeine Zeitung*, West Germany's influential daily newspaper, published an article that treated *Es Geht seinen Gang* as an indication of deep discontent in the GDR. The Party leaders, always sensitive to embarrassing publicity in the West, issued formal reprimands to Günther and Duty for having failed to keep adequate control over the MDV's publications. Meanwhile, Loest drafted an autobiographical memoir in which he recounted his difficulties with the Party. Günther would not consider it. It could not be published in East Germany, he warned; and if it appeared in the West, Loest's career in the GDR would be finished.

Soon afterward, he delivered more bad news: the HV had refused to permit the publication of a second edition of *Es Geht seinen Gang*. The interdiction might be lifted, he suggested, if Loest agreed to still more cuts; but Loest refused. As the first edition continued to circulate, the HV tried to mitigate its effect on public opinion by commissioning hostile reviews in two leading GDR periodicals. It also ordered the Copyright Office to refuse Loest's request for a West German edition of his short stories. Years later, when he read through his thirty-one hefty dossiers in the Stasi archives, Loest discovered that these measures represented a large-scale campaign by the Stasi and the HV to incriminate him as an enemy agent. By March 1981, he had had enough. He realized that he could not continue as a writer in the GDR; and when he left on his next trip to the FRG, he remained there.

By that time, West Germany had accumulated a large population of East German expatriates. The most famous of them was Wolf Biermann, the nonconformist poet and singer with a razor-sharp wit. He had been permitted to leave on a concert tour of the FRG in November 1976. Then, after he had given a performance in Cologne, the Party's Politburo dramatically stripped him of his citizenship and refused to let him return. Twelve prominent East German writers—including Christa Wolf, Stefan Heym, Franz Fühmann, and Volker Braun—signed a letter of protest, which was diffused by Agence France-Presse and was later supported by one hundred other intellectuals. A wave of unrest swept over the GDR, followed by a wave of repression. Students were arrested, writers blacklisted, dissidents silenced. Sarah Kirsch, Jurek Becker, Günter Kunert, and other prominent authors went into exile. Jürgen Fuchs was imprisoned for nine months and then left for the FRG. Robert Havemann was put under house arrest and remained there for two and a half years. Stefan Heym was expelled from the Authors Union and excluded from East German publishing houses. Christa Wolf resigned from the central committee of the Authors Union, and her husband, Gerhard Wolf, was expelled from the Communist (SED) Party, as were Becker, Ulrich Plenzendorf, and Karl-Heinz Jakobs. Rudolf Bahro, the author of *Die Alternative*, a Marxist critique of GDR society published surreptitiously in West Germany, was arrested, sentenced to eight years in prison, and ultimately exiled. Other writers went into "internal exile." Instead of attempting to negotiate with publishers, they wrote, as the current saying put it, "for the desk drawer" and lost hope in the promise of liberalization. Erich Honecker had seemed to make that promise six months after he assumed power, when he declared at the Eighth Party Congress, in December 1971, that there would be "no more taboos in art and literature."[95] The Biermann affair exposed the hollowness of that statement and suggested that writers would have to cope with a severe variety of censorship as long as they remained in the GDR.[96]

Yet the writers who remained never abandoned their socialist convictions. Despite the recurrent episodes of repression, they generally held on to their determination to work within the system. Of course, most of them had no other choice and therefore continued to pursue their careers, making compromises as necessity arose. But to describe them as careerists would be to ignore the constraints built into their world. They accepted the reality of what they knew as "real socialism"—a term they often used to describe the imperfect but superior character of East German society— and as far as one can tell, they retained their belief in its fundamental legitimacy. Christa Wolf, who never deviated from her commitment to the socialist ideals of the GDR, expressed this position when she was interviewed during a trip to Italy. According to a transcript of her remarks that was entered in the Party archives, she had accepted the censors' cuts in sixty pages of *Kassandra*, because she understood literature to play a particular role in real socialism:

> Literature in the GDR has a special function, far more than in Western countries. It must perform tasks that in the West are fulfilled by journalism, social criticism, and ideological debate. People expect answers from authors about a whole range of things that are the concern of institutions in Western countries.

She therefore embraced a relativistic notion of censorship itself:

[...] Die Einsicht, daß unser aller physische Existenz von den Verschiebungen im Wahndenken sehr kleiner Gruppen von Menschen abhängt, also vom Zufall, hebt natürlich die klassische Ästhetik endgültig aus ihren Angeln, ihren Halterungen, welche, letzten Endes, an den Gesetzen der Vernunft befestigt sind. An dem Glauben, daß es solche Gesetze gebe, weil es sie geben müsse. Eine tapfere, wenn auch boden-lose Anstrengung, zugleich der frei schwebenden Vernunft und sich selbst ein Obdach zu schaffen: in der Literatur. Weil das Setzen von Worten an Voraus-setzungen gebunden ist, die außerhalb der Literatur zu liegen scheinen. Auch an ein Maß, denn die Ästhetik hat doch ihren Ursprung auch in der Frage, was dem Menschen zumutbar ist.

Die Homeriden mögen die ihnen zuhörende Menschenmenge durch ihre Berichte von lange vergangenen Heldentaten vereinigt und strukturiert haben, sogar über die sozial gegebenen Strukturen hinaus. Der Dramatiker des klassischen Griechenland hat mit Hilfe der Ästhetik die politisch-ethische Haltung der freien, erwachsenen, männlichen Bürger der Polis mitgeschaffen. Auch die Gesänge, Mysterienspiele, Heiligenlegenden des christlichen mittelalterlichen Dichters dienten einer Bindung, deren beide Glieder ansprechbar waren: Gott und Mensch. Das höfische Epos hat seinen festen Personenkreis, auf den es sich, ihn rühmend, bezieht. Der frühbürgerliche Dichter spricht in flammendem Protest seinen Fürsten an und zugleich, sie aufrührend, dessen Untertanen. Das Proletariat, die sozialistischen Bewegungen mit ihren revolutionären, klassenkämpferischen Zielen inspirieren die mit ihnen gehende Literatur zu konkreter Parteinahme. – Aber es wächst das Bewußtsein der Unangemessenheit von Worten vor den Erscheinungen, mit denen wir es jetzt zu tun haben. Was die anonymen nuklearen Planungsstäbe mit uns vorhaben, ist unsäglich; die Sprache, die sie erreichen würde, scheint es nicht zu geben. Doch schreiben wir weiter in den Formen, an die wir gewöhnt sind. Das .heißt: Wir können, was

110

Two pages from the East German edition of Christa Wolf's Kassandra with a passage from the uncensored West German edition that circulated secretly in the GDR. The passage was to be inserted at the top left of page 110 in the space

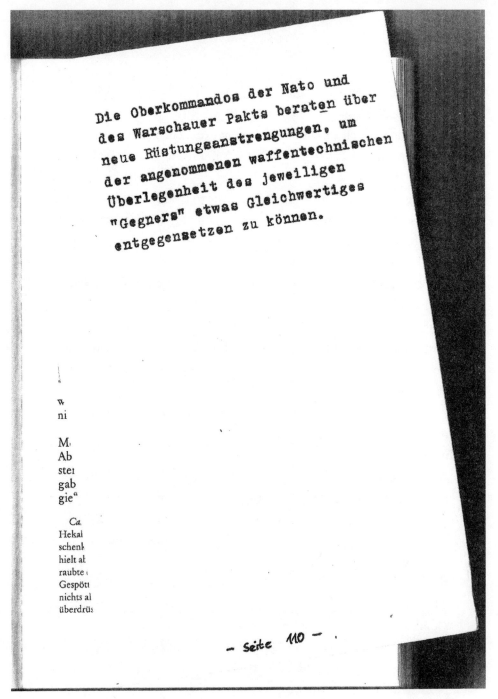

Die Oberkommandos der Nato und des Warschauer Pakts beraten über neue Rüstungsanstrengungen, um der angenommenen waffentechnischen Überlegenheit des jeweiligen "Gegners" etwas Gleichwertiges entgegensetzen zu können.

w
ni

M
Ab
ste
gab
gie"

Ca
Hekal
schenl
hielt ak
raubte
Gespöt
nichts al
überdrüs

— Seite 110 —

indicated by the ellipsis dots between the square brackets. Wolf agreed to the cuts made by the censors but had enough authority to require that they be indicated by the ellipsis dots.

I do not know of any country in the world in which there is no ideological censorship or censorship of the market. I don't consider myself
a victim. I would be one if censorship turned into self-censorship. I
consider myself a fighter who wants to extend boundaries, who wants
to expand the range of what one is permitted to say.[97]

Having committed themselves in this way to the system, the most famous
writers of the GDR received special treatment.[98] They usually published
their work simultaneously in both Germanys, always with permission,
which the East German authorities were happy to give, because the GDR
desperately needed West German marks and took the lion's share of
the royalties. Of course, the Western editions often contained passages
that the censors cut from the copies they permitted to circulate in the
East. But the excised material reached readers in the GDR by means of
smuggled copies or typed and photocopied reproductions of the relevant
pages—that is, in effect, samizdat circulation.

Christa Wolf had so much influence with the authorities that she
required the HV to put ellipsis dots in seven passages where they had
made cuts in *Kassandra* (1983).[99] The dots signaled to GDR readers that
censoring had occurred, and it did so at a time when the Soviet bloc
countries were protesting about the installation of medium-range American rockets in Western Europe. Then the full versions of the offending
passages, typed out from the West German edition, circulated on slips
of paper that could be inserted at the correct places. I was given a set of
the inserts. After larding them into an East German copy of *Kassandra*,
I found that the text came alive in unexpected ways. Here, for example, is a sentence that had been purged from the top of page 110: "The
supreme commanders of NATO and the Warsaw Pact are discussing new
increases in armaments in order to be able to counter their 'opponent's'
presumed superiority in weapons technology with something of equal
strength."[100]

To a Western eye, this sentence looks surprisingly *un*provocative. Even
an East German might slip past it without noticing anything suspicious.
But the typewritten insert highlights it in a manner that brings out an

implicit message: the powers of destruction on both sides of the Cold War are pursuing the same policies; both are bent on destroying the "opponent"—that is, they are morally equal, or equally immoral. Klaus Höpcke was perfectly aware of this interpretation. In fact, he discussed it with Wolf in 1983. She defended her position, which he found incomprehensible, but he permitted the printing of the ellipsis dots.[101]

In its last years, therefore, the regime retreated quite a distance from its earlier Stalinism. It gave ground in negotiation after negotiation, just as the authors did from the opposite side, so that a middle ground emerged in which GDR literature developed an identity of its own. But there were always limits. What happened when authors pushed the boundaries of the permissible to the breaking point? A case study shows how far the system could be stretched until it ceased to be effective and in 1987—that is, before the fall of the Wall—censorship was abolished, at least in principle.

A PLAY: THE SHOW MUST NOT GO ON

Volker Braun stood out as one of the most talented and provocative writers in the generation that came of age in the 1970s.[102] Born in 1939, he became a literary associate (dramaturge) in the Berliner Ensemble in the 1960s, where he assimilated the Brechtian tradition under the encouragement of Brecht's widow, Helene Weigel. By 1976, when he signed the protest letter against the expatriation of Wolf Biermann, he had published enough poetry and drama to command a large following among German readers, to be closely watched by the Stasi, and to have constant conflicts with the censorship at every level, from editors and publishers to the HV and ultimately the head of the state.

To follow Braun's career through the Party archives is to observe the negotiating process between an author and the authorities at its most tortuous. The earliest document, from 1969, shows Braun in an angry, ultra-leftist mood, railing against the Party bureaucracy for the refusal to permit a performance of his play *Hans Faust* in Jena after its premiere in Weimar: "And by the way, what kind of lily-livered cowards are they, who are afraid of their own [Communist] ideas when they no longer remain in the form of documents but become a performance or even life. They are only office workers of the revolution, who tremble before it in fear, like an official before his own bureaucracy."[103] A year later, Braun's editors in the MDV and the censors in the HV insisted that he rewrite many passages in a volume of poetry, *Wir und nicht sie* (Us and not them) and that he abandon several poems altogether, including one entitled "Die Mauer" (The wall). He had managed to get a copy of the manuscript to Suhrkamp in West Germany, which published it in full, and for this act of insubordination, the HV refused a request he had made for permission to travel to Paris. It also turned down a proposal by the Academy of Arts that he be awarded the Johannes R. Becher Prize in 1971.[104] By this time, Braun had established himself as a promising playwright, but his plays addressed ideological issues in a provocative manner, which caused mounting difficulties with the Party. During the 1970s, three of them, *Lenins Tod*, *Tinka*, and *Guevara, oder Der Sonnenstaat* (Guevara, or the sun state), were suppressed in various ways—performances forbidden, texts cut, and publication refused. Braun continued to protest and push for concessions, while proclaiming his loyalty to the Party line; and the Party leaders continued to parry his thrusts, while trying to manipulate him for their own ends. Hager explained their tactics in a letter to Ragwitz ordering her to prevent performances of a fourth play, *Dmitri*, in 1983: "I take the position that in the present circumstances the play *Dmitri* cannot be performed in any of our theaters, since it undoubtedly could be misunderstood on the part of Soviet comrades as well as by the Poles. . . . That said, this play also shows that Volker Braun is a great talent and that it is necessary for comrades in the Berliner Ensemble as well as those in the Ministry and whoever deals closely with him to look after him."[105]

The Party's handling of Braun came to a climax in 1976–77, the years of the Biermann affair and of Braun's failure to stage *Guevara* as well as to publish an expanded version of *Unvollendete Geschichte* (Incomplete story), a short story that he had published in *Sinn und Form*, the literary review of the GDR Academy of Arts. The story had created a sensation by recounting an unhappy love affair—one that evoked *The Sorrows of Young Werther* as well as an actual incident in Magdeburg—in a way that exposed the small-mindedness of apparatchiks and disillusionment with the unfulfilled promises of socialism as it existed in the daily lives of East Germans. On January 7, 1976, Ragwitz, Höpcke, Hoffmann, and five other Party leaders held a meeting—in effect, a war council—about how to deal with Braun and to clamp down on the growing insubordination of GDR authors, which was epitomized by *Unvollendete Geschichte* and an early draft of *Guevara*. In a report on their deliberations, they stressed the danger of Braun's concept of literature. He saw it, they claimed, as a substitute for the state-controlled press and a force that could inspire the working class to seize power. In his view, the workers had executed the socialist revolution in East Germany after the war, but power remained in the hands of apparatchiks. Therefore, by sharpening readers' consciousness of the realities in "real socialism," literature could complete the process of revolution. They could easily silence Braun, they noted. But they did not want to make a dissident of him. Instead, they should "bind him to us" by a carefully orchestrated strategy: banish all discussion of him from the press; compel him to declare his stand on key issues; give him tempting commissions with a publishing house; publish an edition of his collected plays; promise to arrange a production of *Guevara*; and send him on a trip to Cuba, accompanied by a trustworthy Party member, so that he could gather material for the final version of his play.[106]

With Hager's approval, Ragwitz began to execute this strategy two days later. According to a report that she prepared for Hager, she confronted Braun in the office of a colleague, Manfred Weckwerth. Feeling unsure of himself and fearful of jeopardizing his standing in the Party, she explained, Braun had asked to see her. They dealt with him according to a prearranged scenario. Weckwerth turned on Braun as soon as he arrived and delivered a threat—he had better consider whether he could remain a Party member—then left the room. For the next hour, Ragwitz gave Braun a scolding. His latest writings were an attack on the Party and the state, she warned him, and they provided ammunition to the anti-Communist enemies of the GDR. If he did not want to be branded as a dissident, he had better declare his loyalty to the Party and repair the damage in his future publications. Braun seemed shaken. He was horrified, he said, at the way

Unvollendete Geschichte had been exploited by the enemies of the state. He offered to rewrite it, but he could not give up his conviction that a writer's duty under socialism was to criticize the social order. Ragwitz replied that it would not do for him to touch up his text. He would have to change his attitude and his behavior from top to bottom. Then he confessed that he worried about being considered a Maoist and compared to Biermann. He had heard that Hager had doubts about his ideological correctness, and that troubled him deeply, as Hager was "a kind of idol for him." They ended the conversation at that point, after agreeing to keep it confidential and to continue it in further meetings, because Braun asked to have regular contact with Kultur and especially with Ragwitz. In assessing Braun's reaction at the end of her report, Ragwitz stressed that he seemed naïve and unsure of himself, but that he would doggedly hold on to his erroneous view of socialism. Although they should not expect a sudden change of behavior, they could keep him on a short leash by the threat of expelling him from the Party and by the prospect of the trip to Cuba.[107]

Braun went to Cuba in February 1976, but his experience there did not lead to an unproblematic production of *Guevara*. Like his earlier work, it could be interpreted as an attack on the ossification of the revolutionary spirit, for it made a hero of Guevara, who continued to foment revolution as a guerrilla in Bolivia, while Castro remained in charge of the bureaucracy at home. To rearrange history as literature and to present a sacrosanct figure on the stage was a delicate business, as Braun had learned from his failed attempt to dramatize Lenin's death in *Lenins Tod*—a daring enterprise, which had called down upon him the wrath of the Authors Union in 1971.[108] As a way of signaling his departure from a strict historical narrative, he opened *Guevara* with the hero's death in Bolivia, then switched back in time to his career alongside Castro, and ended the play with a scene in which he turned away from the established Cuban state, clutching a rifle and striking out for the new revolutionary frontier. A trial performance at the University of Leipzig in July 1976 did not go well. Some students from Cuba and Bolivia were horrified at the portrayal of Castro and denounced the play to the Cuban embassy. They also did not appreciate a subplot, entirely fictitious, which made Guevara out to be the lover of Tamara Bunke, popularly known as Tania, the daughter of East German–Polish parents who had been born in Argentina and fought with Guevara as a guerrilla in Bolivia in 1966–67. Soon afterward, Hager received a memo recommending that the play be forbidden unless Braun made substantial changes.[109]

Braun spent the next nine months negotiating with the authorities while trying to rewrite his script. At a meeting in July, Hager warned him about the necessity of modifying the characters and the plot in order to resolve "a host of ideological problems."[110] Braun eventually revised the role of Castro, toned down the love story, eliminated passages that made the Communist Party look bad, and transformed Guevara into a Don Quixote who died of asthma instead of in battle.[111] With the agreement of the Party leaders, Ragwitz and Kultur gave permission for the play to be performed at the Deutsches Theater in the spring season of 1977 and also for the text to be published as a book.[112] Rehearsals went into high gear. But thirteen days before opening night, the Cuban ambassador protested vehemently, complaining that among many historical inaccuracies the play made Guevara out to be an opponent of Castro and "the Trotsky of the Cuban Revolution."[113] Meanwhile, Nadja Bunke, Tamara's Polish mother, who was then living in the GDR (like Guevara, Tamara had been killed in Bolivia), stormed into the Deutsches Theater, protesting that the play besmirched the memory of her daughter; and a directive from the foreign office warned that it contradicted "the international line of our Party."[114] By then, the political and institutional pressure had reached such a point that Honecker had to intervene. He received a full briefing from the Culture Division of the Party's Central Committee, underlined key points in the dossier with his green felt pen (the pen that he used to record his reading of documents by initialing them in the upper-right corner), and on March 23 he decreed that the performance would be suspended indefinitely.[115]

Braun dashed off a letter to Honecker on the same day:

Esteemed Comrade Honecker,

I am turning to you at a moment in which there could be a turning point in my life. I say that in all seriousness.

The cancellation of the rehearsals for "Guevara" at the Deutsches Theater and at the Staatstheater Dresden is an arbitrary act, which calls all of my work for the Party into question. . . .

I have kept silent about the impediment to my work for the theater that has occurred for many years (a dozen of the best directors could confirm this). I have kept silent about the prohibition of "Lenins Tod" (and the conflict of conscience fought out in my heart). I could not accept a prohibition of "Guevara" without feeling uprooted from the society in which I write. I consider it my duty to inform the Party about it. If one doesn't feel his ground beneath him, how can one stand? Even if I had the strength to give up the positive effect of my work here and in the communist movement throughout the world, I am not capable of sharing responsibility for the negative effect of this suppression (on the ensembles, on the public).[116]

Honecker turned the matter over to Hager, who met with Braun on the following day and then reported back on the state of the playwright's psyche. It was bad. Braun regretted the impulsive, "harsh and impolite" character of his letter (Honecker underlined those words in the report), but it expressed his despair. If foreign policy could determine what plays were performed, then culture would lose its moorings, art would become divorced from the Party, literature would sacrifice its mission to develop a critical dialogue with power, and Braun would have to renounce literature altogether. "He fears that his work will become meaningless" (a phrase underlined by Honecker). By abandoning it, he would be forced into another mode of existence, that of an "unperson."[117]

More meetings and memos followed. Hager and his assistant, Erika Hinkel, heard out Braun's continued lamentations.[118] The Cuban ambassador, who failed to appreciate Hager's explanation of Brechtian dramaturgy, kept up a barrage of protests about the misrepresentation of history on the stage. The players of the Berliner Ensemble, Brechtian to the core, bewailed their loss of time and money, and the Western press, fairly well informed, reveled in the political-diplomatic-cultural debacle. But the show did not go on. *Guevara* went the way of *Lenins Tod*, and Braun, once he had recovered from the disaster, shifted his attention to other works, especially a novel, *Hinze-Kunze-Roman*, which turned out to be even more contentious than *Guevara*.[119]

A NOVEL: PUBLISH AND PULP

The publishing history of *Hinze-Kunze-Roman*, even more than the struggle over *Guevara*, shows how censorship operated at all levels during the final years of the GDR.[120] The text evolved through many stages and formats, going back to the play *Hans Faust*, which was performed in Weimar in 1968.[121] When it assumed final form as a novel in 1981, it expressed the culmination of a theme that runs through most of Braun's work. By contrasting Kunze, a high-level apparatchik, with Hinze, his chauffeur, it dwelt on the distance that separated the privileged Party elite from the dreary lives of ordinary people. Kunze inhabits a lavishly furnished house (it even has an atom-bomb shelter) and spends his time attending closed-door meetings and representing the Party at official ceremonies, although his dominant passion is skirt-chasing. Hinze lives in a run-down apartment and helps Kunze chase the skirts by pursuing them in an official Tatra with Kunze directing him from the back seat. It is predatory lust, not revolutionary ardor, that propels Kunze on his rounds. As his faithful servant, Hinze shares in the abuse of power and even goes so far as to share his wife, Lisa. Lisa lets herself be used but ultimately triumphs over both men, thanks to Party patronage supplied by Kunze and her determination to seize control of her own life.

Put so baldly, the plot could seem to be a frontal attack on the Communist (SED) Party and its monopoly of power. But Braun leads the reader away from such a straightforward conclusion by employing elaborate stylistic devices—unorthodox punctuation and sentence structure, shifts in the narrative voice, and the intervention of the narrator himself, who becomes an actor in the story and addresses the reader in such a way as to disclaim responsibility for what takes place in it: "I don't understand it, I describe it," he insists throughout the text, and repeats disingenuously that everything is happening "in the interest of society." To complicate things further, Braun cloaks the action in literary allusions. The servant-master relation echoes themes from *Don Quixote*, *Don Giovanni*, and especially Diderot's *Jacques le fataliste*, the model invoked explicitly at several points. Following Diderot, Braun presents his work as a "Galantroman," a philosophical-erotic fantasy. Moreover, Hinze and Kunze can be construed as different aspects of the same man, rather like "Moi" and "Lui" in Diderot's *Neveu de Rameau*. The term means everyman in German, analogous to Tom, Dick, and Harry in English; and the interchangeability of the pair undercuts the idea of reducing their relationship to that of servant and master.

Therefore, Braun could argue, nothing would be more misleading than to interpret his book as a political satire aimed at the East German regime. He had composed it in the spirit of "real socialism," a progressive kind of literature, dedicated to depicting life as lived by ordinary people and capable of critical observations, though always, of course, "in the interest of society." The modernist literary technique was also progressive. It brought GDR literature into dialogue with advanced writing everywhere. To remain confined to the outmoded conventions of socialist realism would be to condemn GDR culture to obsolescence. This argument could (and did) shield Braun from attacks by conservative hard-liners within the Party. But it failed to account for three episodes that broke through the rhetorical patina disguising the narrative's seditious thrust. The first depicted Kunze on a mission to a West German city (Hamburg in an early draft). Pursuing his obsession, he went straight to a brothel, where he learned that capitalism had certain advantages, because it offered sex directly, for money.[122] The second described a fantasy of Kunze's as he sat behind the Politburo on the reviewing stand at an SED demonstration in honor of Rosa Luxemburg and Karl Liebknecht. He imagined a spontaneous uprising of the masses, inspired by the ghosts of "Karl and Rosa" and all the revolutionaries of the heroic past, aimed against the old apparatchiks on the stand, who represented the fossilization of the revolutionary spirit.[123] The third was a dialogue between Hinze and Kunze about the arms race and the peace movement, which challenged the military and foreign policies of the GDR. When Kunze defended the investment in armaments as a way to deter aggression from the United States, which had recently set up medium-range missiles in Western Europe, Hinze replied that this way of assuring "peace" by diverting resources to arms was ruinously expensive: "It eats up progress and shits on prosperity."[124] These were the three parts of the book that seemed most reprehensible to the censors and that Braun refused most tenaciously to excise as the manuscript worked its way up through the system, from the publishing house to the Politburo.

The text passed through all the institutions that constituted GDR literature and came into contact with all the roles distributed within them—author, editor, publisher, outside readers, censors in the HV, ideological guardians in the Party's Central Committee, members of the Authors Union, reviewers for literary journals, and ultimately the head of the state. The whole process took four years. It went through three phases of negotiation: in the publishing house, in the HV, and in the upper ranks of the Party. Volker Braun was drawn into all of them, but much of the maneuvering took place behind his back, among individuals who were more intent on defending themselves than on purging his text.

Braun submitted his manuscript to the MDV in Halle on July 16, 1981. For a year, the director, Eberhard Günther, and various editors negotiated with him over cuts, and he continued to make revisions, drawing on criticism from some trusted friends, notably two literary scholars, Dieter and Silvia Schlenstedt, and two prominent writers, Franz Fühmann and Christa Wolf. In July 1982, the editors produced two in-house reports on a rewritten version. They expressed considerable respect for Braun, who by then had gained a reputation as one of the GDR's greatest literary talents, but they found the manuscript problematic. Even after making allowances for his sophisticated narrative technique, which cloaked his satire in ambiguity, they emphasized that they could not accept his account of "GDR reality."[125] They persuaded him nevertheless to eliminate some "politically and ideologically . . . unacceptable" passages,[126] and by December they had a manuscript that they considered sound enough to warrant inclusion in the Plan for 1984, even though it was not yet sufficiently expurgated to be sent to the HV for a final printing authorization. Braun's principal editor, Hinnerk Einhorn, summarized the situation in a publisher's report, which was guardedly positive, but warned that the book was "too weak in social-ist Party-ness."[127]

If the manuscript were to make it past the censors in the HV, that weakness had to be repaired. Therefore, Einhorn tried to wring more con-cessions from Braun in a series of meetings that stretched from January until October 1983. Braun agreed to make some changes in phrasing, but he refused to yield on anything substantive, notably the three key epi-sodes that Einhorn considered unacceptable. There seemed to be no way to resolve the disagreement until two of Braun's friends, Dieter Schlenstedt and Hans Kaufmann, intervened. They were distinguished literary schol-ars who admired the first draft of the novel and also understood the pre-dicament of the publisher. On October 10, they negotiated a compromise at a meeting in Braun's apartment. He agreed to tone down the brothel scene and to rework several other passages; and the MDV, represented by its director, Eberhard Günther, its chief editor, Helga Duty, and Einhorn, let him have his way with the other two episodes. They committed them-selves to accepting the revised text for publication; and to make it more acceptable to the HV—while protecting themselves against criticism from within the Party—they asked Schlenstedt and Kaufmann to write two more reader's reports.

Braun's friends came up with exactly what the publisher needed. After coordinating their strategy in advance, they made the case for publication in a way that reinforced the arguments of the editors and that anticipated potential objections by the censors in the HV. They also produced mas-terly interpretations of *Hinze-Kunze-Roman* as a work of literature, paying tribute to Braun's virtuosity as a writer and suggesting just enough cuts—the kind that he could tolerate—for him to get the novel that he wanted. Schlenstedt acquitted himself so well at this task that he and Braun agreed to include a reworked version of his report as a postface to the text. It would orient the book's reception in a desirable direction, because it would func-tion as a "reading aid," which would help readers understand that Braun's sophisticated artistry was meant to strengthen the cause of socialism while satirizing aberrations and abuses.[128]

Censorship as practiced in East Germany required this kind of maneuvering when it came up against difficult cases. It involved brokering deals behind closed doors rather than following standard procedures inside offices. In fact, *Hinze-Kunze-Roman* reached this advanced stage in the negotiations only as a result of a confidential agreement that had been negotiated between Höpcke and Braun a year earlier. At a private meeting in Schlenstedt's apartment, Höpcke had agreed to favor the book's publication; and in exchange, Braun had promised to blunt some of the sharpest phrases, although in the following months he did not follow through with enough self-censoring to satisfy Einhorn and the other ideological guardians in the MDV.[129] The deal struck on October 10 resolved this last difficulty, and in January 1984 Helga Duty completed the formalities required of the publisher and sent *Hinze-Kunze-Roman* on to the next stage in the process: approval by the censors in the HV.

The dossier that she prepared for them conformed to standard procedure. In addition to the reworked text, it included all four readers' reports and a covering publisher's report, which she wrote in a way that emphasized the editors' "hard, long struggle with the author."[130] Although they had persuaded Braun to make many cuts, she explained, they had failed to get him to expurgate important passages, which she cited in detail. Therefore, his intransigence left them with a difficult decision. Braun was one of the GDR's most important authors, one whose work was followed closely outside the country, and they could not extract any more concessions from him. Nonetheless, supported by the persuasive arguments of Schlenstedt and Kaufmann and "despite the objections that still existed," they reluctantly recommended publication.[131] The defensive character of the report made its message clear: the professionals in the publishing house had done their job with exemplary professionalism, and from this point on, *Hinze-Kunze-Roman* was the HV's problem.

The person in charge of the dossier at the HV was Klaus Selbig, the head of the belles-lettres section. He had received a letter from Günther warning that the MDV could not assume responsibility for the difficulties that the book would cause;[132] and after submitting the manuscript to several of his fellow censors, Selbig wrote a similar letter to Höpcke. As they read the text—and as they read the readings of the text submitted by

their predecessors—they realized that it confronted the HV with a difficult "political and cultural-political" decision.[133] In fact, the decision was
too difficult for the ordinary censors in belles-lettres. Höpcke would have
to take it.

By this time, as he had promised Braun, Höpcke had already resolved
to publish the book. The argument in favor of publication seemed strong,
because GDR watchers in the West were ready to pounce on any sign of
repression in the East, and Suhrkamp was prepared to produce an unexpurgated edition in the FRG, which would only further inflame the scandal if the East German edition were suppressed. Moreover, a humiliation of
Braun, after so many earlier conflicts, would alienate him and the talented
young authors who looked up to him. But while an increasingly impatient
Braun was pressing Höpcke to issue a printing authorization, the Party's
Central Committee had issued an order to prevent the publication of anything controversial in 1984, a "Jubilee Year," which should be kept free
from dissent while East Germans celebrated the thirty-five years of tri-
umphant socialism that had occurred since the founding of the GDR in
1949. *Hinze-Kunze-Roman* had been tentatively scheduled for the Plan of
that year. Therefore, Höpcke stalled its approval in the HV by requesting
yet another outside reader's report, this one from a Party hard-liner, Werner Neubert, a literary expert in the Academy for State and Legal Studies. Although Höpcke may have wanted to cover himself by consulting
the conservative wing of the Party, he probably miscalculated, because
Neubert produced such a blistering condemnation of the text that its fate
seemed more problematic than ever. Despite the sophisticated exegeses by
Schlenstedt and Kaufmann, he argued, there was no way to get around the
book's fundamental flaw: its lack of commitment to "socialist Party-ness."[134]

When Neubert's report arrived in the HV, Selbig considered it so damaging that, as he advised Höpcke, the book could not be published. But
Höpcke decided to use the report as a way to extract more concessions
from Braun, working through Günther and Einhorn in the MDV. Back
went the manuscript for more changes; once more did Braun and Einhorn wrestle over the contested episodes; yet again did Braun refuse to
make more cuts; and in the end another deal took place at a private meet-

ing between Braun and Höpcke. As a result, Braun agreed to make some additional changes, and Höpcke granted the printing authorization, which was finally issued on January 4, 1985, clearing the way for publication in the summer. The editors, publishers, and censors took care to document each of these steps, and all the documents conveyed the same messages: Braun should not be alienated; a scandal should be avoided; and, above all, no one in the system should be blamed for failing to uphold the Party line, because as Helga Duty emphasized in yet another publisher's report, "Despite long, hard struggle, we could not bring the author to make the further changes that seemed essential to us."[135]

It remained to be seen whether that defense would persuade the most powerful figures in the Party, because at this point the history of *Hinze-Kunze-Roman* entered a new and brutally political phase. The first copies of the book arrived on July 22 in the wholesale distribution center for all GDR publishers (the Leipziger Kommissions- und Grossbuchhandels) located near Leipzig, and they began to appear in bookstores a few weeks later. Höpcke tried to cushion the shock by publishing a two-part review essay in *Die Weltbühne*, a cultural weekly, on August 13 and 20. As in Schlenstedt's "Reading Aid," he attempted to orient the book's reception by emphasizing its literary qualities and downplaying its social criticism.[136] The Party's hard-liners were not impressed. Several of them sent denunciations of the book to Günter Mittag, the powerful secretary for the economy in the Central Committee. One attack, dated August 21, came from Kurt Tiedke, the rector of the Party Academy (Parteihochschule Karl Marx), a bastion of Communist orthodoxy. It described the novel as a shoddy, shameless misrepresentation of the Party's policies and deplored the decision to permit its publication.[137] Three diatribes in the form of memoranda also reached Mittag, and similar protests probably were sent to other members of the Politburo.[138] They may have been part of a concerted campaign, because they contained the same arguments phrased in nearly the same manner.

The memoranda raked over the text of the book in detail, quoting the most objectionable passages and adding exegesis from the Party's point of view. How should the novel be read? they asked. Not as a lighthearted satire inspired by Diderot, but as an all-out attack on the Party and its policies. Braun used sophisticated literary devices to disguise his fundamental message; but by portraying Kunze as an immoral apparatchik, he made his meaning clear: "Such people rule over us."[139] Everything about the novel—its account of sordid living conditions, empty lives, and pervasive pessimism—added up to an indictment of socialism as practiced in the GDR. Braun's satirical asides could not be dismissed as jests. What, for example, should a reader make of the following joke about the mentality and privileges of the Party elite: "They thought for everyone else, so they should also think of themselves. They were personally the best; they could have the best"?[140] It was not funny. It was defamatory. Similar remarks, scattered through the text, built up a picture of the GDR as a class society: the Party members at the top exploited the working masses below them. If read rightly, they amounted to an argument that the GDR had betrayed its revolutionary origins: "In general, Braun conveys the impression that the socialist Revolution has spent itself and at present is meaningless."[141] A right reading contradicted the defense of Braun by Schlenstedt and Höpcke. It could also be turned against other writers such as Franz Fühmann, Günter de Bruyn, and Christa Wolf, who took advantage of the permissiveness inherent in late-bourgeois literature to challenge Party orthodoxy in the same way as Braun.[142] Far from being limited to the peculiarities of one novel, therefore, *Hinze-Kunze-Roman* should be taken as symptomatic of a general problem, a struggle over meaning that went to the heart of the GDR's ideological foundation. The memos that circulated within the Central Committee warned the Party leaders that this struggle was ultimately a question of power. To resolve it, they would have to shift the ground of debate from hermeneutics to politics, and they would have to take political action.

In the face of the gathering storm, the censors did their best to defend themselves. The MDV produced a long memorandum to justify its conduct by describing the four-year struggle of its editors to sanitize Braun's text. Thanks to their efforts, it argued, the social criticism in *Hinze-Kunze-Roman* was essentially constructive—that is, in Marxist terms, limited to "non-antagonistic contradictions" and therefore ultimately *parteilich*, or true to Party principles.[143] Klaus Selbig wrote a similar memo (it even contained some of the same phrasing) to defend his colleagues in the HV. They had purged the book of many "disputable and unacceptable political-ideological" elements,[144] but Braun had refused to accept all their demands. After much hesitation, they had decided it would be better to publish the book in its imperfect form than to reject it, because a rejection would be likely to undercut Braun's future creativity and to produce damaging publicity about the GDR's cultural politics. This memo went to Hager via Hoffmann. But at the same time, Hager received a memo from another source, probably Mittag, which developed the opposite argument: "This is a case of a nasty, shoddy piece of work in which the overall policies of our Party and our state are distorted in the worst way and are attacked in many areas."[145] All the memos converged in Hager's office during the first week of September, when he had to reach a decision. He had long considered Braun a "great talent" who should be encouraged and looked after by protectors within the Party.[146] Yet the constant conflicts over the inadmissible passages in his works had made Hager realize that Braun often overstepped the permissible limits of satire.[147] *Hinze-Kunze-Roman* far exceeded those limits, and it had enraged some powerful members of the Party's Central Committee. What to do?

On September 9, Hager ordered a halt to the distribution of the book. All the copies (4,295) that remained in the Leipzig distribution center were blocked, and all those still in the bookstores (6,670) were removed from the shelves.[148] About 3,700 copies had been sold, and they included 250 put up for sale at a "book premiere" on September 26 in which Braun was permitted to make some carefully self-censored remarks to a public composed mostly of "young intellectuals."[149] The authorities allowed this event to take place and claimed that the edition had been sold out, in order to avoid admitting that they had repressed it. They probably pulped all the confiscated copies, as normally happened when they banned a book that had already been printed; but the Suhrkamp edition appeared in West Germany, as had been arranged with the permission of the HV. It was therefore impossible to deny or disguise the repression, despite the transparent fiction that the edition had been sold out; and once the sales had been stopped, the Party leaders had to decide what further measures to take.

On September 9, while the order went out to block the sales, Ursula Ragwitz sent another memorandum to Hager. She and her colleagues in Kultur had studied the text carefully, she explained. They were not taken in by its sophisticated wordplay. Braun refused to accept the leading role of the Party, the progressive policies of the state, and the legitimacy of socialism itself as practiced in the GDR. Certain episodes—especially the fantasy of a popular uprising in the spirit of Luxemburg and Liebknecht and the dialogue about armaments and the peace movement—would stick in the craw of the Party faithful. Having confronted Braun with his devi-ational tendency long ago, Ragwitz recognized *Hinze-Kunze-Roman* as the culmination of the anti-apparatchik themes that ran through all his work. He should be called on the carpet and forced to defend himself in front of the executive board of the Authors Union and the Berlin branch of the SED. They could recommend that he be expelled from the Party, and further disciplinary action should be taken by Hans-Joachim Hoffmann, the minister of culture. Meanwhile, all reviews of the novel should be for-bidden in the daily press, and full-scale attacks on it should be published in two influential journals, *Neue Deutsche Literatur* and *Weimarer Beiträge*.[150]

According to the memorandum, Höpcke's behavior was even more unforgivable than Braun's, because he was responsible for ensuring that correct literature reached the masses. In discussions with Kultur about the Plan for 1985, he had been warned about the objections to the book. But he withdrew it from the Plan and issued the printing authorization on his own authority, without consulting either Kultur or the Ministry of Culture. As grounds for this irregular behavior, Höpcke cited the read-er's reports of Schlenstedt and Kaufmann, but he ignored the damning report by Neubert and then went on to defend Braun (but really, in fact, himself) by his article in *Die Weltbühne*, which also did not have clear-ance from Kultur. All these actions added up to a "serious political error," which "defamed real socialism and gave ammunition to our enemies for their attacks against us."[151] Such misbehavior could not be ignored. It was up to the Party to decide how to punish it.

On September 16, Hager summoned Höpcke to defend himself at a meeting that also included Hoffmann and Franz Hentschel, Ragwitz's deputy in Kultur. How, Hager asked, could Höpcke justify permitting such a defamatory work to be published, especially at a time when they were preparing the Eleventh Party Congress? Höpcke replied with a long account of the attempts to get Braun to modify the text. After the last round of negotiations, which led to some important cuts, he said that he finally had to make a critical decision: either break with Braun and accept all the negative consequences, or publish the book and face up to the criticism. Hager rejected that argument, citing many passages from the book that demonstrated Braun's hostility to socialism as it existed in the GDR. The dominant theme of the novel, he insisted, was an attack on the Party elite, which Braun derided for enjoying its privileges at the top of society while a powerless population suffered at the bottom. That was not acceptable social satire; it was rank defamation of the state. The report on the meeting ended with a series of resolutions, which called for a campaign in the press to discredit *Hinze-Kunze-Roman* and for measures to heighten vigilance in the HV and to enforce Party discipline in matters of culture.[152] Hager sent the report to Honecker, who underlined crucial passages in it and filed it away, presumably for use in a future meeting of the Politburo.[153] In the following days, Höpcke received a strong reprimand from the Party (a setback that could badly damage an apparatchik's career); Selbig was fired from his position in the HV; and Braun was required to confront his critics in the Authors Union. But *Hinze-Kunze-Roman* was not formally forbidden, and Braun was spared public punishment, presumably because the regime wanted to avoid any further scandal.

The confrontation between Braun and the Authors Union took place at two meetings of the union's executive board, which were attended by large numbers of militant members. On September 26, Hager himself appeared before eighty members and delivered a general report about the critical situation of GDR literature. He referred to *Hinze-Kunze-Roman* as an example of the issues that needed to be resolved, especially relations between authors and the Party in the light of correct cultural politics. Most of those present had not yet read the novel, but several spoke up about the importance of reinforcing socialist realism and of rejecting a tone of "resignation and pessimism" that had crept into recent publications. As the target of those objections, Braun replied that he had consulted the authorities at every stage and that he refused to accept the claim by some of his critics that his writing amounted to a rejection of socialism. Hager summarized the debate in a memo to Honecker, which ended with a recommendation that they do more to undercut the impact of *Hinze-Kunze-Roman* by exposing its "political deficiencies."[154] On December 12, Braun faced a more hostile gathering of fifty-four union members. Twenty speakers, led by Klaus Jarmatz, a Party hard-liner, attacked *Hinze-Kunze-Roman*; but this time Braun sat silently, letting the vituperation wash over him. When challenged to reply by Hermann Kant, another hard-liner, who was chairman of the board, he declined to answer the criticisms and merely said in self-defense that he had cooperated with the publisher and the Ministry of Culture. Evidently, he was determined to avoid polemics and to ride out the attacks, which continued unabated in the GDR press.[155] Once calm had been restored, there was a possibility that the HV would permit a new edition. It had done so in the case of earlier literary scandals: that was what the censors meant when they told me that, after the publication of "hot" works, they would wait for time to pass—"let some grass grow"—until a new edition could be safely permitted.

While the polemics died down, Braun took care to avoid saying anything inflammatory. He gave a reading in the Academy of Arts in Berlin without raising a storm, and with the permission of the GDR authorities he also made some appearances in West Germany, where the press tried to play up the *Hinze-Kunze-Roman* as "a German-German bomb" ["eine deutsch-deutsche Bombe"].[156] Braun kept the press at bay while he gave readings at the Frankfurt Book Fair and in Cologne. Hager's office—and, no doubt, the secret police—received reports about all of his public appearances.[157] Everything indicated that the East German authorities had successfully minimized damage from the "bomb." By refraining from punishing Braun and permitting him to travel in West Germany, they seemed to demonstrate their willingness to tolerate controversy. After all, they had never banned *Hinze-Kunze-Roman*; they had merely tried to stifle it. They did so in secret, and insofar as they succeeded, they even opened up the possibility of tolerating a new edition.

How Censorship Ended

While the afterlife of *Hinze-Kunze-Roman* hung in the balance, the world started to change. In March 1985, Mikhail Gorbachev took over the leadership of the Communist Party in the Soviet Union and began implementing a policy of glasnost (openness) and perestroika (restructuring). In 1986, after the Twenty-Seventh Party Congress and the Chernobyl nuclear disaster, glasnost—an ambiguous term that at first merely connoted open debate in the management of public affairs—turned into a movement for freedom of information. By June 1988, the Party had ceased to dominate political life in the USSR. Solidarity had transformed the power structure in Poland; samizdat publications were spreading everywhere; and the Soviet empire was beginning to break up, yet the GDR remained ossified in a Party dictatorship derived from the system of Stalin.

So much had occurred that when a printing authorization for the second edition of *Hinze-Kunze-Roman* was issued on January 27, 1988 (for a relatively small pressrun of 10,000 copies), it was a nonevent.[158] Hager granted permission for the edition after receiving a recommendation from Höpcke, who in turn had received a request from the MDV. After the book finally appeared on the shelves of bookstores, no tremors ran through the Party apparat and no one paid a great deal of attention to it.[159] Meanwhile, other books—notably *Horns Ende* (Horn's End), by Christoph Hein, and *Neue Herrlichkeit*, by Günter de Bruyn—had produced similar scandals. Their publishing histories followed the same course, a struggle with censors at every stage in their production and distribution.[160] By the end of 1987, the struggle shifted to censorship itself.

For three days, from November 24 to 26, a large assembly of authors discussed every aspect of their profession at a congress of the Authors Union in Berlin. It was an important occasion. Honecker, six members of the Politburo, and delegates from thirty countries attended the opening session. Despite the presence of Hager, Höpcke, Ragwitz, and numerous observers from the Stasi, things did not go as planned. On November 25, de Bruyn used his place on the agenda to read a letter from Christa Wolf, who had remained at her retreat in Mecklenburg. It reminded the union members of the Biermann affair, the exclusion of dissidents, the emigration of talented authors, and the restrictions that inhibited those who remained in the GDR. Speaking for himself, de Bruyn denounced the greatest restriction of them all: censorship. As the GDR refused to acknowledge that it existed, he said he would avoid a useless dispute over terminology and refer to it as "the practice of granting printing authorizations" (*Druckgenehmigung-spraxis*).[161] He demanded its abolition, if not immediately at least within a few years. No longer should the fate of books be determined behind closed doors. The responsibility for them should fall entirely on authors and publishers. Literature should take place in the open.

In a separate session earlier that day, Christoph Hein delivered an even more audacious speech:

> The printing-authorization procedure, supervision by the state, or to put it briefly and no less clearly, the censorship of publishing houses and books, of publishers and authors, is outmoded, useless, paradoxical, hostile to humanity, hostile to the people, illegal, and punishable.[162]

Hein called for the immediate abolition of censorship—and in its place for a new set of institutions: autonomous publishing houses, honest book reviews, independent theaters, a free daily press, and freedom to travel abroad. He did not advocate the kind of publishing that prevailed in the West, because he considered it dominated by monopolistic market forces, which favored cheap bestsellers and trash. He cherished the GDR as a "land of reading" (*Leseland*), especially of "book reading" (*Buchleseland*), where literature served higher cultural purposes.[163] The GDR should remain true to its socialist principles and support its cultural institutions, but it should free them from state control.

Never before had East German intellectuals spoken out so boldly. Of course, it was one thing to deliver speeches, another to transform institutions. The institutional structure of GDR literature remained in place after the congress dissolved. The Berlin Wall—still called the "antifascistic Protection Wall" (*antifaschistischer Schutzwall*) in official documents[164]—still stood strong, marking the divide between hostile camps in a Cold War that seemed likely to go on indefinitely. Yet the surrounding climate of opinion had changed, partly in response to the fresh winds that blew from Moscow, and the Party leaders realized that they had to make adjustments.

Höpcke and Hager met on February 18, 1988, to decide what measures to take. They agreed that the main responsibility for vetting manuscripts should shift from the HV to the publishing houses, but that could cause problems. Overall output would still have to be coordinated in a yearly Plan, which would include the annual Plans submitted by each publisher. The HV would direct this operation and continue to control the availability of paper and presses. Everything should take place in such a manner as to avoid "cumbersome . . . bureaucratic measures." But how? Höpcke and Hager only agreed that things should run smoothly, because, according to their estimate, 99 percent of the proposed publications would pose no difficulty. Problem cases could usually be resolved at the level of the publishers, they asserted, and the publishers should be directed to work closely with certain authors, avoiding loose talk about "censorship." Of course, some authors had to be excluded from the system. For example, nothing by Lutz Rathenow and Monika Maron should be allowed to appear in print. And despite the relative autonomy of the publishing houses, the ultimate decisions about printing authorizations must remain with the HV.[165]

The minutes of this meeting give the impression that the men in charge of the system accepted the need for change and also rejected it. They continued to deny the existence of "censorship" in principle and to enforce it in practice. Above all, they could not release their grip on power. Their inability to resolve these contradictions also showed through the minutes of a meeting that took place nine months later. Hager told Höpcke that no "liberalization" should be allowed:

The state should not give up its rights, and the director of a publishing house is responsible to the state. It is incumbent on him to take relevant problems to the HV, just as [the HV] can demand manuscripts from the publisher. The cultural-political line [of the Party] is assured by long-term Plans and by the responsibility of the publisher and editors. Each publishing house must be aware that great demands will be made on it and that its responsibility will grow. Through this approach, a democratic method will be applied and excessive centralization avoided.[166]

Höpcke interpreted these directives as best he could. At a meeting with the Authors Union on June 28, 1988, he gave a report on the Plan for 1989, stressing the new procedures for obtaining printing authorizations. The final decision was to remain in the hands of the HV, but it would act quickly and would no longer require the publishers to submit a full dossier with the manuscript and readers' reports. A carefully argued request would suffice. Some union members expressed doubts about putting too much power in the hands of the publishers, but Volker Braun, who was present at the meeting, welcomed the new policy as "an exemplary case of the distribution of power . . . social democracy in action."[167]

By this time, Braun was having his way in negotiations with the authorities, although the conflicts over drafts of texts and productions of plays did not end with the crisis over *Hinze-Kunze-Roman*. They came to a head in 1987, when Braun insisted on publishing a relatively unexpurgated edition of *Langsamer knirschender Morgen* (Slow, grinding tomorrow), a volume of poems that contained enough contentious material to have occupied the editors in the MDV and the censors in the HV for four years. A printing authorization was granted and then suspended, owing to its "political aspect," as Braun put it in a letter of protest to Hager. When he threatened to publish an uncensored edition with Suhrkamp in West Germany, Hager finally gave in.[168] Braun also protested to Hager when the authorities refused to permit a performance of his play *Nibelungen* by an East German troupe in West Germany in May 1987. In this case, Hager did not put up any resistance, but the production had to be canceled, because the actors, from the National Theater in Weimar, were not *Reisekader*—that is, personnel authorized to travel outside the GDR—and the state was doing everything possible to stop its citizens from escaping to the West.[169] By February 1988, the tables had been turned. Braun was unhappy with the first performances of another play, *Transit Europa*, and wanted to cancel the continuation of its run. But this time Hager objected to the proposed cancelation. Why? In a memo to a fellow member of the Politburo, Günter Schabowski, he explained that he wanted to prevent their enemies in the West from seizing on the cancellation and construing it as another case of cultural repression. He appealed to Braun in a phone call, and Braun consented to allow a few more performances.[170]

Episodes such as these, however trivial in themselves, indicated that a new tone had crept in to the relations between authors and the authorities, even though censorship continued and the power system remained the same. Braun's letters to Hager always remained respectful, but they became fairly casual, and Braun switched from the formal *Sie* to an intimate *Du* in his mode of address—a far cry from the deferential style he had adopted in 1971, when he first appealed for favorable treatment from the "Most esteemed Comrade Professor Hager."[171] By 1988, however, letters from other writers sometimes sounded almost cheeky. Rainer Kerndl, a leading member of the Authors Union, negotiated long and hard with his publisher and the HV over *Eine gemischte Gesellschaft* (A disreputable crowd), an adventure novel set in the Near East. They finally refused to issue a printing authorization, because the text did not correspond to the Party line on foreign affairs; and Kerndl sent an impertinent letter to Hager: "It would be important for me to know whether I must toss away the work of many months merely because an employee in some special department takes it upon himself to decide what people in this country are and are not permitted to read."[172] Hans Schneider, a specialist in military novels, protested in the same way, when someone in the Ministry of Defense blocked a second edition of *Der Fall Tessnow* (The Tessnow case), because it contained an episode involving a GDR border guard that was unacceptable on "political-ideological" grounds. How could a bureaucrat prevent the publication of a book that had cost him two years of work? he

asked in a letter to Hager. "This unfeeling injustice" infuriated him, and he
wished that he could confront his opponent, who had assumed the role of
a "censor."[173] It would have been unthinkable a decade earlier for an author
to protest about censorship, which supposedly did not exist, in a letter to
a member of the Politburo. Things had changed in the GDR by the end
of the 1980s. The change occurred invisibly, in the informal system of
human relations, which determined the way things were done, while the
old institutional structure remained in place. Censorship had not been
abolished, but authors and censors alike expected new liberties to prevail.

At a meeting on March 1, 1989, the PEN organization in the GDR
passed a resolution protesting the imprisonment of Václav Havel in
Czechoslovakia. Klaus Höpcke attended the meeting and signed the resolution. Five days later, he was called on the carpet by his old opponents
in the Culture Division of the Party's Central Committee. According to a
report on the confrontation that Ursula Ragwitz submitted to Hager, Höpcke defended his action and offered to explain the reasons for it to the
Czech ambassador. But, Ragwitz insisted, there was no denying that he had
interfered with the internal affairs of a fellow socialist country and that his
endorsement of the PEN protest would be exploited in the propaganda of
their common enemies.[174] Höpcke must have expected to receive some kind
of punishment. In fact, he later said that he had an informant among Ragwitz's colleagues in Kultur.[175] But the sanctions against him were relatively
light, perhaps because he assumed full responsibility for his behavior in a
forthright letter to Erich Honecker. The protest against the mistreatment
of Havel was fully justified, he argued, and by supporting it he had not
implied that there was anything incorrect in the way writers were treated
in the GDR. In the end, Höpcke was merely suspended from his office for a
few weeks, while the Politburo put out the story that he was ill.[176]

Did the new aura of permissiveness mean that censorship had ceased
to exist de facto in the GDR? No: the authorities continued to prevent
the publication of books on "political-ideological grounds," as they often
expressed it in letters and memoranda to one another.[177] In April 1987,
Hager and Honecker stopped the publication of *Mir fehlte Spanien* (I miss
Spain), the memoirs of Dolores Ibárruri, known as La Pasionaria, because

they were said to be tainted with right-wing Eurocommunism.[178] In May, Hager and Höpcke blocked the distribution of 4,100 copies of *Widerstand 1939 bis 1945* (The resistance 1939 to 1945), by Klaus Mammach, because censors in the HV had failed to spot its heresies about the Communist resistance to the Nazis during World War II.[179] In July 1989, the HV refused to give a printing authorization to *Schreibt die Menschheit ihr letztes Kapitel?* (Is mankind writing its last chapter?), by Erich Hanke, not because it was inadequately Marxist, but rather because its dogmatic Marxism exaggerated the imperialistic and militaristic nature of the NATO powers to such an extent that it contradicted the Party line on peaceful coexistence.[180] Daniil Granin's *Sie nannten ihn Ur* (published in English as *The Bison*), circulated freely in the Soviet Union after its publication in 1987, although it recounted the career of the geneticist Nikolay Timofeeff-Ressovsky in a way that reflected badly on the connections between science and politics in the Soviet system. But what could be tolerated in the USSR was too much for the authorities in the GDR. It received a printing authorization from the HV and was produced at a pressrun of 15,000 copies. Then, in June 1988, its distribution was frozen, and it remained blocked in the Leipzig warehouse until well into 1989, when at last it was released.[181]

No, censorship never stopped, not even during the relatively tolerant last years of the GDR. Authors continued to complain about manuscripts rejected for "political-ideological" reasons. Publishers still declined to take chances with "hot" works. The HV refused printing authorizations, and the Party leaders intervened to block the publication of works that failed to conform to the Party line even when the Party began to lose its grip on power. The process of negotiation, accommodation, resistance, and compromise went on at all levels, as it had done in earlier years, as if it could go on indefinitely. What, then, finally brought an end to censorship in East Germany? The fall of the Wall. Soon after the Wall was breached on November 9, 1989, the government fell apart, the Party splintered, the state collapsed, and nothing remained of the censorship system, except the censors themselves, who sat at their desks with nothing to do, trying to make sense of it all and to explain their experience to a naïve outsider, when I showed up in their office at 90 Clara-Zetkin-Strasse.

Conclusion

———◆◆◆———

Having got to know censorship in three authoritarian regimes, it now seems opportune to revisit a question that was left hanging at the beginning of this book: What is censorship? The question is legitimate, but it belongs to a category of conceptual traps that the French call *questions mal posées*—badly put questions, which can point the search for an answer in the wrong direction. If censorship were defined too rigidly, it might be understood as an autonomous phenomenon, which operates everywhere in the same way, no matter what the context. In that case, the historian would be tempted to treat it as a thing-in-itself and to try to follow it through a body politic as if it were analogous to a radioactive substance being traced through a bloodstream. An ethnographic approach avoids that danger, and it also serves as a way to avoid trivializing the concept of censorship by associating it with constraints of every kind.

The trivialization of censorship as a concept contrasts with the experience of censorship among those who suffered from it. Authors, printers, booksellers, and middlemen have had their noses sliced, their ears cut off, and their hands amputated; they have been exposed in stocks and branded with hot irons; they have been condemned to row for many years in galleys; they have been shot, hanged, beheaded, and burned at the stake.[1] Most of these atrocities were inflicted on book people during the early modern period. Nothing comparable appears in the sources consulted for this study. Yet examples from the preceding pages show that milder punishments could cause severe suffering: Mlle Bonafon, thirteen years of imprisonment in a convent for writing a political fairy tale (*Tanastès*); Mukunda Lal Das, three years of "rigorous imprisonment" for singing suggestive songs ("The White Rat"); Walter Janka, five years of solitary confinement for publishing an author who fell out of favor (Lukács). Those punishments might be considered as constraints and lumped together with all the other impediments and inhibitions that set limits to expression. But the constraint of imprisonment operates differently from the forces of the marketplace. It is inflicted by the state, which has a monopoly of power. If one publisher refuses my manuscript, I can try to sell it to another. I may fail and feel oppressed by the sheer weight of capitalism, but autocratic states close off such alternatives. There was no appeal from the Bastille, the sweltering prisons of Mandalay, or the gulag.

Not that all states imposed sanctions in the same way. Their actions might be arbitrary, but they clothed them in procedures that had a tincture of legality. One of the striking aspects of the dossiers from the Bastille is the effort by the police to ferret out clues and establish guilt by rigorous interrogations, even though the prisoners had no legal defense. Under the pressure of circumstances, trials in the British Raj returned the expected verdicts, yet they adopted elaborate ceremonies to act out the rule of British law and affirm the fiction of freedom of the press. Janka's conviction in Berlin was a ceremony of a different kind: a show trial orchestrated in Stalinist fashion to launch a purge and to signal a change in the Party line. The line determined legitimacy in a system that had no room for civil rights. East German censors had to hew to it when they went over manuscripts. In doing so, however, they had to make interpretations—of the Party line, the text, and the compatibility between the line of the Party and the lines in the text. When they argued with authors and with one another over specific passages, they were drawn into hermeneutical battles. Censorship in all three systems was a struggle over meaning. It could involve decoding references in a roman à clef or wrangling over Sanskrit grammar or reading between the lines of a picaresque novel; but it always involved interpretive debates.

The debates required consideration of reader response—a favorite subject among literary theorists today and a practical problem for the censors at all times.[2] Reading was an essential aspect of censoring, not only in the act of vetting texts, which often led to competing exegeses, but also as an aspect of the inner workings of the state, because contested readings could lead to power struggles, which sometimes led to public scandals, as in the case of De l'Esprit, Nil Durpan, and Hinze-Kunze-Roman. Scandals occurred often enough for those in power to constantly calculate the effects a book might produce when it reached the public, whether sophisticates in le monde or planters in the mofussil or students in Prenzlauer Berg. The archives contain reports on those effects and the ways readers responded, discussing, declaiming, and performing texts. Some of the documents reveal how readings were refracted within different sectors of the state and how they were superimposed on one another—for example when Kurt Hager read Ursula Ragwitz's account of her reading of Klaus Höpcke's reading of Dieter Schlenstedt's reading of Hinze-Kunze-Roman.

In one of the most influential studies of censorship, Leo Strauss, who was a refugee from Nazi Germany as well as a distinguished philosopher and literary scholar, claimed that censors are by nature stupid, because they lack the ability to detect meaning hidden between the lines of unorthodox texts.[3] The studies in this book prove the opposite. Not only did censors perceive nuances of hidden meaning, but they also understood the way published texts reverberated in the public. Their sophistication should not be surprising in the case of the GDR, because they included authors, scholars, and critics. But eminent authors also functioned as censors in eighteenth-century France, and the surveillance of vernacular literatures in India was carried out by learned librarians as well as district officers with a keen eye for the folkways of the "natives." To dismiss censorship as crude repression by ignorant bureaucrats is to get it wrong. Although it varied enormously, it usually was a complex process that required talent and training and that extended deep into the social order.

It also could be positive. The approbations of the French censors testified to the excellence of the books deemed worthy of a royal privilege.
They often resemble promotional blurbs on the back of the dust jackets on
books today. Column 16 in the secret "catalogues" of the India Civil Service sometimes read like modern book reviews, and they frequently lauded
the books they kept under surveillance. While acting as censors, East German editors worked hard to improve the quality of the texts they vetted.
So did the experts who wrote the readers reports and the full-time censors
in the HV, who defended the annual Plans against the apparatchiks in the
Culture Division of the Party's Central Committee, whom they despised
as philistines. Despite its ideological function, the reworking of texts had
resemblances to the editing done by professionals in open societies.

It also led to collaboration between censors and authors, often closer
than in the author-editor relations that exist today in the publishing houses
of Paris, London, and New York. Some French censors worked so closely
with writers that they were drawn into virtual co-authorship. The texts of
their approbations, printed in the book, cannot be divorced from the body
of the texts that they recommended. Approbations, privileges, and dedications all received a careful going-over from the administration in charge of
books, and all appeared inside the books as parts of a single whole. While
keeping a critical eye on vernacular literature, officials in the India Civil
Service sometimes intervened to encourage it, giving subsidies and prizes
to writers who, they believed, might someday produce something like a
European novel.[4] From start to finish, the novels of the GDR bore the
marks of intervention by the censors. They resulted from a collaborative
process of writing and rewriting—to such an extent, that some censors
complained that they had done most of the work.

Collaboration took place through negotiation. In authoritarian systems, writers understood that they operated in a real world, where agents
of the state held the power to control and repress all publications. Most
controls were directed at newspapers and other news media, not at books,
which are the subject of this study. But books often threatened to upset the
monopoly of power, and they were taken seriously by the authorities, even
those at the top of the system, including ministers in Versailles, London,

and Berlin. Negotiation occurred at every level, but especially at the early stages when a text began to take shape. That did not happen in the Raj, where censorship was restricted to post-publication repression, nor did it affect the literature that circulated outside the system in eighteenth-century France. But even Voltaire, when he published legal or quasi-legal works, negotiated with censors, their superiors, influential intermediaries, and the police. He knew how to manipulate all the gears and levers of the power apparatus, and he was an expert in using it for his benefit.[5] For East German authors like Erich Loest and Volker Braun, negotiation was so important that it could hardly be distinguished from the publication process. They sometimes spent more time haggling over passages than writing them. The parties on both sides understood the nature of the give-and-take. They shared a sense of participating in the same game, accepting its rules, and respecting their opposite number.

Far from being helpless victims, authors could sometimes play a strong hand. In eighteenth-century France, they used protectors to lobby the *directeur de la librairie*. If they failed to get at least a tacit permission, they could send their manuscripts to presses in Holland or Switzerland, much to the chagrin of the French authorities, who deplored the losses inflicted on the domestic economy by competition from abroad. Indian writers had no equivalent outlet, but they sometimes appealed for support from backbenchers in Parliament or the secretary of state for India in London, who frequently crossed swords with the viceroy in Calcutta. East German authors used similar tactics, especially if they attracted enough attention to be known as dissidents. They could threaten to publish books in West Germany, and they could stir up enough controversy to expose the GDR's pretention to favor a progressive variety of culture, free of repression and censorship. Yet the adversarial nature of author-censor relations should not be exaggerated. The opponents often became friends. In the course of their negotiations, they were absorbed into a network of players and a system of relations that operated within the boundaries of official institutions. It was a human system, which mitigated the rigidity of censorship as the direct expression of reason of state. The legal loopholes in France, the support of accomplices like James Long in India, the *Spielraum*, or room for maneuver, in East Germany (including the blank spaces left in the annual Plans) combined in different ways to make censorship work.

Because complicity, collaboration, and negotiation pervaded the way authors and censors operated, at least in the three systems studied here, it would be misleading to characterize censorship simply as a contest between creation and oppression. Seen from the inside, and especially from the censor's point of view, censorship can appear to be coextensive with literature. Censors believed that they made literature happen. Instead of doubting their good faith, it would be more effective to treat it as an ingredient of the system. No system can operate by sheer coercion, not even in North Korea today or the Soviet Union in the 1930s or England at the height of the tyranny of Henry VIII. All systems need true believers. Insofar as they erode belief, authoritarian regimes impair their own functioning: that, too, is a historical process, which in the case of the Soviet empire can be measured by the growing cynicism of the intelligentsia. I was surprised to find that the censors of the GDR remained committed to its principles even after its collapse. The censors under the Ancien Régime in France certainly subscribed to its values, above all the principle of privilege, even when they deviated from them, as in the case of Crébillon fils, who wrote novels of the kind that he would never have approved in his capacity as a proud *censeur royal*. To the judges of the British Raj and the Indian librarians who prepared its catalogues, liberalism was perfectly compatible with imperialism. To perceive compatibility among the contradictory elements of a cultural system is, I believe, to testify to the power of its hold on the "natives." It can be argued that religions draw strength from their ability to confront contradictions and to mediate them—for example, by helping their adherents to reconcile the belief in a beneficent creator with the experience of evil and suffering.

Without minimizing the disaffection and disbelief that also developed under authoritarian systems, I think it important to recognize that censors and authors often shared a commitment to the kind of literature they produced together. Literature, in the three cases studied here, was not confined to the creation of imaginative works of fiction. It involved all sorts of writing and all kinds of roles in the process of producing, distribut ing, and consuming books. Authors played only one role at the beginning of the process (authors wrote texts; editors, designers, and printers made books); and readers often determined the outcome at the other end. In between, all sorts of middlemen intervened, each with connections outside the system—to coachmen, for example (*Tanastès* reached readers in Paris by being smuggled in coaches from Versailles), or district officers (they supplied the information that went into the "returns" on books in India), or periodical editors (they published the reviews used to manipulate the reception of *Hinze-Kunze-Roman*). Beyond them all, literature took place within a larger context: the cosmopolitanism of Enlightenment and French culture in the eighteenth century, the competition of imperial powers and the resistance to them by nationalist movements in the nineteenth century, and the power struggles on both sides of the Cold War in the second half of the twentieth century. In each case, the nature of literature itself was culturally specific. Literature inhered in cultural systems with configurations of their own and core principles around which they crystallized: privilege, in the case of Bourbon France; surveillance, in British India; and planning, in Communist East Germany.

Those shorthand descriptions hardly do justice to the abuses of power that occurred in all three systems. In each one, power assumed many forms, pervading all aspects of literary life and constituting literature as a subsystem within the social order. Should we therefore go as far as some post-structuralist theorists and see censorship in every expression of power and in constraints of every kind, including the marketplace as understood by Marxists and the subconscious as studied by Freudians? I think not. If the concept of censorship is extended to everything, it means nothing. It should not be trivialized. Although I would agree that power is exerted in many ways, I think it crucial to distinguish between the kind of power that is monopolized by the state (or other constituted authorities such as religious organizations in some cases) and power that exists everywhere else in society. Censorship as I understand it is essentially political; it is wielded by the state.[6]

Having ventured dangerously close to relativism, therefore, I would back away from it—just as ethnographers do in the field when they encounter

"native" practices that violate their own principles. Can an anthropological approach to censorship be reconciled with commitment to culturally
distinct categories such as the right to freedom of speech enshrined in
the First Amendment to the U.S. Constitution? Anthropologists often feel
pulled in opposite directions, like the two dogs who crossed paths at the
Polish–Czech border, according to a joke recounted by Poles in the 1970s.
"Why are you going to Czechoslovakia?" the Czech dog asked. "I want
to eat," the Polish dog answered, "and why are you going to Poland?" "I
want to bark," said the dog from Czechoslovakia. Freedom of speech has
to accommodate contrary urges, including the need to make one's way in a
harsh world and the need to protest against the harshness.

For help in sorting out this problem, one can consult the testimony
of writers who experienced censorship fairly recently under autocratic
regimes. Older evidence, such as the famous *Diary of a Russian Censor*
from the mid-nineteenth century, and documents leaked from Communist
countries, such as *The Black Book of Polish Censorship*, provide supplementary information;[7] but the memoirs of accomplished authors give access to
insiders' understanding of how censorship affected them, especially in the
psychological realm that is most difficult to penetrate: self-censorship.

Consider Aleksandr Solzhenitsyn's account of his experience in *The
Oak and the Calf*, published in 1975, a year after his expulsion from the
Soviet Union. When you open it, you expect to encounter the voice of a
prophet, crying in the wilderness; and you won't be disappointed, for Solzhenitsyn casts himself as a Jeremiah. Yet he recounts much of his story in
a surprising register: shrewd, precise, ironic, and sociologically rich observations of how literature functioned as a power system in a Stalinist society.
We meet him first in the gulag. During eight years of labor in the prison
camps, he writes about the misery around him, and he continues writing
after his release while living miserably as a teacher. He writes in isolation
and with total freedom, because he knows he cannot publish anything. His
words will not be read until long after his death. But he must keep them
secret. He memorizes them, writes them in a minute hand on thin strips
of paper, and rolls the paper into cylinders, which he squeezes into a bottle
and buries in the ground. As manuscript follows manuscript, he continues

to hide them in the safest, most unlikely places. Then, to his amazement, Khrushchev denounces the excesses of Stalin at the Twenty-Second Party Congress in 1961, and Aleksandr Tvardovsky, the editor of *Novy Mir*, the most important review in the USSR, proclaims a readiness to publish bolder texts. Solzhenitsyn decides to take a risk. He rewrites, in milder form, the work that will eventually break through the wall of silence about the atrocities of the gulag under the title "A Day in the Life of Ivan Denisovich"; and he submits it to *Novy Mir*.

At this point, Solzhenitsyn's narrative turns into a kind of sociology. He describes all the editors at the review, their rivalries, self-protective maneuvers, and struggles to stifle the bomb that he has planted in their midst. Aleksandr Dementyev, the intelligent, duplicitous agent of the Central Committee of the Party, sets traps and erects barriers during editorial conferences, but Tvardovsky is torn. As a genuine poet with roots in the peasantry, "[h]is first loyalty was to Russian literature, with its devout belief in the moral duty of the writer." Yet he also felt compelled by "the Party's truth."[8] In the end, he prevails over his own doubts and the doubters on the staff, and he goes over the manuscript line by line with Solzhenitsyn, negotiating changes. Solzhenitsyn is willing to make them, up to a point, because he understands that the text must be modified enough to pass through the obstacle course that constitutes literary reality. The course itself is described—leaked copies, huddled conversations in corridors of power, a reading before Khrushchev in his dacha, and approval by the Presidium (Politburo). The official censors, kept in the dark, are horrified when they see the proofs. But they praise the book when it goes to press, having been informed at the last minute that it received the approval of the Central Committee. The work creates a sensation, and it could have been followed by the other books that Solzhenitsyn has prepared; but he holds them back, unwilling to make the necessary modifications—a strategic mistake, he sees in retrospect, because the window of opportunity will close when Brezhnev succeeds Khrushchev in 1964 and a new wave of Stalinization shuts down genuine literature, driving Solzhenitsyn, now notorious, into exile. For all its vivid detail, backed up by a great deal of documentation, the story does not come across as a journalistic exposé.

Nor does it invoke a Western view of freedom of speech. In a specifically Russian idiom, it proclaims a prophetic view of literature as a vehicle of truth.[9]

Milan Kundera writes in a different idiom—ironic, sophisticated, steeped self-consciously in centuries of European literature. He, too, confronted censorship at a moment when Stalinism opened up long enough to expose its fault lines, then closed again, eventually driving him into exile. Literature and other arts, notably film, revived in Czechoslovakia during the 1960s, despite the heavy-handedness of the Communist regime. The Party itself succumbed to reformers determined to install "socialism with a human face" in January 1968, when Alexander Dubček became its first secretary. Censorship was abolished during the wave of reforms known as the Prague Spring, and it was restored soon after the Soviet invasion in August. A year earlier, in June 1967, the Authors Union held a congress, which in retrospect looks like a prelude to the Prague Spring. Kundera and other writers used it as a forum to demand greater freedom. In his address to the congress, Kundera invoked literature as the vital force behind "the very existence of the nation," "the answer to the nation's existential question," and he denounced censorship, after quoting Voltaire, in the language of natural rights:

> For the truth can only be reached by a dialogue of free opinions enjoying equal rights. Any interference with freedom of thought and word, however discreet the mechanics and terminology of such censorship, is a scandal in this century, a chain entangling the limbs of our national literature as it tries to bound forward.[10]

Could such a statement appear in print? *Literární noviny*, the Czech equivalent of *Novy Mir*, intended to publish it with the proceedings of the congress, including a resolution to abolish censorship. This was too much for the censors in the "Central Publishing Board," which resembled the HV of East Germany. They refused to let the issue go to press and summoned the editor of *Literární noviny*, Dusan Hamsík, along with members of its editorial board to meet with them and Frantisek Havlícek, head of the Central Committee's Ideological Department, the Czech counterpart to Kultur in the Central Committee of the GDR. According to Hamsik's account, the meeting turned into a hard-fought struggle over every article in the issue, above all the text of Kundera's speech. Kundera himself was present, and he wrangled with Havlícek, line by line, fighting over every clause and comma. He could not simply refuse to negotiate, because the writers wanted their manifesto to be published and to reinforce the public's resistance to Stalinism. He won some points and lost others, insisting all the while on "the absurdity of censoring a text that protested against all censorship."[11] In the end, he managed to save nearly everything that he had written. But when he left the meeting, he was miserable. "Why did I knuckle under?" he complained to Hamsik. "I let them make a complete idiot of me. . . . Every compromise is a dirty compromise."[12] Soon afterward, the Party Central Committee phoned to say that it could not accept the compromise after all. The proceedings were never published. And Kundera was enormously relieved.

In Hamsik's description of this episode, Kundera appears as "a difficult customer,"[13] a writer of such unbending commitment to his art that he felt sickened by any degree of complicity with the political authorities. When the crisis came, however, he was willing, like Solzhenitsyn, to trim his prose in order to break the Party's hold on literature. He, too, understood literature as a force that forged the national identity, although he associated it more broadly with the rise of European civilization.[14] It had such transcendent importance for him, in fact, that he could not stomach the negotiation and compromise that determined literary life in all Stalinist regimes. By making him complicit in its tyranny, even when he resisted, it violated his sense of his self.

The inner sense of wounded integrity also comes through Norman Manea's account of his dealings with the censors in Communist Romania during the 1980s, when Nicolae Ceauşescu had established a totalitarian regime outside the sphere of the Soviet Union. Manea insists on the "human reality"[15] on both sides of the power divide—corrupt and canny officials pursuing their own ends within the state and ambitious authors, trying to advance their careers in a system dominated completely by the

Party. As one of the authors, Manea hoped to make a breakthrough with his novel *The Black Envelope*, which contained some carefully oblique criticism of the totalitarianism around him. Owing to the fiction that censorship had been abolished, he did not receive the censor's report on his book, only a copy of the text that the censor had vetted. About 80 percent of it was marked for deletion or revision, without any accompanying explanations. Manea struggled to puzzle out the objections and rewrote the text extensively, then submitted it through his publisher, as before. The rewritten version was rejected, again without an explanation. There seemed to be no way out of this impasse, until the publisher took a chance. He sent the text to an "outside" reader, a retired veteran of the censorship system whom he knew through his contacts in the human network that got things done behind the façades of the official institutions. Coming from a noncensor, this censor's report could be shown to Manea. It gave a penetrating and intelligent reading of the book and proposed major changes. Painful as they were, Manea adopted the recommendations of his "shrewd censorteacher,"[16] for they represented his only hope of continuing to exist in the world of literature. The strategy worked, the edition sold out, and in the wake of its success, Manea was forced into exile. In 1988, he emigrated to America, where he discovered "freedom"—not an order unbound by constraints, but a complex system that required compromises of its own, including some imposed by "the harsh laws of the marketplace."[17] While acknowledging the hard realities of exercising freedom in a democracy, Manea insisted on the distinctions that made it fundamentally different from what he had experienced in Romania. When he looked back on the cuts he had accepted in *The Black Envelope*, he did not regret the excision of critical passages so much as the whole process of compromise and complicity, and the toll it took on him. In the end, he concluded, "The censor's office won."[18]

Danilo Kiš underwent a similar experience in Communist Yugoslavia, although Stalinism there took a milder form than in East Germany, Czechoslovakia, or Romania. When he reflected on his attempts to cope with censorship, he stressed its invisible character—the informal pressures exerted by publishers and editors, who acted as censors while exercising their professional functions, and, above all, the pervasive power of self-censorship. The inner, self-appointed censor, he wrote, is the writer's double, "a double who leans over his shoulder and interferes with the text *in statu nascendi*, keeping him from making an ideological misstep. It is impossible to win out against this censor-double; he is like God, he knows all and sees all, because he comes out of your own brain, your own fears, your own nightmares."[19]

Czeslaw Milosz carried this argument further by describing how intellectuals in Poland subjected themselves to censorship as "involuntary subjective control"[20]—that is, an internalized assimilation of Communist doctrine inflicted not by force but by a need to find significance in the wake of World War II and the conquest of their country by its old enemy, Russia, with a new weapon, Stalinist dialectics. They had experienced the horrors of history up close, so close that it undid their sense of reality. How could someone who had seen friends massacred and Warsaw leveled maintain a belief in the meaningfulness of the squabbles of the literary avant-garde before the war or believe in the cheerful, postwar view of the world that existed in parts of the West—the kind, for example, that was then being painted by Norman Rockwell for covers of the *Saturday Evening Post*? Dialectical materialism, Soviet style, explained how history was transforming reality in great waves, which had engulfed Central Europe, soon would flood Paris and London, and eventually would drown the philistines in America. Authors like "Alpha," Milosz's fellow traveler through literary circles in the 1930s and 1940s, found psychological relief and material support by embracing the official certainties. Milosz described the trajectory of their inner and outer lives, using artificial names, in order to explain their submission to total state control. For them and for him, the turning point came with the imposition of "socialist realism," which he understood not merely as an aesthetic directive but as a totalizing doctrine "concerned with the beliefs which lie at the foundation of human existence. In the field of literature it forbids what has in every age been the writer's essential task—to look at the world from his own independent viewpoint, to tell the truth as he sees it, and so to keep watch and ward in the interest of society as a whole."[21] Milosz committed himself to this mission of literature in 1951, at the height of Stalinism, when he went into exile. His decision to cut himself off from his country and his culture was, as he put it, more visceral than philosophical, "a revolt of the stomach." Yet it expressed a determination "to keep alive freedom of thought."[22]

When exiles from the Soviet system invoked "freedom" and "truth," they were not appealing to the protection of the First Amendment or speaking as philosophers. They were using words to describe their experience of censorship as a force operating in specific circumstances, a force that determined the nature of literature in an oppressive political system. "Freedom of speech" served as a standard against which to measure the oppression. It did not apply to constraints of all kinds, although many kinds had weighed on the lives of the writers. Freedom for them was a principle made meaningful by the experience of its violation. Experiences varied, of course, and the variations make it hopeless to search for a general proposition that would encompass all of them, including some that have been studied up close, such as censorship under apartheid in South Africa.[23] Even within the Soviet system some writers wrote, rewrote, cut, and spliced accounts of their experience, including forced labor in the prison camps of Siberia, according to detailed directions from the censors, and they did so willingly, convinced of the Party's capacity to guide them to the truth.[24]

Terms like "truth" and "freedom" may seem misplaced in a discussion of the complexities that constituted censorship in the Soviet empire. In using such abstractions, the exiles from the system did not minimize the historical contingencies in which they found themselves. On the contrary, they emphasized the constant need for negotiation and compromise as the Party line shifted and authors changed tacks while attempting to make their way through the hard realities of the world they knew as literature. They also understood that literature in what Westerners called the "free world" suffered from constraints. Does their experience argue for a relativistic notion of freedom?

Hegel notwithstanding, I doubt that absolutes exist in history. All events occur in contexts, and all actions are hedged in with constraints. To take seriously the testimony of writers who were silenced or who silenced themselves under Stalinist regimes is not, however, to equate their experience with that of anyone who finds it difficult to publish a book. Nor is it to conflate twentieth-century modes of silencing with ways of stifling voices in other times and places. Historians are not equipped to tote up degrees of iniquity in different periods of the past. But we cannot avoid making value judgments, and we should be able to recognize the way our values shade our understanding, just as we acknowledge the conceptual framework that shapes it. In describing approaches to the history of censorship, we can string together opposites—the normative versus the relative, the empirical versus the theoretical, the liberal versus the poststructural—but they fail to do justice to the complexities of experience. Rather than facing either/ or alternatives, I would prefer to shift the ground of the debate.

An ethnographic view of censorship treats it holistically, as a system of control, which pervades institutions, colors human relations, and reaches into the hidden workings of the soul. By taking such a broad view, ethnographic history can do justice to the different ways that censorship operated in different societies. It can avoid reifying censorship and reducing it to any formula, including even violations of declarations of rights. Far from contesting the validity of those declarations, it takes them seriously as elements in cultural systems. Yet it doesn't flatten out all distinctions in an attempt to create a level playing field for scientific investigation.

Anthropologists learned long ago that to understand an alien point of view they must enter into dialogue with the "natives" in a way that sharpens their consciousness of their own viewpoint.[25] Fieldwork in the archives brings the historian up against appalling examples of oppression. In describing some of them, this book is meant to explain how censors did their job, how censorship actually operated, and how it functioned within authoritarian systems. In studying its operations, I have learned to acquire greater respect for principles that I share with other citizens in our peculiar part of the world and our moment in history. I understand that the First Amendment does not extend beyond the jurisdictional limits of the U.S. Constitution, but I believe in the right to freedom of speech with all the fervor of my fellow citizens, despite the scorn of sophisticates who deride "First Amendment pieties."[26] While attempting understanding, one must take a stand, especially today, when the state may be watching every move we make.

ACKNOWLEDGMENTS

—◆◆◆—

This book is a much expanded version of the Panizzi Lectures, which I delivered at the British Library in January 2014 and dedicated to the memory of the first Panizzi lecturer, D. F. McKenzie. I would like to thank the Panizzi Foundation and my hosts at the British Library for their kind invitation. I also would like to express my gratitude to the librarians and staff at the Bibliothèque de l'Arsenal and the Bibliothèque nationale de France who have helped me track censors, authors, and police agents through their manuscript collections ever since the 1960s. The Wissenschaftskolleg zu Berlin provided me with a fellowship in 1989–90 and again in 1992–93. I shall always be grateful to the WiKo, its rector, Wolf Lepenies, and its staff. Solveig Nester helped me find my way through the labyrinthine complexities of the papers of the Central Committee of the Communist or Sozialistische Einheitspartei Deutschlands in East Berlin. And Graham Shaw offered expert guidance through the archives of the India Civil Service at the British Library in London. My thanks go to them; to Steven Forman, my excellent and sympathetic editor at W. W. Norton; and to Jean-François Sené, who improved my text while translating it into French for Editions Gallimard. The French edition includes a discussion of some theoretical issues, which was eliminated from the English edition. It can be consulted for the original French in quotations from manuscript sources, and the German edition contains the original German quotations. All translations into English are my own.

NOTES

----◆◆◆----

INTRODUCTION

1. John Palfrey, "Four Phases of Internet Regulation," *Social Research* 77 (Fall 2010): 981–96. As an example of the free-spirited view of cyberspace, see John Perry Barlow, "A Declaration of the Independence of Cyberspace," available online at barlow@eff.org.

2. See Marc Bloch, "Pour une histoire comparée des sociétés européennes," in Marc Bloch, *Mélanges historiques*, vol. 1 (Paris, 1963), 16–40.

3. Aleksandr Solzhenitsyn, *The Oak and the Calf: Sketches of Literary Life in the Soviet Union* (New York, 1980; first published in 1975), 33.

4. For a survey of the literature, see *Censorship: A World Encyclopedia*, ed. Derek Jones, 4 vols. (London and Chicago, 2001).

5. See Reinhold Niebuhr, *The Children of Light and the Children of Darkness: A Vindication of Democracy and a Critique of Its Traditional Defence* (New York, 1944).

6. The First Amendment reads, "Congress shall make no law respecting an establishment of religion, or prohibiting the free exercise thereof, or abridging the freedom of speech, or of the press; or the right of the people peaceably to assemble, and to petition the Government for a redress of grievances."

7. Stanley Fish, *There's No Such Thing as Free Speech, and It's a Good Thing, Too* (New York, 1994), 111.

8. Robert Bellah, *The Broken Covenant: American Civil Religion in Time of Trial* (Chicago, 1992).

9. *The Correspondence of John Locke. Electronic Edition*, Intelex Past Masters, vol. 5, p. 78.

10. John Milton, *Areopagitica* (Rockville, Md., 2008), 57 and 61.

11. As a free thinker, Diderot certainly favored freedom of expression, but as an author caught between the danger of imprisonment by *lettre de cachet* (an arbitrary order of the king) and the pressures of a literary market controlled by the Parisian guild of booksellers and printers, he expressed a disabused view of the contemporary publishing industry, one that had much in common with that expressed by Milton a century earlier, except that Diderot depended more heavily on powerful publishers. See Denis Diderot, *Lettre sur le commerce de la librairie*, ed. Jacques Proust (Paris, 1962).

12. The Whig interpretation of history, as characterized by Herbert Butterfield, stresses the inevitable advance of progress over reaction toward a present that looks like the triumph of liberalism: Herbert Butterfield, *The Whig Interpretation of History* (London, 1931). Because of its apparent, culture-bound, political bias, "Whig history" has become a pejorative, but in a recent article, William Cronin argues that it is worth reconsidering: "Two Cheers for the Whig Interpretation of History," *Perspectives on History* 50, no. 6 (Sept. 2012), online edition, ISSN 1556-8563. Of course, a view of history that opposes censorship to the continuous pursuit of truth need not be Whiggish or limited to liberals. One of the best-known studies of censorship was written by the conservative historian of ideas Leo Strauss: *Persecution and the Art of Writing* (Glencoe, Ill., 1952). It explicitly rejects the kind of "historicism" that I am advocating in this book.

13. Fish, *There's No Such Thing as Free Speech*, 102–19. Legal scholars sometimes emphasize distinct uses of the adjective "free" as illustrated by the distinction between free speech and free beer. The former refers to an action that is protected by law and limited by legal constraints; the latter, to a product that involves costs. To advocate freedom of speech—or free access to material on the Internet—is not, therefore, to ignore economic and social realities or to retreat to an uninformed idealism of the sort that Fish derides. See Lawrence Lessig, *Free Culture: How Big Media Use Technology and the Law to Lock Down Culture and Control Creativity* (New York, 2004).

14. Among studies of censorship that take account of postmodernist theories, see Michael Holquist, "Corrupt Originals: The Paradox of Censorship," *Publications of the Modern Languages Association* 109 (1994): 14–25; the essays collected in *Censorship and Silencing: Practices of Cultural Regulation*, ed. Robert C. Post (Los Angeles, 1998); the essays in *Censorship and Cultural Regulation in the Modern Age*, ed. Beate Müller (New York, 2004); the essays in *The Administration of Aesthetics: Censorship, Political Criticism, and the Public Sphere*, ed. Richard Burt (Minneapolis, 1994); and Sophia Rosenfeld, "Writing the History of Censorship in the Age of Enlightenment," in *Postmodernism and the Enlightenment: New Perspectives in Eighteenth-Century French Intellectual History*, ed. Daniel Gordon (New York, 2001).

15. On thick description, see Clifford Geertz, *The Interpretation of Cultures: Selected Essays* (New York, 1973), 3–30.

PART ONE

1. As examples of this tendency among the best-known works on the Enlightenment in English, see Kingsley Martin, *French Liberal Thought in the Eighteenth Century* (London, 1962; 1st ed., 1929), 95–102; George R. Havens, *The Age of Ideas: From Reaction to Revolution in Eighteenth-Century France* (New York, 1955), 9 and 27–28; Peter Gay, "Voltaire against the Censors," in Peter Gay, *Voltaire's Politics: The Poet as Realist* (New Haven, 1959); and Peter Gay, *The Enlightenment: An Interpretation* (New York, 1969), vol. 2, pp. 69–79.

2. These questions are especially pertinent to the history of books, a field of study that is only beginning to influence the understanding of history in general. For a broad view of book history, see the first of the Panizzi lectures: D. F. McKenzie, *Bibliography and the Sociology of Texts* (Cambridge, 1999).

3. Bibliothèque nationale de France, ms. fr. 22137–22152. The first three of these large registers contain "judgments" submitted by censors to Malesherbes and grouped according to the names of the censors. The other twelve have an admixture of different kinds of documents, including many "judgments." Rich as they are, the documents pertain only to the period 1750–63, when Malesherbes was *directeur de la librairie*. A friend or protector of several *philosophes*, he was noted for his tolerant and flexible rule; but he consistently asserted the authority of the state against attempts by the clergy, the university, and the parlements to interfere with the surveillance of the book trade. Malesherbes's successor, Antoine de Sartine (1763–74), generally continued his liberal policies, but there were periods of repression under later *directeurs*, notably Le Camus de Néville (1776–84). The following discussion is limited to the Malesherbes years, although I have sampled all the material in this general "Anisson-Duperron" collection and have tried to read everything in it for the years 1769–89. For a full account of this collection, see Ernest Coyecque, *Inventaire de la Collection Anisson sur l'histoire de l'imprimerie et la librairie principalement à Paris (manuscrits français 22061–22193)*, 2 vols. (Paris, 1900). Among the studies of censorship in eighteenth-century France, the best in my opinion is Raymond Birn, *Royal Censorship in Eighteenth-Century France* (Stanford, 2012). Nicole Herrmann-Mascard, *La Censure des livres à Paris à la fin de l'Ancien Régime, 1750–1789* (Paris, 1968), is heavily derived from the groundbreaking work of J.-P. Belin, *Le Commerce des livres prohibés à Paris de 1750 à 1789* (Paris, 1913). But there is much of value in more-recent work, notably William Hanley, "The Policing of Thought in Eighteenth-Century France," *Studies on Voltaire and the Eighteenth Century* 183 (1980), 265–93; Barbara Negroni, *Lectures interdites: Le*

travail des censeurs au XXVIIIe siècle, 1723–1774 (Paris, 1995); Georges Minois, *Censure et culture sous l'Ancien Régime* (Paris, 1995); and Edoardo Tortarola, *Invenzione della libertà di stampa: Censura e scrittori nel Settecento* (Rome, 2011). Two publications connected with my own research in the papers of the Direction de la librairie are "Reading, Writing, and Publishing in Eighteenth-Century France: A Case Study in the Sociology of Literature," *Daedalus* (Winter 1971), 214–56, and "Censorship, a Comparative View: France, 1789–East Germany, 1989," *Historical Change and Human Rights: The Oxford Amnesty Lectures 1994* (New York, 1994), 101–30.

4. Abbé Geinos, Nov. 24, 1750, Bibliothèque nationale de France, ms. fr. 22137, document no. 103.

5. Lagrange de Chécieux, Sept. 6, 1759, ms. fr. 22138, no. 2.

6. Simon, May 2, 1752, ms. fr. 22139, no. 113. "This manuscript, preceded by a preliminary discourse, lacks the grand and florid style that is warranted by its subject matter. But although simple, it is written soundly, and it can make known the advantages and the perfections to be provided to all men in general by the virtues that are analyzed therein. As a whole, it is full of interesting historical touches that are relevant to the virtues being analyzed and also of anecdotes that can amuse the reader while instructing him by edifying maxims. Not having found anything in this manuscript that could be an obstacle to its printing, I believe I must approve it."

7. For example, de Mareille, May 4, 1752, ms. fr. 22138, no. 111, on a *Vie de Grotius.*

8. Lagrange de Chécieux, Nov. 6, 1757, ms. fr. 22152, no. 190.

9. Undated report by abbé Foucher, ms. fr. 22137, no. 90.

10. Undated report by Déguignez, ms. fr. 22137, no. 135.

11. Le Blond, Oct. 2, 1752, ms. fr. 22138, no. 38. In a similar report, undated, de Parcieux rejected a mathematical work as "a confused mishmash of a prodigious quantity of arithmetical questions in which one cannot find any order or method. . . . The author resolves his questions the way a worker from Limousin mixes plaster. . . . You can't learn a thing from one end [of the manuscript] to the other; or if you could learn something, it would be very badly. We already have far too many of these books that teach poorly." Ms. fr. 22139, no. 3.

12. An unsigned and undated report, ms. fr. 22140, no. 12.

13. Delaville, Nov. 23, 1757, ms. fr. 22138, no. 19. "It's a compilation done without taste and discernment. . . . I found this work detestable in its substance and in its form."

14. Foucher, Jan. 17, 1754, ms. fr. 22137, no. 94.

15. Rémond de St. Albine, April 29, 1751, ms. fr. 22138, no. 78, refusing to give an approbation to a play. "The substance of this play is too trivial, and this fault is not offset by any charm in the dialogue. In general, the work is faulty in its style, and the author is even guilty of several grammatical errors. The large number

of false rhymes, which are everywhere in the play, will especially give offense to everyone of any delicacy. I don't see any other reason to forbid the printing of this play, aside from the damage that is being done to the honor of French literature by the excessive profusion of works that are not worthy of the readers' attention."

16. Guiroy, July 24, 1753, ms. fr. 22137, no. 136. An unsigned and undated rejection of an anti-Jansenist work was equally blunt. Its substance was perfectly orthodox, but "[t]here is throughout the work a great deal of gibberish, good arguments developed in a very weak manner, verbiage, innumerable sentences that are not even French." Ms. fr. 22140, no. 17.

17. Undated report by Simon, ms. fr. 22139, no. 107. "This novel is poorly written, bad in its style, most of its terms being incorrect and not proper French. This little tale is without any verisimilitude, and the puerile adventures it relates are not interesting enough to amuse the reader. Not having found the slightest usefulness or instruction for the public, I find I must refuse to approve it."

18. De Bougainville, Aug. 26, 1751, ms. fr. 22137, no. 33.

19. Ibid.

20. C. G. de Lamoignon de Malesherbes, *Mémoires sur la librairie et sur la liberté de la presse* (1809, written in 1788; reprint, Geneva, 1969), 300.

21. The regulations governing the book trade issued on Aug. 30, 1777, created a new category, the "permission simple," which permitted the nonexclusive right to republish a text whose privilege had expired. It made explicit the right of an author to obtain a privilege, which he and his heirs could possess forever. But authors normally transferred their privileges to the booksellers who published their works. In such cases, the edicts of 1777 limited the duration of a privilege to the life of the author and a minimum of ten years. See *Arrêt du Conseil d'Etat du Roi, portant règlement sur la durée des privilèges en librairie. Du 30 août 1777*, reprinted in Antoine Perrin, *Almanach de la librairie* (Paris, 1781), which itself is available as a reprint: *Almanach de la librairie* (Aubel, Belgium, 1984; preface by Jeroom Vercruysse).

22. The correspondence and reports concerning this affair are scattered through ms. fr. 22138, nos. 151, 160, 161, and 168, and ms. fr. 22149, nos. 18–24.

23. Marquis de Marigny to Poncet de La Grave, April 17, 1755, ms. fr. 22149, no. 65. "To accept the dedication of a work would be to give it a public approbation." The documents concerning this affair are in ms. fr. 22149, nos. 59–74.

24. Moncrif to Poncet, Oct. 13, 1755, ms. fr. 22149, no. 67: "I can only repeat what I had the honor to tell you concerning my practice of not approving any work about the arts without the consent of persons whom the king has charged with their administration. I do not solicit them, nor do I resist them when they make their views known about such works."

25. Poncet to Malesherbes, Oct. 21, 1755, ms. fr. 22149, no. 69, reporting the conversation in which Moncrif told him, "I know it is my duty as a censor. But I would

disoblige M. de Marigny, who indicated to me that he does not want this book to be published."

26. Ibid.

27. Given the incomplete and uneven nature of the sources, it may be nearly as difficult to do a full-fledged, sociological study of censors as it is to write a social history of authorship in eighteenth-century France. But the censors are listed in the annual volumes of the *Almanach royal*, and they left many traces of their careers in the Collection Anisson-Duperron of the Bibliothèque nationale de France. Using these and other documents, William Hanley is preparing a rigorous biographical dictionary, which will make it possible to develop a prosopography or collective profile of all the censors during the last five decades of the Ancien Régime. See William Hanley, *A Biographical Dictionary of French Censors, 1742–1789* (Ferney-Voltaire, 2005), vol. I (A–B).

28. On the social and professional character of the contributors to Diderot's *Encyclopédie* and its immediate successor, the *Encyclopédie méthodique*, see Robert Darnton, *The Business of Enlightenment: A Publishing History of the Encyclopédie, 1775–1800* (Cambridge, Mass., 1979), 437–47.

29. "Mémoire sur l'état ancien et actuel de la librairie, présenté à M. de Sartine, directeur général de la librairie et imprimerie, par les syndic et adjoints en charge au mois de mars 1764," Bibliothèque nationale de France, Collection Anisson-Duperron, ms. fr. 22063, fol. 136 verso.

30. Terrasson to Malesherbes, March 5, 1758, ms. fr. 22146, no. 61: "Moreover, Monsieur, at present I am in no rush to examine books. The Chancellor d'Aguesseau, on his own initiative and in connection with his intention of favoring me, put me on the list [of censors], owing to several reasons, one of which was that my father had been a censor for a long time. As that [intention] has not been fulfilled, I now am in a situation in which I can devote myself to other work."

31. These figures are based on the names listed in the annual *Almanach royal*, but censors continued to be listed after they had ceased to function; so the numbers are approximate. The closest study of the censors as a group is the thesis by Catherine Blangonnet, "Recherche sur les censeurs royaux et leur place dans la société au temps de M. de Malesherbes" (Ecole des Chartes, 1975). Not having had access to this typescript, I have relied on the summaries of Ms. Blangonnet's findings in Daniel Roche, "La Censure," in *Histoire de l'édition française: Le livre triomphant, 1660–1830*, ed. Roger Chartier and Henri-Jean Martin (Paris, 1984), 91, and Raymond Birn, *La Censure royale des livres dans la France des Lumières* (Paris, 2007), 101–31, which contains a great deal of additional material. My own research in the same sources confirms many of Birn's conclusions. For slightly different statistics on the numbers of censors, see Robert Estivals, *La Statistique bibliographique de la France sous la monarchie au XVIIIe siècle* (Paris, 1965), 50.

32. Estivals, *La Statistique bibliographique de la France sous la monarchie*. Different registers of requests for different types of permission to publish inevitably lead to different statistical conclusions. For a discussion of this problem and further quantitative analysis, see the essays collected in *Livre et société dans la France du XVIIIème siècle*, ed. François Furet (Paris, 1965 and 1970). For a summary of requests for privileges and tacit permissions that takes account of these complexities, see Henri-Jean Martin, "Une croissance séculaire," in *Histoire de l'édition française*, vol. 2, *Le livre triomphant 1660–1830*, ed. Roger Chartier and Henri-Jean Martin (Paris, 1984), 97–100.

33. Act 5, scene 3: "Provided that in my work I do not discuss authority, nor religion, nor politics, nor morality, nor men in power, nor influential organizations, nor the Opera, nor any other theatrical productions, nor anyone of any importance, I may print everything freely, under the inspection of two or three censors."

34. Max Weber, "The Development of Bureaucracy and Its Relation to Law," in *Max Weber: Selections in Translation*, ed. W. G. Runciman (Cambridge, 1978), 341–56. According to *Le Grand Robert de la langue française* (Paris, 2001), vol. 1, p. 1755, the word *bureaucratie* was coined by the economist J.-C.-M.-V. de Gournay, who died in 1759. See also Ferdinand Brunot, *Histoire de la langue française des origines à nos jours* (Paris, 1966), vol. 6, pt. 1, 445–47. Louis-Sébastien Mercier in his *Tableau de Paris* (Amsterdam, 1783 ed., reprinted and edited by Jean-Claude Bonnet, Paris, 1994), vol. 2, p. 572, included a chapter called "Bureaucratie," which emphasized the arbitrary power exercised by state employees hidden from the public view: "Bureaucracy. A word created recently to designate in a concise and forceful manner the extensive power of ordinary clerks who, in the various offices of the ministry, promote a multitude of projects which they make up or often find under the dust of their office, or promote because of their personal taste or mania."

35. For analyses of the dysfunctional aspects of the administration in eighteenth-century France, see Marcel Marion, *Les Impôts directs sous l'Ancien Régime: Principalement au XVIIIème siècle* (Paris, 1910); Herbert Lüthy, *La Banque protestante en France, de la Révocation de l'Edit de Nantes à la Révolution* (Paris, 1959); and J. F. Bosher, *French Finances, 1770–1795, from Business to Bureaucracy* (Cambridge, 1970).

36. Pierre Grosclaude, *Malesherbes: Témoin et interprète de son temps* (Paris, 1961). According to references in Malesherbes's correspondence, the Thursday audiences were crowded affairs, which involved all sorts of business related to the book trade. See, for example, Malesherbes to the archbishop of Toulouse, August 17, 1763, ms. fr. 22150, no. 62, and Malesherbes to Semonville, Feb. 14, 1760, ms. fr. 22146, no. 87.

37. On these terms, see Brunot, *Histoire de la langue française*, vol. 6, pt. 1, p. 445.

38. Moncrif to Malesherbes, Nov. 4, 1775, ms. fr. 22138, no. 159.

39. This *billet de censure* with the *jugement* in reply is in Boze to Malesherbes, Feb. 28, 1751, ms. fr. 22137, no. 38. See also the similar documents in Secousset to Malesherbes, Jan. 2, 1752, ms. fr.22139, no. 98.

40. This account of the process of censoring relies on remarks scattered throughout the correspondence of Malesherbes and the censors. See especially Millet to Malesherbes, Feb. 28 and May 26, 1755, and Millet to the archbishop of Paris, Dec. 9, 1755, ms. fr., 22138, nos. 137, 138, 139; unsigned letter to Malesherbes, March 24, 1753, ms. fr. 22137, no. 91; Rassicod to Malesherbes, Dec. 24, 1750, ms. fr. 22139, no. 18; Simon to Malesherbes, Oct. 1, 1755, ms. fr. 22139, no. 135; Le Blond to Malesherbes, Oct. 2, 1752, ms. fr. 22138, no. 37; Boussanelle to Malesherbes, Feb. 21, 1761, ms. fr. 22146, no. 43; Malesherbes to Buret, June 22, 1762, ms. fr. 22150, no.103; and the series of "Rapports et décisions" in ms. fr. 22140, nos. 80–109. There is also a description of the formal process for obtaining a privilege in 1781 in Perrin, *Almanach de la librairie*.

41. Buret to Malesherbes, July 9, 1762, ms. fr. 22150, no. 115.

42. Abbé de La Ville to Malesherbes, Aug. 8, 1756, ms. fr 22138, no. 12. "Such a large number of historical and political memoirs come across my desk—and most of them are so unworthy, both in substance and in form—that it is hardly surprising that I pay only quick and superficial attention to them."

43. Foucher, Aug. 25, 1754, ms. fr. 22137, no. 97: "I am occupied with the examination of a fairly lengthy work on the soul and the origin of its knowledge directed against M. Locke. . . . The substance seems very good to me . . . but nonetheless I am requiring many cuts and corrections, which involves me in rather taxing labor and writing. Long live history books and anthologies."

44. Simon, Aug. 30, 1752, ms. fr. 22139, no. 134.

45. La Palme, undated, ms. fr. 22138, no. 11; Tercier, Feb. 1, 1751, ms. fr. 22139, no. 144; Barthélemy, undated, ms. fr. 22137, no. 8; Cahusac, undated, ms. fr. 22137, no. 45.

46. Cotteret, Sept. 9, 1756, ms. fr. 22137, no. 57.

47. For examples of how Voltaire manipulated the legal and illegal systems of publication, see René Pomeau, *Voltaire en son temps*, new ed., vol. 1 (Oxford, 1995), 799–800 and 810–11.

48. Malesherbes to d'Aubert, March 18, 1759, ms. fr. 22142, no. 17. A similar case concerned the choice of a censor for a *Chronologie historique militaire* by an official in the war ministry. At the request of the maréchal de Belle-Isle, Malesherbes issued a *billet de censure* to an official in the ministry of foreign affairs: Malesherbes to Belle-Isle, undated, ms 22143, no. 87. A professor in the University of Strasbourg who had written a book about Alsace asked Malesherbes to give the manuscript to an Alsatian capable of understanding the local themes. Malesherbes replied with a list of Alsatians and an offer to send the *billet de censure* to the one whom the author preferred: Malesherbes to Schoepflin, April 6, 1761, ms. fr. 22142, no. 1.

49. Fontenelle, Oct. 2, 1750, ms. fr. 22137, no. 85.

50. Note on a decision in the *bureau de librairie* entitled "Travail du 30 septembre 1754," ms. fr. 22140.

51. Picardet, canon of Saint-Jean-de-Dijon, Aug. 2, 1763, ms. fr. 22148, no. 51. A note on top of this letter said, "Sent the *billet de censure* to M. Michault."

52. Moncrif, undated, ms. fr. 22138, no. 167

53. Moncrif, undated, ms. fr. 22143, no. 81, complaining that the abbé de La Baume had learned that Moncrif was censoring his *La Christiade*: "Censors can no longer be free in their judgments once they are known to the authors. M. l'abbé La Baume has written to me that his fate is in my hands."

54. Déparcieux, Nov. 29, 1753, ms. fr. 22152, no. 109.

55. Millet, July 16, 1756, ms. fr. 22138, no. 144.

56. Malesherbes explained his principle of tolerance and neutrality in a long letter to d'Alembert in which he refused to take action against the work of Elie-Catherine Fréron, the arch-enemy of the *philosophes*, because he did not want to restrict debate at the level of ideas. It is quoted in full in de Negroni, *Lectures interdites*, 60–61.

57. In his *Mémoires sur la librairie*, Malesherbes explained that in administering the censorship, he was guided by commitment to the free exchange of ideas, provided they did not attack the church, crown, morals, or individuals. See his "Second mémoire," in *Mémoires sur la librairie*, especially pp. 83–90.

58. Sénac to Malesherbes, undated, ms. fr. 22143, no. 36; Baron to Malesherbes, Dec. 31, 1755, ms. fr., 22143, no. 35.

59. Marcilly, Nov. 7, 1755, ms. fr. 22138, nos. 111 and 112.

60. Tanevot, Oct. 12, 1752, ms. fr. 22139, no. 141.

61. Unsigned and undated report on a *Histoire de la Rochelle* by M. Arcere, ms. fr. 22140, no. 16: "This work is dominated in general by an oratorical style that is at times very inflated, precious, and full of neologisms—one that does not correspond to the simple and noble manner in which history should be written. Although it is not the censor's job to rework the style of a book he examines, nevertheless there are some places where the expressions have seemed so extraordinary to me that I marked the main ones by pencil, and the author has promised to pay attention to them."

62. In rejecting a *Histoire de l'Opéra*, Moncrif explained to Malesherbes in a note of Aug. 18, 1751, ms. fr. 22138, no. 150, "I cannot approve it, and I beg you to name another examiner. I proposed several changes to the author, and he would not consent to them."

63. Moncrif, Nov. 4, 1755, ms. fr. 22138, no. 159. Moncrif found the eulogy of Louis XV in the prologue of a libretto to an opera, *Picus et Canente*, to be unsatisfactory. He informed the author, Rivoire de Terralbe, that he "would cut this prologue, and he accepted with good grace this innocent criticism on my part."

64. Malesherbes intervened to get a sympathetic censor to approve an almanac, "in order to be helpful to a poor devil": undated letter, ms. fr. 22141, no. 151. See also Moncrif's note to Malesherbes of April 1, 1751, ms. fr. 22138, no. 149, approving the manuscript of *Dialogues et fables allégoriques*: "This work, thanks to some cuts that I made, has nothing offensive to morals. That's the best I can say for it. Still, the author is without means. He is getting 300 livres for his fables. Please be good enough to grant him a tacit permission to have them printed. The poems in general are so bad and the subjects of the fables are usually so unsubstantial that it would be ridiculous to sign off on an approbation to the manuscript. But this book will disappear like so many others that are bad yet have readers." Claude-Prosper Jolyot de Crébillon, known as Crébillon fils, an important novelist as well as a censor, was particularly sympathetic in his treatment of authors, but he normally handled only *permissions de police* for short and ephemeral works. See the somewhat touched-up account of Crébillon's "audiences" by Louis-Sébastien Mercier in *Tableau de Paris*, vol. 1, pp. 804–8.

65. Foucher, Aug. 24, 1762, ms. fr. 22148, no. 110.

66. Foucher, Dec. 20, 1755, ms. fr. 22137, no. 98. Foucher explained to Malesherbes that the manuscript had come in two parts. As to the first, "I initialed it with pleasure. But the second brought me up short. In it I found various passages that I could not approve; and as the author decided he was not inclined to accept what I demanded, I returned his manuscript to him, saying that I would not approve it and that I no longer could take it upon myself to intervene with you for the permission that he desires."

67. Cotteret, Sept. 9, 1756, ms. fr. 22137, no. 57; Malesherbes to Salmon, May 23, 1760, ms. fr. 22148, no. 23.

68. Chevalier Du Plessis to Malesherbes, July 10, 1763, ms. fr. 22150, no. 131, complaining about his censor: "I offered to delete the verse that offended my energetic censor in order to have his approbation, thereby satisfying the condition for it as he had agreed. But this gentleman then pestered me further by saying that he did not want to approve the deletions and that I must soften more [passages that offended him]. I won't soften anything more. . . . I feel stung by this persecutor." See also Du Plessis to Malesherbes, undated, ms. fr. 22150, no. 132.

69. Author of a *Traité démonstratif de la quadrature du cercle* to Malesherbes, undated, ms. fr. 22138, no. 71.

70. Daniel Roche, "La Censure," in *Histoire de l'édition française : Le livre triomphant, 1660–1830* (Paris, 1984), vol. 2, p. 83.

71. See J.-P. Belin, *Le Commerce des livres prohibés à Paris de 1750 à 1789* (Paris, 1913); Robert Darnton, *The Forbidden Best-Sellers of Pre-Revolutionary France* (New York, 1995).

72. This concern, which appears everywhere in the archives of the Direction de la librairie and the Chambre syndicale de la Communauté des libraires et des imprimeurs de Paris, was made explicit by Malesherbes in his *Mémoires sur la librairie*, pp. 86 and 177. As an example of similar views held by the censors themselves, see Sallier to Malesherbes, Dec. 28, 1750, ms. fr. 22139, no 80. The censor argued that a moderate Protestant work should be given an informal *tolérance* on economic grounds: "Every day considerable sums of money are sent for the acquisition of books printed in Holland. If one tolerated works that did not openly attack morality or religion, one would, I believe, render a great service to the state."

73. Many of these exchanges are in a series "Rapports et décisions," in ms. fr. 22140, nos. 80–109. See also comte d'Argenson to Malesherbes, Feb. 11, 1755, ms. fr. 22140, no. 72; Machault to Malesherbes, July 19, 1756, ms. fr. 22143, no. 138; Malesherbes to the duc de Praslin, Jan. 3, 1763, ms. fr. 22144, no. 142; and Malesherbes to comte d'Argenson, undated, ms. fr. 22147, no. 54.

74. See the series of documents classified as "Acceptations et refus d'éloges et de dédicaces" in ms. fr. 22140, nos. 18–54.

75. Unsigned and undated report on *Mélanges philosophiques par M. Formey*, ms. fr. 22140, no. 3.

76. Undated note by Millet, ms. fr. 22140, in "Rapports et décisions."

77. In *Lectures interdites*, p. 195, Barbara Negroni estimates that of all books condemned by different varieties of post-publication censorship, 64 percent were related to Jansenism and 8 percent were philosophical works.

78. Ladvocat, Nov. 16, 1757, ms. fr. 22138, no. 33. A Protestant refutation of deism was acceptable to one censor: Millet, Nov. 6, 1758, ms. fr. 22138, no. 141. But another drew the line at Protestant works that argued for religious toleration: undated and unsigned rejection of *Questions sur la tolérance*, ms. fr. 22149, no. 121.

79. Depasse, Oct. 19, 1757, ms. fr. 22139, no. 12, on Jean-Henri-Samuel Formey's *Les Principes du droit naturel*: "There are are some principles about marriage which will have to be modified, but the author expresses himself in accordance with the doctrine received in his faith, and I do not think that what he says in this respect makes the reading of his book dangerous."

80. De Lorme, April 13, 1752, ms. fr. 22138, no. 61. An undated note on a memoir about a Jesuit's request to reprint *Réfutation d'un livre publié par feu M. l'évêque de Mirepoix sous le titre de Défense de la grâce efficace par elle-même* said that it had been refused, because "Monseigneur [i.e., the chancellor] does not consider it advisable to permit the publication of new books on this subject": ms. fr. 22140 in the file "Rapports et decisions," no. 80–109. It is difficult to specify the location of documents in this disorderly file.

81. Unsigned and undated memorandum by Rousselet, ms. fr. 22139, no. 70. In a note on a meeting of the censors dated Aug. 17, 1745 ("Rapports et décisions," unpaginated), the rejection of a manuscript concerning Jansenism was explained as follows: "These books serve only to heat up tempers."

82. Tamponnet, undated rejection of *Exposition des vérités chrétiennes et des moeurs de ce siècle*, ms. fr. 22139, no. 150: "The intention of the author is praiseworthy, but unfortunately his execution does not fulfill it. He wants to do battle with the deists. But he does so without any order, without principles, without diction. I consider his work useless, even harmful, because to produce a weak defense of religion is inadvertently to expose it."

83. Cotteret, May 26, 1751, ms. fr. 22137, no. 54. In refusing to approve a manuscript entitled *Théologie curieuse, ou questions recherchées extraites des Saintes Ecritures*, Cotteret remarked, "In it the author deals with questions concerning religion in a weak manner. His arguments are feeble and are not presented in a way that would enlighten the mind. Moreover, the work is badly written. I don't think it could produce any good." The abbé Le Rouge rejected *Exhortations sur l'Eucharistie* for the same reasons in a report of March 4, 1751, ms. 22138, no. 45: "It has no divisions into substantial sections, no order, no connections. Its [chapters] are stuffed with repetitive passages, which are irrelevant to their subject, and with trivial expressions, which are far below the grandeur of [religious] mystery. . . . One must not burden the public with useless works, which could be harmful to religion."

84. Moncrif, Nov. 4, 1755 ms. fr. 22138, no. 159. In an undated report, ibid., no. 162, Moncrif insisted on cutting passages of a book about French military victories, because it used unacceptable language in praise of the king.

85. Tercier, March 25, 1758, ms. fr. 22141, no. 2.

86. Salley, April 11, 1759, ms. fr. 22139, no. 94.

87. Malesherbes to the duc de Praslin, Jan. 3, 1763, ms. fr. 22144, no. 142.

88. Maréchal de Belle-Isle to Malesherbes, Aug. 25, 1760, ms. fr. 22147, no. 188.

89. Jean-Baptiste Machault d'Arnouville to Malesherbes, May 5, 1753, ms. fr. 22149, no. 110. In Aug. 1750 Machault tried to impose a "twentieth" tax that would fall on the nobility and clergy as well as commoners. This crucial attempt at reforming the tax system aroused enormous controversy and ultimately was defeated, owing primarily to opposition by the clergy.

90. An exceptional case was a tacit permission for a *Vie de Clément XI* recommended to Malesherbes by Rousselet, Dec. 23, 1751, ms. fr. 22139, no. 67, "In it the author has carefully avoided anything that could offend the parlement. . . . I have found only three small sections to be reworked."

91. Bonamy, Dec. 18, 1755, ms. fr. 22137, no. 23.

92. In an undated note to Malesherbes, ms. fr. 22141, no. 96, a censor named Lavaur rejected one volume in a *Bibliothèque amusante* "because of several anecdotes

that I consider contrary to good morals." Malesherbes assigned it to another censor, who then approved it.

93. De Passe, July 16, 1753, ms. fr. 22139, no. 9: "Several parts of this manuscript are indecent and grossly obscene without the slightest disguise. The rest of it, a ridiculous work of fiction, is full of reflections lacking all charm and utility. It must be by mockery that the author submitted to the censorship a work that, I believe, is as offensive to morality as it is poorly written and lacking in any intrinsic interest."

94. De La Haye, undated, ms. fr. 22138, no. 11.

95. Abbé Boudot, Sept. 10, 1754, ms. fr. 22137, no. 27.

96. Tercier, undated, ms. fr. 22144, no. 203.

97. Delagarde, Jan. 2, 1758, ms. fr. 22143, no. 93.

98. De Silhouette, May 5, 1753, ms. fr. 22140, no. 26.

99. Abbé Guiroy, apparently to Malesherbes's secretary, Oct. 25, 1751, ms. fr. 22137, no. 135.

100. Simon, Feb. 23, 1752, ms. fr. 22139, no. 128.

101. Malesherbes, *Mémoires sur la librairie*, 91–92. See the similar remarks on pp. 58, 101–2, and 206.

102. For example, in a report of Oct. 30, 1751, ms. fr. 22139, no. 69, Rousselet approved a novel, *Le Mot et la chose*, as follows: "Everything in it is sage and measured, and it seems to me that there are not any applications to be made concerning personages who are introduced in the plot and who could give rise to some complaints. Moreover, it is up to the author to respond to them, because I myself do not know anyone who could have had the adventures, whether true or false, recounted in the manuscript." For a discussion of the obsession with "applications" among the police, see "Vies privées et affaires publiques sous l'Ancien Régime" in my *Bohème littéraire et Révolution* (Paris, 2010), 113–34.

103. For a survey of all aspects relating to the production and control of books during the early modern era, see *Histoire de l'édition française*, ed. Roger Chartier and Henri-Jean Martin, 2 vols. (Paris, 1982–84).

104. Among the many accounts of the *De l'Esprit* affair, see especially Didier Ozanam, "La Disgrâce d'un premier commis: Tercier et l'affaire de *De l'Esprit* (1758–1759)," *Bibliothèque de l'Ecole des Chartes* 113 (1955), 140–70, and David W. Smith, *Helvétius: A Study in Persecution* (Oxford, 1965). Malesherbes expressed his views, stressing the Parlement's attempt to make inroads into the authority of the state, in *Mémoires sur la librairie*, 58–74.

105. On the general context of the time, see Dale Van Kley, *The Damiens Affair and the Unraveling of the Ancien Régime, 1750-1770* (Princeton, 1984).

106. Isambert, Jourdan, and Decrusy, *Recueil général des anciennes lois françaises* (Paris, 1821–33), vol. 22, pp. 272–74.

107. I have discussed the economic aspects of the successive editions of the *Encyclopédie* in *The Business of Enlightenment*, especially chaps. 2 and 7.

108. See, for example, his *Mémoires sur la librairie*, 85–86.

109. Malesherbes outlined his general view of the crisis surrounding *De l'Esprit* and the *Encyclopédie* in his *Mémoires sur la librairie*, "Premier Mémoire," pp. 57–74.

110. The most notorious affair that took place after 1759 was the publication of a Voltairean treatise, *De la Philosophie de la nature*, by J.-B.-C. Isoard, known as Delisle de Sales in 1770. Hoping to get a privilege, Delisle submitted the text to a sympathetic censor, abbé Chrétien, but they quarreled over Delisle's attempts to slip an unexpurgated version past him. Delisle managed to procure and to dupe a second censor, while writing supplementary volumes. In the end, the scandal led to a highly publicized polemic in which Chrétien justified his role as censor and denounced Delisle's deceptive maneuvers. The book was condemned by the General Assembly of the Clergy and by the Châtelet court, and it was burned by the public hangman in 1775. See Pierre Malandain, *Delisle de Sales philosophe de la nature (1741–1816)* (Oxford, 1982).

111. All these small towns had booksellers who corresponded with a Swiss publisher and wholesaler, the Société typographique de Neuchâtel, yet none of them appears in the *Almanach de la librairie* (Paris, 1781), which supposedly listed all the booksellers in France. For a discussion of the STN and its network of correspondents, see my *Forbidden Best-Sellers of Pre-Revolutionary France* and its companion volume, *The Corpus of Clandestine Literature in France, 1769–1789* (New York, 1995).

112. The information in this paragraph is drawn from the excellent work by Thierry Rigogne, *Between State and Market: Printing and Bookselling in Eighteenth-Century France* (Oxford, 2007), and from my research in the papers of the Société typographique de Neuchâtel in the Bibliothèque publique et universitaire of Neuchâtel, Switzerland.

113. For information about police raids, see *The Forbidden Best-Sellers of Pre-Revolutionary France* and also my *Edition et sédition: L'Univers de la littérature clandestine au XVIIIe siècle* (Paris, 1991), which contains a great deal of information that I have not published in English. I have discussed the literary police work of d'Hémery in "A Police Inspector Sorts His Files: The Anatomy of the Republic of Letters," in *The Great Cat Massacre and Other Episodes in French Cultural History* (New York, 1984).

114. Among contemporary accounts of the Parisian police, see Jean-Baptiste-Charles Le Maire, *La Police de Paris en 1770: Mémoire inédit composé par ordre de G. de Sartine sur la demande de Marie-Thérèse d'Autriche*, ed. Antoine Gazier (Paris, 1879); Nicolas de La Mare, *Traité de police, où l'on trouvera l'histoire de son établissement, les fonctions, et les prérogatives de ses magistrats . . .* (Amsterdam,

1729); and Jacques Peuchet, *Encyclopédie méthodique: Jurisprudence tome neuvième: Contenant la police et les municipalités* (Paris, 1789 and 1791).

115. The following account is based on a rich dossier in the archives of the Bastille: Bibliothèque de l'Arsenal, Archives de la Bastille, ms. 11582.

116. The following quotations come from the transcriptions of Mlle Bonafon's three interrogations: Ibid., folios 55–57, 79–80, and 115–16. As indicated in the text above, I have summarized parts of the dialogue (those not set off by quotation marks), but I have kept close to the original, which, like all interrogations, was written in the past tense: "Asked . . ."; "Answered that . . .", etc.

117. Ibid., fol. 20. I consulted the copy of the book in the Bibliothèque de l'Arsenal: *Tanastès: Conte allégorique par Mlle de xxx* (The Hague, 1745), 8 B.L. 19489, which includes a manuscript key to the names of the personages hidden behind the characters in the fairy tale.

118. Pierre-Auguste Goupil, inspector of the book trade, to Jean-Charles-Pierre Lenoir, lieutenant general of police, Dec. 14, 1774, Bibliothèque de l'Arsenal, Archives de la Bastille, ms. 12446. The following account is based on this exceptionally voluminous dossier.

119. Ibid.

120. Goupil to Lenoir, Jan. 18, 1775, ibid.

121. Ibid.

122. "Interrogatoire de la nommée Manichel dite la Marche à la Bastille," Jan. 27, 1775, ibid.

123. La Marche to Lenoir from the Bastille, Jan. 28, 1775, ibid.

124. Goupil to Lenoir, Jan. 25, 1775, ibid.

125. Chevalier, major de la Bastille, to Lenoir, Feb. 2, 1775, ibid.

126. For a detailed account of raids executed in Caen, Rouen, Alençon, and Saint Malo by Goupil's predecessor, Joseph d'Hémery, in April and May 1771, see Bibliothèque nationale de France, ms. fr. 22101.

127. "Procès verbal" of the raid by Goupil and Chénon, Feb. 20, 1775, Archives de la Bastille, ms. 12446.

128. "Procès verbal" of the raid by Goupil and Chénon, Feb. 23, 1775, ibid.

129. La Londe to Lenoir, Feb. 26, 1775, ibid.

130. See Desauges's letters to Walle, who supplied him with forbidden books, dated April 22, June 24, July 24, and Aug. 6, 1773. In a letter to Desauges of July 20, 1773, Walle said he had sent a shipment for Desauges to pick up at a secret entrepôt in the royal château of Saint-Germain-en-Laye. It contained 16 copies of *Histoire de dom B . . ., portier des Chartreux*, 148 copies of *La Putain errante*, and 148 copies of *L'Ecole des filles*, worth a total of 448 livres. All these documents are in the Archives de la Bastille, ms. 12446.

131. "Description des livres saisis sur le sieur Manoury," Feb. 25, 1775, ibid. (This document is full of holes, and its bottom section is missing, possibly because

of the trampling it received after the storming of the Bastille.) The last three works on the following list allude to the superior courts (*conseils supérieurs*) that Maupeou had installed in the judicial system designed to destroy the political power of the traditional parlements. Louis XVI restored the parlements after his accession to the throne in 1774.

132. Undated note by Joseph d'Hémery, Bibliothèque nationale de France, ms. fr. 22100, fol. 244.

133. D'Hémery's mission of 1771, which warrants a study in itself, is extensively documented in Bibliothèque nationale de France, ms. fr. 22101. Manoury referred to it and the losses it caused him in several letters to the Société typographique de Neuchâtel, notably those of Dec. 16, 1771, Sept. 27, 1778, and Nov. 26, 1781. He cited a different figure each time, however, and probably exaggerated the extent of his losses in order to demonstrate the underlying solidity of his business. In his letter of Nov. 26, 1781, he wrote, "In 1771 I showed that I had lost more than 40,000 livres, owing to the vexations of our Maupeou government." These letters, which contain a great deal of information about his affairs, can be found in Manoury's dossier in the archives of the Société typographique de Neuchâtel, Bibliothèque publique et universitaire de Neuchâtel.

134. Circular in Manoury to Mme l'Ecorché, Jan. 20, 1775, Archives de la Bastille, ms. 12446.

135. Gabriel Regnault to Manoury, Feb. 7, 1775, ibid.

136. Manoury's letters to the Société typographique de Neuchâtel are full of references to his dealings with booksellers in France and abroad. I have discussed this aspect of his business in my *Edition et sédition*, 98–104.

137. Le Baron to Manoury, March 22 and June 6, 1774, Archives de la Bastille, ms. 12446. Le Baron was a friend of Manoury's from Caen. After emigrating to London, he found employment in a printing shop that produced some of Beaumarchais's memoirs in his famous judicial affair with Louis-Valentin Goesman under the title *Mémoires pour servir à l'histoire du Parlement de Paris* and also the violent libel against Mme du Barry by Charles Théveau de Morande, *Mémoires secrets d'une femme publique*. Morande later destroyed the edition in return for a payment by the French government, which was negotiated by Beaumarchais.

138. Gabriel Regnault to Manoury, Feb. 7, 1775, ibid. The books Regnault mentioned were: *Traité des trois imposteurs*, a notorious irreligious work, which maligned Moses, Jesus, and Mohammed as the "three impostors"; *Histoire de dom B . . ., portier des Chartreux*, the pornographic and anticlerical bestseller; *Pensées théologiques relatives aux erreurs du temps*, an irreligious tract; *La Gazette de Cythère*, a scandalous libel against Mme du Barry, which Regnault reprinted under the title *Précis historique de la vie de Mme la comtesse du Barry*; *Maupeouana, ou correspondance secrète et familière de M. de Maupeou . . .*, an anthol-

ogy of essays against the Maupeou ministry; and *La Fille de joie*, a translation of John Cleland's *Memoirs of a Woman of Pleasure*.

139. Manoury to the Société typographique de Neuchâtel, Oct. 4, 1775, papers of the Société typographique de Neuchâtel, Bibliothèque publique et universitaire de Neuchâtel.

140. Batilliot l'aîné to the Société typographique de Neuchâtel, Nov. 7, 1777, ibid.

141. Desauges to Manoury, Jan. 11, 1775, Archives of the Bastille, ms. 12446. Even after the accession of Louis XVI, attacks on the Maupeou ministry, which was dissolved after the death of Louis XV on May 10, 1774, continued to sell widely and to be fiercely repressed by the police.

142. Desauges to Manoury, Jan. 15, 1775, ibid.

143. La Marche to her father, March 5, 1775, ibid. All of the letters in her dossier and in those of the other prisoners were never delivered to the intended recipients.

144. Goupil to Lenoir, Jan. 24 and 25, 1775, ibid.

145. Lenoir to La Vrillière, undated letter, ibid. La Vrillière forwarded it to the Bastille with a note in a margin, "I agree to this," and an official added, "Good, according to the order of 26 mars 1775." Although this case concerned a humble *bouquiniste*, it was followed by the king himself. On Jan. 26, 1775, the duc de La Vrillière, who was head of the King's Household (Maison du roi) and responsible for the Bastille, wrote to the lieutenant general of police Lenoir, "I reported to the king that the woman La Marche had been arrested. His Majesty strongly approved of this and desires that this affair be [actively] pursued and that, if possible, it can serve as an example."

146. Chevalier, major de la Bastille, to Lenoir, March 30, 1775, ibid.

147. Lenoir recounted the arrest and death of Goupil in a draft of a work that he intended to publish as his memoirs and that is among his papers in the Bibliothèque municipale d'Orléans, ms. 1422. I have discussed Goupil's career extensively in *The Devil in the Holy Water, or the Art of Slander from Louis XIV to Napoleon* (Philadelphia, 2010), chap. 9.

PART TWO

1. As an example of how liberalism and imperialism are described as distinct and virtually incompatible "isms," see the influential textbook by R. R. Palmer and Joel Colton, *A History of the Modern World*, 2nd ed. (New York, 1965), 432–33 and 615–22. In the case of the British Raj, I want to argue that they were inseparable aspects of the same phenomenon. This essay is based on long stints of research in the Oriental and India Office Collections of the British Library in 1994 and 1995. I would like to thank Graham Shaw for his hospitality and help during that period. Earlier versions of the essay were published as "Literary Surveillance in the British Raj: The Contradictions of Liberal Imperialism," *Book History* 4

(2001): 133–76, and "Book Production in British India, 1850–1900," *Book History* 5 (2002): 239–62. Among those who offered helpful criticism of early drafts, I would like to thank Gyan Prakash, Priya Joshi, Michael Katten, and Anindita Ghosh. I learned a great deal from Anindita Ghosh's excellent *Power in Print: Popular Publishing and the Politics of Language and Culture in a Colonial Society, 1778–1905* (New Delhi, 2006), which covers many of the themes discussed here. For a masterfly discussion of the relevant scholarship in the field of the history of the book, see Graham Shaw, "The History of Printing in South Asia: A Survey of Research since 1970," *Leipziger Jahrbuch zur Buchgeschichte* 7 (1997), 305–23.

2. See the classic article by Ranajit Guha, "The Prose of Counter-insurgency" in *Subaltern Studies*, ed. Ranajit Guha (Delhi, 1983).

3. James Long, "Returns Relating to the Publications in the Bengali Language in 1857, to Which Is Added a List of the Native Presses, with the Books Printed at Each, Their Price and Character, with a Notice of the Past Condition and Future Prospects of the Vernacular Press of Bengal, and the Statistics of the Bombay and Madras Vernacular Presses" (Calcutta, 1859), in Oriental and India Office Collections, British Library, V/23/97. All subsequent references are to these papers unless indicated otherwise. For information about Long, see the article on him in the Indian *Dictionary of National Biography* (Calcutta, 1973), vol. 2, pp. 416–17, and Geoffrey A. Oddie, *Missionaries, Rebellion and Proto-nationalism: James Long of Bengal, 1814–87* (London, 1999). His investigation of Bengali literature is discussed in Tapti Roy, "Disciplining the Printed Text: Colonial and Nationalist Surveillance of Bengali Literature," in *Texts of Power: Emerging Disciplines in Colonial Bengal*, ed. Partha Chatterjee (Minneapolis, 1995), 30–62.

4. Long, "Returns," vi.

5. Ibid., quotations from xii and xiv.

6. Ibid., xx–xxi.

7. Ibid., xlviii.

8. Ibid., xlix.

9. Ibid., xxvi.

10. Ibid., 31.

11. Ibid., xv.

12. Ibid., xiv.

13. Ibid., xv.

14. Donald Serrell Thomas, *A Long Time Burning: The History of Literary Censorship in England* (London, 1969), and *The Cambridge History of the Book in Britain*, vol. 5, *1695–1830*, ed. Michael F. Suarez, S.J., and Michael L. Turner (Cambridge, 2009), 128–29 and 834–36. Of course, after the passage of the Libel Act of 1792, the British authorities repressed a great deal of literature, which they considered dangerous and sympathetic to Jacobinism, but the Treasonable

and Seditious Practices Act of 1795 justified the repression of radical publications on the grounds of treason rather than seditious libel.

15. On John Wilkes and the radical agitation of the 1760s, see John Brewer, *Party Ideology and Popular Politics at the Ascension of George III* (Cambridge, 1976).

16. *Trial of the Rev. James Long, for the Publication of the Nil Darpan, with Documents Connected with Its Official Circulation* (London, 1861), India Office, W 977. On the *Nil Durpan* affair, see also "Tracts. Indigo, 143" and related documents scattered through V/23/95 in the archives of the India Office as well as *The History of the Nil Darpan, with the State Trial of J. Long* . . . (Calcutta, 1861), British Library 5318.c.4. The title of the drama is sometimes translated as *Nil Darpan*.

17. *Nil Durpan, or the Indigo Planting Mirror by Dinabandhu Mitra. Translated from the Bengali by a Native* (Calcutta, 1972), introd., xxxiv. For reasons of convenience, all citations are to this edition, which includes extensive reprints of documents from James Long's trial. The originals are in the archives of the India Office cited in the preceding note. For a persuasive interpretation of the play in relation to the peasant uprising of 1859–60, see Ranajit Guha, "Neel-Darpan: The Image of a Peasant Revolt in a Liberal Mirror," *Journal of Peasant Studies* 2 (Oct. 1974): 1–46.

18. As an example of the English disdain for the babu, which was heavily laced with racism, see the essay from *Vanity Fair* of 1880 reprinted as "H. E. The Bengali Baboo," in George R. Aberigh-Mackay, *Twenty-One Days in India* (London, 1914), 37–45.

19. *Nil Durpan*, 101.

20. Ibid., cvi.

21. The following account is based on the proceedings of the case, "Queen vs. Long," in the Supreme Court of Calcutta, printed in ibid., 103–86.

22. Ibid., 107.

23. Ibid., 113.

24. Ibid., 155.

25. Ibid., 167.

26. Michel Foucault, *Power/Knowledge: Selected Interviews and Other Writings, 1972–1977*, ed. Colin Gordon (New York, 1980), and Foucault, *Surveiller et punir: Naissance de la prison* (Paris, 1975). *Surveiller* has been mistranslated as "discipline" in the English translation of the latter: Foucault, *Discipline and Punish: The Birth of the Prison* (New York, 1995).

27. The following account cannot do justice to the complexities of the British Raj and the enormous literature about it. For an overview of the subject, see Stanley Wolpert, *A New History of India* (New York, 1993), and the older but more detailed work by Percival Spear, *The Oxford History of Modern India, 1740–1975* (Delhi, 1989). For more interpretive and conceptual approaches, see Ranajit Guha, *Elementary Aspects of Peasant Insurgency in Colonial India* (Delhi, 1994),

and *Selected Subaltern Studies*, eds. Ranajit Guha and Gayatri Chakravorty Spivak (New York, 1988).

28. C. A. Bayly, "Knowing the Country: Empire and Information in India," *Modern Asian Studies* 27 (1993): 3–43; C. A. Bayly, *An Empire of Information: Political Intelligence and Social Communication in North India, c. 1780–1880* (New York, 1997).

29. Although some historians dispute the role of the Enfield rifle cartridges in provoking the Sepoy Rebellion, there seems to be a consensus that they were an important factor, at least as a rumor. See Wolpert, *A New History of India*, 233–34, and Guha, *Elementary Aspects of Peasant Insurgency in Colonial India*, 262–63.

30. Of course, many agents of the Raj, especially among district officers, made great efforts to understand the people under their authority and sympathized with the lot of the poor. For a vivid account of the frustrations of a district officer with an impressive knowledge of Indian languages, see John Beames, *Memoirs of a Bengal Civilian* (London, 1984).

31. Bernard S. Cohn, "The Census, Social Structure and Objectification in South Asia" in Cohn, *An Anthropologist among the Historians and Other Essays* (Delhi and Oxford, 1987).

32. "An Act for the Regulation of Printing Presses and Newspapers, for the Preservation of Copies of Books Printed in British India, and for the Registration of Such Books," Act No. XXV of 1867 in India Office, V/8/40. The act was often referred to in the papers of the ICS as the "Press and Registration of Books Act."

33. *Bengal Library Catalogue of Books* (hereafter cited as BLCB), printed as an appendix to the *Calcutta Gazette*, second quarter, 1879, Z Y CH.

34. All quotations come from the BLCB for 1879, where they can be found under the titles of the books.

35. "Testimony of John Stuart Mill before the Select Committee of the House of Lords, 21 June 1852," *Parliamentary Papers, 1852–53*, vol. 30. On the liberal and utilitarian ingredients of British imperialism in India, see Ronald B. Inden, *Imagining India* (Oxford, 1990), and Eric Stokes, *The English Utilitarians and India* (Oxford, 1959).

36. For a fuller account of these complex topics, see standard histories, such as those mentioned in n. 26, and for more information on specific subjects, see monographs such as David Kopf, *British Orientalism and the Bengal Renaissance* (Berkeley, 1969), Sudhir Chandra, *The Oppressive Present: Literature and Social Consciousness in Colonial India* (Delhi, 1994), and Homi Bhabha, *The Location of Culture* (London, 1994).

37. The quotations, cited in the order of their appearance in the text, come from the BLCB for 1871, prepared by John Robinson, librarian at that time. They concern the following works, whose titles are given as transliterated and trans-

lated in the catalogue: *Brujeshwuree Kabuy*, or *Poem entitled Brujeshwuree*; *Rujuneekantu*, or *The Moon*; *Kabyukoosoom*, or *The Flower of Poesy*.

38. The Bengal catalogues, the most voluminous by far of those in all the presidencies, were published every quarter and signed by the librarians in their capacity of "Librarian of the Bengal Library and Keeper of the Catalogue of Books": John Robinson from 1867 to Oct. 1878 (except for brief periods when he was replaced by R. J. Ellis and Robert Robinson), William Lawler from Oct. 1878 to June 1879, Chunder Nath Bose from June 1879 to Oct. 1887, Haraprasad Shastri from Oct. 1887 to Jan. 1895, and Rajendra Chandra Sastri from Jan. 1895 to March 1907. The column of remarks was eliminated in 1901, and the format was simplified somewhat in 1902 and in 1905, when titles appeared in native characters instead of in transliteration.

39. *BLCB*, 1880. Owing to the lack of continuous pagination in the catalogues, quotations must be found following the title of the work in the volume for the appropriate year, in this case *Surendra-Binodini Nátak*. In some cases the references have "pro. nos." or progress numbers, which also are given.

40. The son of a government official in Raipur, Central Provinces, Harinath De had been educated at Raipur High School, Presidency College, Calcutta, and Christ's College, Cambridge, where he got a first class in the classical tripos, and a second in the tripos in medieval and modern languages. As librarian of the Imperial Library in Calcutta, his responsibilities extended over the entire Raj, and therefore, unlike the librarian of the Bengal Library, he did not prepare the catalogue of a particular presidency. See Oriental and India Office Collections, British Library, P/7587, pro. nos. 201 and 237–43.

41. *BLCB*, 1874.

42. *BLCB*, 1879: *Hita-shiksha*, or *Useful Instruction*.

43. *BLCB*, 1878. It may be, of course, that the book really was incoherent. The Indian librarians could be just as uninhibited as their British predecessors in expressing scorn for incomprehensible writing. Thus the remarks by Rajendra Chandra Sastri in the *BLCB* for 1900 on *Astray Siddhanta Chandrodaya Va Svarup Damodar Gosvamir Karcha*: "A metrical discourse on some of the most abstruse and esoteric doctrines of Vaishnavism. The work is full of unintelligible technicalities and mysticisms."

44. Sympathetic remarks about native medicine can be traced back to the *BLCB* of 1878, where John Robinson had nothing but praise for *Deshiya prakriti o chikitsa*, or *The Constitution and Medical System of the Country*: "The European system of medicine and treatment not adapted to the constitution of natives of the country. Reference is made to their being so tender about the spleen." On polygamy see the remarks on *Buhoobibahu Rahityarahityu Neernuyu*, or *A Determination of Whether Polygamy Ought to Be Abolished or Not*, in the *BLCB* of 1871. On religion, see the favorable review of *Krishna Bhakti Sar*, or *The Truths of the Devotion*

to Krishna, as contrasted with the condemnation of "idolatrous" Hindu devotion in *Assamya Larar Ditya Shikhya*, or *The Second Lesson Book for Assamese Children*, in the *BLCB* for 1874.

45. Remarks on *Moonlight of the Worship of the Goddess Kali*, BLCB, 1879.

46. BLCB, 1878. For remarks on the *Ramayana* and the *Vedanta*, see the reviews of *Nirbasita Seeta*, or *The Banished Seeta*, in the BLCB for 1871, and *Sriyukta Babu Srigopal Basu Malliker Phelosiper Lekchar*, or *Srigopal Basu Mallick's Fellowship Lectures*, and *Nigurha Atma-darsan*, or *Esoteric Self-Perception*, both in the BLCB for 1900.

47. As an example, see *Bhubudeb Puddhuti*, or *The Institutes of Bhubudeb*, in the BLCB for 1871. There is a vast amount of information on chapbook literature in the catalogues. Unlike its European counterparts, it has not, as far as I know, been studied, except in Anindita Ghosh, *Power in Print*.

48. BLCB, 1875.

49. Ibid.

50. *Rama-vanavas-natak*, or *The Residence of Rama in the Forest*, BLCB, 1879.

51. For example, the following remarks from the BLCB for 1900: "*Thakur-Jhi*, or *Father-in-Law's Daughter* . . . is a story of everyday life relating how a young man of good education and character named Hiralal was well nigh ruined by his drinking habit, and how his rescue and reformation were due to the self-sacrificing efforts of his sister. . . . A sincere devotion to her brother is the principal trait in her character, and it is this devotion which sustained Hiralal in his days of trial and adversity and ultimately reawakened his dormant moral nature."

52. Several of these crime thrillers published by the manufacturers of Kuntalin and Mohiya hair oil appear in the BLCB for 1908.

53. *Ranga Bau Va Sikshita Malila*, or *Beautiful Daughter-in-Law or the Education of a Lady*, BLCB, 1900.

54. See, for example, *Galpa-guchchha*, or *A Cluster of Stories*, in BLCB, 1900.

55. *Swarnalata* (a proper name), in BLCB, 1881.

56. *Paramartha Prasanga*, or *Discourses on the Highest Truth*, in BLCB, 1900.

57. The catalogue included a separate section for periodicals. In 1873 it welcomed the appearance of a new literary review, *Bangadarshan*, or *The Mirror of Bengal*, as follows: "A very superior literary magazine and review, both the editors and contributors being among the ablest of Bengali writers."

58. *Vina*, or *Lyre*, in BLCB, 1900.

59. The remarks on Vidyasagar's *Sankhya Darsan*, or *Sankhya Philosophy*, in the BLCB for 1900 indicate reservations about the attempt to mix Western ideas with traditional Indian philosophy: "It is an extremely interesting and original exposition of the principles of Sankhya Philosophy, based mainly on the aphorisms of Kapila and differing fundamentally from the views of standard authors on the subject. This attempt to look beyond the traditional interpretation and

to substitute in place of it views and ideas which are possibly suggested by the writings of European authors must always be looked upon with suspicion. . . . There is no denying that the book contains evidence of clear thinking, close reasoning and an honest and fearless devotion to truth, which is rarely met with in an equal degree in the writings of any other Bengali author of the present day. The writer's untimely death has been a great loss to Bengali literature."

60. *BLCB*, 1900.

61. Ibid.

62. Ibid. See also the comments in this catalogue on *Sachitra Gris Turaska-Yuddha,* or *Graeco-Turkish War with Illustrations,* and *Tetavatar Ramachandra,* or *Ramachandra, the Incarnation of the Treta Era.* Similar remarks can be found in the earlier catalogues, notably the one for 1878.

63. On the broadly political aspect of the vernacular literatures in nineteenth-century India, see Sudhir Chandra, *The Oppressive Present: Literature and Social Consciousness in Colonial India* (Delhi, 1994).

64. *Kavitavali,* or *Collection of Poems,* in *BLCB*, 1879.

65. See, for example, the remarks on *Jel Darpan Natak,* or *Mirror Depicting the Jail,* in *BLCB*, 1876: "The work commences with a dialogue between two of the principal actors in the case of the Guikwar of Baroda, in which unfavorable comments as to the action taken therein by Government. A little further on, and forming the main part of the book, the immunities permitted in the civil jail are contrasted with the heart-rending treatment by the jail authorities of prisoners in the criminal jail. The native doctor is depicted as kind and sympathetic, whilst the civil surgeons and the magistrates are, on the other hand, represented as heartlessly cruel, especially in flogging the prisoners. The drama comprises scenes in the Alipore, Jessore, Burdwan, Narail and Bankoora jails. The Jessore jail stands out most prominently in the cruel treatment of its prisoners, one of whom is represented as having died from the effects of the lashes administered to him whilst in prison." Other examples include *Baranabater Lukochuri,* or *Hide and Seek at Baranabat,* in *BLCB*, 1874; *Surendra-Binodini Natak* (proper names), in *BLCB*, 1875; and *Sharat Sarojini, Natak* (proper names), in *BLCB*, 1876.

66. *Cha-kar Darpan Natak,* or *The Mirror of a Tea Planter,* in *BLCB*, 1875: "This drama sets forth the dreadful oppressions and cruelties of the tea planters and their amlahs, and taunts the British government with efforts to do away with slavery in other lands, whilst in their own possessions such heart-rending scenes are practised."

67. *Sabhyata Sopan, Drishya Samajchitra,* or *Stepping Stone to Enlightenment,* in *BLCB*, 1878.

68. Some typical examples from the *BLCB* of 1876: *Dasatwa-shrinkhala,* or *The Bonds of Slavery:* "Describes the bondage of the people of India, whose acts

and wills are made subservient to the orders of others." *Manihara-phani Barat janani*, or *Our Mother India is like the Serpent Who Has Lost Its Wonderful Jewel*: "Describes the growing ills of India since it passed into the hands of foreigners." *Gyandipika*, or *The Light of Knowledge*: "Discourse on the law and administration of the country, pointing out existing defects."

69. *Ingraj Goonu Burnun*, or *A Description of the Virtues of the English*, in BLCB, 1871. See also *Satik Pauchali*, or *Metrical Verses*, in BLCB, 1876, which praised the British "for the introduction of the telegraph, the steam boat, the railway, the administration of justice, etc."

70. *Rajputra*, or *The Prince*, in BLCB, 1876. On the anti-Mughal view of Indian history, see *Bharathe Jaban*, or *The Mohammedans in India*, in BLCB, 1874: "The tyrannical acts of the Mohammedans during their rule in India—killing cows and Brahmins and violating the chastity of women, till the English came to the rescue of India."

71. *Inraj Pratibha*, or *Genius of the English*, in BLCB, 1910.

72. *Bharat Kahini*, or *The Story of India*, in BLCB, 1900: "They [the Indians] must be true to the cardinal principles of their religion and set their faces against imitating the mere forms, without spirit, of western civilization and avoid ultra radicalism in the matter of social and religious reform. The Congress movement is no doubt a good thing, but mere political agitation can not save the country. Let the people work more and talk less, and they will rise in the estimation of government. The book is written in an excellent spirit and freely acknowledges the benefit of British rule."

73. See, for example, *Daiva-lata*, or *Creeper of Providence*, in BLCB, 1879: "The writer . . . praises the English for their just administration and hopes that they will long continue to rule the country and that all India should be grateful for the benefits received from English rule." Not surprisingly, this theme also appeared in works written in English, such as *High Education in India*, in BLCB, 1878.

74. BLCB, 1879.

75. Thus *Sarat-Sashi* (a proper name) as described in the BLCB for 1881: "The hero is a young Bengali *Babu*, who knows English, has shaken off the bonds of caste and superstition, is full of patriotic fire, is a practical philanthropist, exposes official corruption and wickedness, writes articles in newspapers, hates tyranny and oppression of all kinds, is in short the author's ideal of what educated Bengalis should be."

76. *Is This Called Civilization?*, a Bengali drama translated into English: BLCB, 1871.

77. In reviewing *Kajer Khatam*, or *The End of the Business*, "a farce written in defense of native theatres," the librarian noted in the BLCB of 1900, "The affectation of Anglicism by 'England-returned' gentlemen forms, as usual, one of the staple topics of ridicule."

78. For example, *Bharat-uddhara, athaba chari-ana matra*, or *The Deliverance of India, or Four Annas Only*, in BLCB, 1878: "The writer ridicules the military aspirations of the so-called educated Bengalis, who, though entirely devoid of courage and strength, are impatient of the abject condition of their country, and always in their speeches express their desire to rid it of foreign domination. . . . The writer refers throughout to the habits of drinking, the timidity, inaptitude for action, and love of speechifying, and the utter shallowness which characterize Bengalis."

79. *Bharat-Ishwari*, or *The Empress of India*, in BLCB, 1877.

80. For example, *Sukhamukur Kavya*, or *The Mirror of Happiness*, in BLCB, 1878: "The present weak and degraded condition of the descendants of the Aryan race, their subjection to a foreign power, and their habits of intemperance are all described in language of some force." See also in the BLCB of 1878: *Manas Kusum*, or *The Flowers of Fancy*, and *Bharate dukh*, or *India in Distress*.

81. *Aryua Jati*, or *The Aryan Race*, in BLCB, 1900: "The influence of Western education on Hindu Society of the present day is pronounced to be distinctly harmful, and the establishment of a Hindu religious association is advocated as a means of combating that influence and fostering a spirit of nationality and brotherhood among the different sections of the Hindus."

82. *Kavi-kahini*, or *Narrations by a Poet*, BLCB, 1876. See also *Swadeshanurag-uddipak Sangita*, or *Songs Stimulating Patriotism*, BLCB, 1878.

83. "Literary Surveillance in the British Raj," 147–49, and "Book Production in British India," 248–62, cited above, in n. 1.

84. Ibid., section on Bengal. Until 1890, publishers received payment for the copies that they deposited for registration in the catalogues. After 1890, the keepers of the catalogues noted an increased tendency to avoid registration, even though it was a legal requirement. Nevertheless, overall book production, as measured by the catalogues, rose constantly throughout the nineteenth century. The exception was 1898, when the cataloguers estimated that production had decreased by almost 5 percent as a consequence of the plague of 1897. I have compiled statistics from the "Report on Publications" of 1878 for the presidencies of Madras, Bombay, Bengal, and the Northwestern Provinces with Oudh. They show a total output of 3,847 titles, as compared with 5,322 titles for 1898. Taken together, those four regions account for the dominant proportion of book production in all of India. There are no statistics for the entire subcontinent, but I would consider 200,000 titles to be a modest estimate of the total output for the nineteenth century.

85. "Publications Registered at Curator's Office, Allahabad during the Year 1869," in "Selections from the Records of Government, North-Western Provinces" (1870), V/23/129.

86. The reports from 1874 illustrate the same complacent and condescending attitude among British authorities in different parts of the subcontinent: "Reports

on Publications Issued and Registered in the Several Provinces of British India during the Year 1874," V/23/28. The report from Oudh (the old colonial spelling of Avadh) stated flatly that almost no literature existed outside the traditional genres of religion and poetry. The report from the Northwestern Provinces (roughly Uttar Pradesh and Uttarancha today) found little, except for school-books. The reports from Mysore and Coorg noted nothing of interest aside from booklets written for a regional variety of street theater. And the report from the Punjab concluded bluntly, "No literary work of any importance has appeared during the year." No one complained of political agitation. The Madras report noted, "The column of Politics is altogether bare this year, owing probably to the very quiet times in which we live." And the report from Bombay found nothing to deplore other than two indecent Urdu prints: "The general tone of the publications under review was unobjectionable as regards morality and loyalty." In 1870 the report from the Northwestern Provinces concluded, "As yet the intellectual culture amounts to little else than patchwork clearances in the jungle": "Publications Received at Curator's Office, Allahabad during the Year 1870," V/23/129.

87. The authorities seem to have been fairly vigilant about the import of seditious literature during the nationalist agitation of the early twentieth century, as indicated in the "confidential" political papers of the Home Department Pro- ceedings of the Government of India: P/7587, P/7590, P/7875, P/8153, P/8430, P/8431. But a careful reading of those papers turned up relatively few cases involving sedition as the British understood it. In Nov. 1906, for example, the police confiscated three boxes of books and periodicals that had been shipped from Cairo to M. A. Jetekar, a bookseller in Bendi Bazaar, Bom- bay. Most of the books were Arabic treatises on religion and law, but one of the journal articles called upon the Egyptians to overthrow their British conquerors. Jetekar was judged to be a "respectable" dealer during his inter- rogation and was released after promising to cancel his subscription to the periodical: P/7587, pro. no. 258. In 1908, Bombay officials received special authority to intercept the mail in order to confiscate copies of a book on the Rebellion of 1857 by V. D. Savarkar: P/8153, pro. nos. 23–27. In 1909 the French authorities in Pondicherry offered to cooperate with the British but tolerated the printing of journals like *India*, which had moved to their territory from Madras. Judging from the confidential correspondence in the India Office, the French enjoyed lecturing the British on "the limits permit- ted by the French legislature on the subject of the liberty of the press": Minto to Morley, April 1, 1809, P/8153, pro. nos. 44–52. But the correspondence does not suggest that Pondicherry functioned as a source of forbidden books in a manner comparable to Amsterdam and Geneva in eighteenth-century Europe.

88. In 1878 the British imposed restrictions on the vernacular press by a "gagging act" (the Vernacular Press Act), which was intended to stifle criticism of the Second Afghan War. It set off vehement protests among the Indians, because it suggested that freedom of the press existed only on one side of the line that divided Britons from "natives." But the act was repealed in 1880, when Lord Ripon succeeded Lord Lytton as viceroy in Calcutta and Gladstone replaced Disraeli as prime minister in London.

89. This account is based primarily on the documents in the Oriental and India Office Collections of the British Library, but it also draws on Sumit Sarkar, *The Swadeshi Movement in Bengal, 1903–1908* (New Delhi, 1973), and Peter van der Veer, *Religious Nationalism: Hindus and Muslims in India* (Berkeley, 1994), as well as on standard histories of India.

90. Dispatch of Denzil Ibbetson, April 30, 1907, P/7590, pro. no. 183: "The Punjabi is no doubt less hysterical than the Bengali. But he is not exempt from the defects of the East. Credulous to a degree which is difficult for us to understand, traditionally disposed to believe evil of his government, difficult to arouse, perhaps, but emotional and inflammable when once aroused, he affords ground admirably adapted to the purposes of the political agitator."

91. Dispatch of Sir Herbert White, Aug. 1, 1907, P/7590, pro. no. 69.

92. Dispatch of H. J. Stanyon, July 28, 1907, P/7590, pro. no. 71.

93. Dispatch of the Commissioner of the Nagpur Division, Aug. 7, 1907, P/7590, pro. no. 71.

94. See the dispatches from the Northwestern Frontier Province, July 29, 1907, P/7590, pro. no. 72; from Eastern Bengal and Assam, March 24, 1908, P/7875, pro. no. 24; and from Mysore, Sept. 1, 1909, P/8430, pro. no. 65.

95. Minto to Morley, July 11, 1907, P/7590, pro. no. 31: "Nothing can be further from our intentions or more opposed to the spirit of our general policy than to interfere in any way with the legitimate functions of the press. But when the public safety is in danger, we claim for the executive government the right to intervene. . . . Here is no question of the liberty of the press. The object is simply to stir up disaffection."

96. Cotton penetrated the weak points in Morley's policy so effectively that Morley came to dread his questions and requested information from India that would provide some protection: Morley to Minto, July 5, 1907, P/7590, pro. no. 31; Morley to Minto, April 25, 1910, P/8430, pro. no. 55. See also the related information in the dispatches of July 29, Oct. 22, and Dec. 17, 1908: P/8153, pro. nos. 15, 21, and 36; and the published version of the Minto-Morley correspondence: *India, Minto and Morley, 1905–1910; Compiled from the Correspondence between the Viceroy and the Secretary of State by Mary, Countess of Minto* (London, 1935).

97. See the reports on the raid in Calcutta of May 2, 1908, in P/7875, pp. 625 and 971.

98. Dispatch from the government of Bombay, July 30, 1909, P/8430, pro. no. 65.

99. Dispatch from the viceroy's office, June 17, 1910, P/8431, pro. no. 159.

100. P/7875, pro. no. 95. The government also refused to allow the import of a translation of an essay by Tolstoy, *Ek Hindu pratye Mahan Tolstoy no Kagal*, or *Great Tolstoy's Letter to a Hindu*, which the young M. K. Gandhi produced as a pamphlet in South Africa. In describing Gandhi, a translator for the government of Bengal warned, "Though he pretends to be a lover of peace and a thorough passive resister, he evidently wants to drive the English out of India, and freely gives utterance to sentiments which are not calculated to teach peace and good will towards the ruling nation": P/18431, pro. no. 69. The police later confiscated a copy of Gandhi's Gujurati pamphlet *Hind Swaraj*, or *Indian Home Rule*. He reacted by sending an English translation to the Government of India, "entirely to assist it. This in no way means that I necessarily approve of any or all the actions of the Government, or the methods on which it is based. In my humble opinion, every man has a right to hold any opinion he chooses, and to give effect to it also, so long as, in doing so, he does not use physical violence": Gandhi to the Government of India, April 16, 1910, P/8431, pro. no. 96.

101. Dispatch of M. W. Fenton in the Punjab, June 11, 1909, P/8153, pro. no. 145.

102. Reports on seditious literature in the Punjab, May–July, 1909, P/ 8153, pro. nos. 145–53.

103. See the cases in P/8431, pro. nos. 117–34 and P/8153, pro. nos. 89–94.

104. The key text in Section 124A, chap. 6, p. 424, of the Indian Penal Code of 1860, reads as follows: "Whoever by words, either spoken or intended to be read, or by signs, or by visible representation or otherwise, excites or attempts to excite feelings of disaffection to the Government established by law in British India, shall be punished with transportation for life or for any term, to which fine may be added . . .": V/8/319. An "Explanation," which followed, attempted, not very successfully, to make clear that disaffection "is not the expression of disapprobation of Government measures by one disposed to be obedient to its authority." In a separate section, pp. 292–93, which had nothing to do with sedition, the code forbade the sale of obscene books and prints.

105. The documentation concerning both Tilak cases was reproduced in *Law Relating to Press and Sedition*, the compilation prepared for the government by G. K. Roy in 1915: V5597. In the first case, the judge construed "disaffection" in a broad way, despite the defense argument that the term was impossibly vague.

106. "Indian Penal Code Amendment Act, 1898," ibid., p. 11. This law also added a new section, 153A, which provided severe punishment for anyone "who promotes or attempts to promote feelings of enmity or hatred between different classes of Her Majesty's subjects." Although intended primarily to prevent hostility between Hindus and Muslims, Section 153A was later used to punish insulting remarks by Indians against Britons.

107. "Indian Press Act of 1910," ibid., p. 45.

108. For the texts of the Dramatic Performances Act and the Newspapers Act, see ibid., pp. 8–10 and 35–38.

109. The text of the poem and the documentation from the case, including the quotations cited below, come from P/8431, pro. nos. 144–64.

110. R. Nathan to Government of East Bengal and Assam, July, 1907: report on disturbances in Mymensingh District, April–May, 1907, P/7590, pro. no. 58.

111. The following account, including all quotations, comes from P/7875, pro. nos. 42–44.

112. P/8153, pro. nos. 110–17.

113. The text and the following account of the two cases comes from P/8153, pro. nos. 112–31.

114. These are Justice Strachey's words as quoted by T. Thornhill, a magistrate in Calcutta, on Feb. 23, 1909, while condemning Babu Kiran Chandra Mukerjee to eighteen months in prison for writing a book entitled *Pantha* in Bengali: P/8153, pro. nos. 89–94. Like many other magistrates, Thornhill had to sort out a good deal of Vedic mythology, but he found it easy to reach a verdict: "I can have no difficulty in coming to the conclusion that the booklet was written and published with the intention of bringing into hatred and contempt and exciting disaffection towards the Government in India."

115. The case involved the publication of another songbook, *Bande Mataram Sangit*, compiled by Ramani Mohan Das, who was declared guilty of violating Section 124A on May 19, 1909: P/8153, pro. nos. 43–47.

116. P/8153, pro. nos. 110–17.

117. P/8431, pro. nos. 60–65.

118. This and the following quotations come from the proceedings of the trial, P/8153, pro. nos. 112–31.

119. P/8153, pro. no. 142.

120. Ibid. and, for similar reports from ICS agents, P/8153, pro. nos. 135–47.

121. P/8153, pro. nos. 112, 115, and 142.

122. P/8430, pro. no. 103.

PART THREE

1. I published a general account of the fall of the Berlin Wall and the collapse of East Germany as *Berlin Journal, 1989–1990* (New York, 1991). Part 3, pp. 193–217, includes my interviews with the censors and reports on writers and literary institutions. An early version of my interview with the censors appeared as "Aus der Sicht des Zensors: Von der Überwachung der Literatur" in *Lettre Internationale* 3, no. 10 (Autumn 1990): 6–9. Throughout this book, I will refer to the German Democratic Republic by its usual English acronym, the GDR,

and to the Federal Republic of Germany as the FRG. Because it had been forci-
bly united with the Social Democratic Party in 1946, the Communist Party was
formally known as the Socialist Unity Party of Germany (Sozialistische Einheitspartei Deutschlands, or SED). I will generally refer to it as the Communist
Party and will occasionally use the common acronym SED.

2. See Theodor Constantin, *Plaste und Elaste: Ein deutsch-deutsches Wörterbuch*
   (Berlin, 1988), 27 and 67.

3. The publishing houses are listed in the official GDR directory *Verlage der
   Deutschen Demokratischen Republik* (Leipzig, 1988).

4. *Zensur in der DDR: Geschichte, Praxis und "Ästhetik" der Behinderung von Literatur*, ed. Ernest Wichner and Herbert Wiesner (Berlin, 1991), 53.

5. Ibid., 75 and 81.

6. See especially Wichner and Wiesner, *Zensur in der DDR* and the other volume
   they edited, *"Literaturentwicklungsprozesse": Die Zensur in der DDR*, ed. Ernest
   Wichner and Herbert Wiesner (Frankfurt am Main, 1993); Siegfried Lokatis,
   "Verlagspolitik zwischen Plan und Zensur: Das 'Amt für Literatur und Verlag-
   swesen' oder die schwere Geburt des Literaturapparates der DDR," *Historische
   DDR-Forschung: Aufsätze und Studien*, ed. Jürgen Kocka (Berlin, 1993); Simone
   Barck and Siegfried Lokatis, *"Jedes Buch ein Abenteuer": Zensur-System und literarische Öffentlichkeiten in der DDR bis Ende der sechziger Jahre* (Berlin, 1997);
   Simone Barck and Siegfried Lokatis, *Zensurspiele: Heimliche Literaturgeschichten
   aus der DDR* (Halle, 2008); and *Das Loch in der Mauer: Der innerdeutsche Lit-
   eraturaustausch*, ed. Mark Lehmstedt and Siegfried Lokatis (Wiesbaden, 1997).
   This essay concerns only the censorship of books and literary institutions, not
   the press and other media.

7. "Protokoll der Sektorenleiterberatung vom 1-/12/84," Abteilung Kultur, ms.
   32704, Archiv der Parteien und Massenorganisationen der DDR. The following
   discussion is based on these extensive archives, which were produced within the
   Central Committee of the Communist (SED) Party, especially by the office of
   Kurt Hager ("Büro Hager") and the Culture Division ("Abteilung Kultur").

8. Ragwitz to Hager, Nov. 11, 1981, and Oct. 11, 1981, ms. 34935.

9. Ragwitz to Hager, July 7, 1983, ms. 34870. The statistics referred only to GDR fiction categorized under belles-lettres. The *Verlage der Deutschen Demokratischen
   Republik* set the total number of titles produced in 1985 at 6,471, with a total
   of 144,600,000 copies. The round figures it gave for 1988 were 6,500 titles and
   150,000,000 copies. Estimating output as more than eight books per person, it
   claimed that the GDR was one of the leaders worldwide in book production.

10. Ragwitz's bureaucratic style is particularly apparent in a memo that she sent to
    Hager on April 18, 1983, entitled "Information zu aktuellen Fragen des thema-
    tischen Plans für die Buchproduktion 1983," ms. 34870.

11. For basic biographical information about public figures in the GDR, including many authors, see *Wer War Wer in der DDR* (Berlin, 2010).

12. Ragwitz to Hager, March 1, 1982, ms. 32709.

13. Another example of informal exchange is a note from Ragwitz to Hager dated April 16, 1984, ms. 32709. It mentioned difficulties that had developed with Christa Wolf, the GDR's best-known author, criticism of the literary review *Sinn und Form*, the need to prevent public discussion of the sensitive subject of requests for travel outside the GDR, and problems with disaffected young authors.

14. Protokoll der Sektorenleiterberatung, March 28, 1984, ms. 32704.

15. Protokoll der Sektorenleiterberatung, Feb. 6, 1984, ms. 32704.

16. Protokoll der Sektorenleiterberatung, April 23, 1984, ms. 32704. See also the Protokoll of May 22, 1984, ms. 32704.

17. "Notiz. Arbeitsbesprechung des Genossen Hager mit Genossin Ursula Ragwitz und Genossen Hans-Joachim Hoffmann am 24-11-82," ms. 42325.

18. Report on a meeting of Hager and Höpcke, Feb. 18, 1988, ms. 42325.

19. Ibid.

20. Höpcke to Hager, Oct. 31, 1983, ms. 30344. Monika Maron implored Hager to grant her permission to travel to the West in a distraught letter dated Feb. 23, 1983, ms. 33512.

21. Höpcke to Hager, Oct. 31, 1983, Oct. 6, 1983, and Oct. 10, 1983, ms 30344. In his long and detailed letter of Oct. 31, Höpcke informed Hager about a wide variety of literary matters so that Hager could consider them before a meeting in which he and Höpcke would reach strategic decisions. Höpcke began the letter with a general statement that typified the way literature was discussed at the highest level of the GDR: "I have given much thought to the experience of reading recent GDR literature from the perspective of ideology and worldview, and I could . . . present some reflections about it." He then discussed delicate questions, such as how to deal with the eminent dissident author Stefan Heym, who published works in the FRG without permission from the authorities of the GDR: "The publishing house Der Morgen has in its possession a manuscript of a novel entitled *Schwarzenberg*. As suggested by the accompanying reviews of comrades in the belles-lettres section of the HV, a publication [of the novel] in our republic is out of the question; it is not even sensible to have a discussion of this with the author. For this is a matter of anti-Sovietism, falsifying the history of certain episodes in the region around Schwarzenberg, which in 1945 was temporarily unoccupied by either the Soviet or U.S. troops."

22. Höpcke to Hager, Oct. 10, 1983, and an undated "Notiz" by Höpcke about his meeting with Hilbig on Oct. 6, 1983, ms. 30344.

23. Höpcke to Hager, Oct. 31, 1983, ms. 30344. A few months earlier, the authorities had refused Braun's request that he be permitted to receive *Die Zeit*. Höpcke proposed rescinding that decision, even though he expected some Party members to object.

24. See, for example, the list and accompanying dossiers filed under the heading "Eingaben, 1985," ms. 42258.

25. Walter Vogt, first secretary of the Verband der Theaterschaffenden der DDR in Berlin to Peter Heldt, undated, ms. 36835/1.

26. Erika Hinkel memorandum to Hager, Dec. 20, 1973, ms. 36835/1.

27. Kirsch to Oberbürgermeister Kraak, March 18, 1975, copy of a letter included in Kirsch to Erika Hinkel, March 18, 1975, ms. 36835/1.

28. Kirsch to Hager, Dec. 31, 1984, and Ragwitz to Hager, Feb. 27, 1985, ms 36835/1. In a letter to Hager of March 3, 1987, ms. 36835/1, Hermann Axen, a member of the Politburo, protested against some poems that Kirsch had recently published in *Neue Deutsche Literatur*, the literary review of the Authors Union: "Some of these 'poems' contain, in my opinion, unmistakably direct attacks on and disparagement of our state and our leadership. . . . Must one publish these attacks in the journal of the Authors Union and then in the Eulenspiegel Press?"

29. Ragwitz to Hager, March 23, 1983, with a report on Hilbig and his volume of poetry, *Stimme, Stimme*, dated Dec. 14, 1982, ms. 38787.

30. Memo to Hager from the Culture Division of the Party's Central Committee, Jan. 12, 1984, ms. 38787.

31. Memo to Hager by Ragwitz, Dec. 14, 1982, ms. 38787.

32. For example, in her report on Hilbig to Hager of March 23, 1983, ms. 38787, Ragwitz said that the Reclam publishing house had been warned that it should not accept a revised version of *Stimme, Stimme* that included "expressions against real socialism."

33. In 1976 the Party had issued a "severe reprimand" to Hermlin for his role in the Biermann affair. On March 20, 1985, Hermann Kant, the president of the Authors Union, wrote to Honecker, suggesting that they revoke that sanction, since Hermlin had been steadfast in defending GDR policies for the past nine years, but he recommended that they do so without any debate in the executive board of the union so as to avoid opening old wounds. Ms. 36835.

34. Hermlin to Hager, March 17, 1983, ms. 38787.

35. Ragwitz to Hager, March 23, 1983, ms. 38787.

36. Höpcke to Hager, March 6, 1985, ms. 38787.

37. Hager to Hoffmann, Aug. 8, 1985, ms. 36835/1. Earlier in 1985, Hilbig had run into further difficulties with Reclam, his East German publisher, concerning *Der Brief*, a collection of his prose writings, and he had had it published without permission by Fischer in the FRG.

38. Hermlin to Honecker, Oct. 19, 1985, ms. 36835/1.
39. Hilbig to Honecker, Aug. 26, 1985, ms. 36835/1.
40. Hager to Hoffmann, Oct. 17, 1985, ms. 36835/1. In a letter to Hager of Sept. 22, 1985, Hoffmann recommended granting the visa, even though Hilbig had published *Der Brief* without permission in the FRG and even though "the content of the text shows that Hilbig until now is not capable of making his literary activities agree with the cultural-political expectations of the GDR."
41. See, for example, the hostile report on Volker Braun's *Hinze-Kunze-Roman*, which Ragwitz sent to Hager on Sept. 9, 1985, quoted below, in n. 150.
42. The term crops up in several of the letters that were addressed to Hager from the general public and that were collected in three dossiers labeled "Standpunkte, Meinungen . . . aus der Bevölkerung," 1987–89, ms. 42280/1, 42280/2, and 42280/3. One of the poems that the HV insisted on deleting from Volker Braun's *Wir und nicht sie* was entitled "Die Mauer." Unsigned report to Hager from the HV, Feb. 15, 1971, ms 36834/1.
43. Ragwitz to Hager, Dec. 23, 1981, which includes the letter of protest, dated Dec. 20, 1981, ms. 32747. The Culture Division of the Party's Central Committee produced a long report on the Anthology and its authors dated Oct. 1, 1981, and it also produced three memoranda recommending measures to be taken. These documents were filed together in ms. 32747.
44. Quotation from an unsigned and undated memorandum from Kultur filed with the documents in ms. 32747.
45. "Conception of a future policy regarding the authors who wish to produce a volume sponsored by the Academy of Arts (as a kind of anthology)," an unsigned memorandum from the Culture Division of the Party's Central Committee, Nov. 6, 1981, ms. 32746.
46. Unsigned report on the Anthology group from the Culture Division of the Party's Central Committee, dated Jan. 27, 1982, ms. 32746.
47. "Information zum Literaturgespräch am 29-10-81," an unsigned report filed with the Anthology documents in ms. 32747.
48. "Conception of a future policy," cited above, n. 45. This memorandum contained similar descriptions of thirty authors connected with the Anthology.
49. The best-documented among the many accounts of Anderson's spying is Joachim Walther, *Sicherungsbereich Literatur: Schriftsteller und Staatssicherheit in der Deutschen Demokratischen Republik* (Berlin, 1996), 639–42.
50. Ragwitz to Honecker, April 3, 1981, ms. 32747.
51. Unsigned memorandum by the Culture Division of the Party's Central Committee, June 29, 1981, ms. 32747. Ragwitz drafted a reply for a rebuttal of the Western broadcasts, which was to be issued in Honecker's name: Ragwitz to Hager April 6, 1981, ms. 32747.

52. Ragwitz to Hager, Dec. 9, 1982, with an accompanying report, ms. 32746.

53. Memorandum of the Culture Division of the Party's Central Committee, Nov. 12, 1982, ms. 32746. This memorandum, clearly intended for Hager and the leading members of the Party, gave a thoughtful but dogmatic diagnosis of GDR literature, its problems, and its relations to the needs of East German readers. In analyzing recent difficulties with writers, it noted, "The authors' insufficient Marxist-Leninist education and very narrowly limited connections to socialist reality are often the reason that the critical element predominates and ultimately works in a destructive manner. Complicated formulations arise in which the authors' explicit commitment to the GDR is linked with views that are alien to socialism, for example petit bourgeois notions of humanism or subjectivism concerning the relation between the ideal and reality."

54. "Conception of a future policy," cited above, n. 45.

55. Memorandum of the Culture Division of the Party's Central Committee, untitled and also dated Nov. 6, 1981, ms. 32746. The "Literaturzentren" were established and usually attracted from eight to fifty members, but they did not seem to be very effective, according to a report by the Culture Division of the Party's Central Committee dated Oct. 12, 1982, ms. 32746.

56. These measures are described in an undated memorandum from Ragwitz to Hager, ms. 32747.

57. This remark, dated June 20, 1983, comes from a handout with excerpts from Braun's notebooks that was distributed at a lecture he gave in Berlin on March 1, 1994.

58. For the wide range of fiction, poetry, essays, "proletarian-revolutionary belles-lettres," light literature, and other genres published by the Mitteldeutscher Verlag, which was the most important publisher of GDR fiction in the 1980s, see *Verlage der Deutschen Democratischen Republik*, 45.

59. Erich Loest, *Der Zorn des Schafes* (Munich, 1993 ed.), 38 and 229.

60. Erich Loest, *Der vierte Zensor: Der Roman "Es geht seinen Gang" und die Dunkelmänner* (Stuttgart, 2003), 30.

61. *Die Schere im Kopf: Über Zensur u. Selbstzensur*, ed. Henryk M. Broder (Cologne, 1976).

62. This is the interpretation of Manfred Jäger in *"Literaturentwicklungsprozesse,"* 28–47. See also the remarks on self-censorship by Christoph Hein in his demand for the abolition of censorship at the congress of the Authors Union in 1987: X. *Schriftstellerkongress der Deutschen Demokratischen Republik: Arbeitsgruppen* (Berlin, 1987), 229. Looking back on his experience before the collapse of the GDR, Uwe Kolbe remarked, "Self-censorship is the actual, the all-mighty censorship": *Fragebogen: Zensur. Zur Literatur vor und nach dem Ende der DDR*, ed. Richard Zipser (Leipzig, 1995), 225.

63. Joachim Seyppel, "Der Porzellanhund," in *Zensur in der DDR*, 25–26. See also the essay by Bernd Wagner in the same volume, 27–28.

64. Ministerium für Kultur, HV Verlage und Buchhandel. The enormous run of dossiers submitted to the HV by the MDV were filed under the general rubrics DRI.2188 and DRI.2189. Each dossier was classified by the name of the author whose work was being submitted by the publisher for a printing authorization (*Druckgenehmigung*). I also sampled the papers of other publishers in the DRI series, and I would especially recommend that other researchers consult the 54-page dossier on Günter de Bruyn and his novel *Neue Herrlichkeit* in DRI.2189.

65. An unsigned, undated memorandum, probably written in the Culture Division of the Party's Central Committee in Sept. 1978, ms. 32747. The memo explained that once they had examined the supposedly finished manuscript, the publisher and chief editor of the Verlag Neues Leben informed Jakobs that they could not accept it, for ideological reasons: "Mentioned in particular were the deficiencies of the basic ideological concept, undialectical opposition of the individual and the social system, a falsified image of socialism, questions of motivation regarding the actions of some of the characters in the novel."

66. Dossier Ahrndt, DRI.2189. As mentioned, the dossiers are identified by the names of the authors.

67. Dossier Flieger, DRI.2189.

68. Dossier Brandstner, DRI.2189.

69. Dossier Hammer, DRI.2189.

70. Dossier Bruns, DRI.2189. In a letter to the HV of May 29, 1984, Helga Duty discussed the literary weaknesses of the manuscript in detail and concluded, "Here on the side of the publisher, many compromises had to be made."

71. Dossier Cibulka, DRI.2189.

72. Dossier Rähmer, DRI.2188.

73. Dossier Reinowski, DRI.2188.

74. See, for example, dossier Ebersbach, DRI.2189.

75. Dossier Höntsch-Harendt, DRI.2189.

76. Dossier Künne, DRI.2189.

77. See, for example, the dossier Kruschel, Heinz, on his crime novel *Tantalus*, DRI.2189, and the dossier Scherfling, Gerhard, on his crime novel *Von einem Tag zum anderen*, DRI.2188.

78. Dossier Herzberg, DRI.2189.

79. For example, her note on the dossier Meinck, Willi, DRI.2188.

80. Dossier Mensching, DRI.2188.

81. Dossier Nowack, DRI.2188.

82. Dossier Püschel, Ursula, on *Der Schlangenbaum: Eine Reise nach Moçambique*, DRI.2188.

83. Dossier Speitel, Ulrich, on *Das Grafenbett*, DRI.2188.

84. Dossier Schulz-Semrau, Elisabeth, on *Suche nach Karalautschi*, DRI.2188.

85. See, for example, the dossier Herold, Ulrich, on *Was haben wir von Martin Luther?*, DRI.2188.

86. *Stasi-Akten zwischen Politik und Zeitgeschichte: Eine Zwischenbilanz*, ed. Siegfried Suckut and Jürgen Weber (Munich, 2003), 161.

87. Loest printed extensive excerpts from the dossiers in *Der Zorn des Schafes*. See especially pp. 84 and 148 and also his further account in *Die Stasi war mein Eckermann: Mein Leben mit der Wanze* (Göttingen, 1991).

88. Among the many works on the Stasi and intellectuals, see Walther, *Sicherungs-bereich Literatur*, 21, which documents the role played by Christa Wolf, and Sonia Combe, *Une société sous surveillance: Les intellectuels et la Stasi* (Paris, 1999). Christa Wolf's collaboration with the Stasi first came to light in an article in *Berliner Zeitung*, Jan. 21, 1993, which was taken up by *Der Spiegel*, Jan. 25, 1993, and then discussed widely in the German press. The Stasi's spying on Wolf herself amounted to forty-two volumes. An East German friend told me in 1992 that I had my own dossier in the Stasi files and quoted a report in which I appeared as "a progressive young bourgeois."

89. The following account is based on Walter Janka, *Schwierigkeiten mit der Wahrheit* (Reinbek bei Hamburg, 1989), and Janka, *Die Unterwerfung: Eine Kriminalges-chichte aus der Nachkriegszeit* (Munich, 1994).

90. Janka's health was severely damaged in prison, but he eventually recovered and found work as a translator and in the film industry. Owing to the danger of further imprisonment, he did not speak openly about his experience until Oct. 28, 1989, when Heiner Müller and others organized a reading in the Deutsches Theater from a text that was later published as *Schwierigkeiten mit der Wahrheit*.

91. *Die Unterwerfung*, 27–28.

92. Ibid., 50–51.

93. The following account is based on Loest's *Der Zorn des Schafes* and *Die Stasi war mein Eckermann*.

94. *Der Zorn des Schafes*, 96.

95. Honecker made his famous "no taboos" remark contingent on a strong commit-ment to socialism: "Wenn man von der festen Position des Sozialismus ausgeht, kann es meines Erachtens auf dem Gebiet von Kunst und Literatur keine Tabus geben": Martin Sabrow, "Der unterschätzte Diktator," *Der Spiegel*, Aug. 20, 2012. The remark resonated through the letters sent by authors to officials in the Party from 1971 until 1989, but in the 1980s it was usually cited to express disappointment at the continuation of repressive censorship. For example, in a letter to Hager, undated but marked as received on Jan. 7, 1988 (ms. 42313), Rainer Kerndle protested against the refusal of the HV to permit his novel *Eine gemischte Gesellschaft*, noting, "I still have partially in memory the conclusion of the Eighth Party Congress according to which there should be no taboos for art

and literature in our society." Ericht Loest recounted his own disillusionment at Honecker's "berühmten Worte" in *Der Zorn des Schafes*, 60.

96. Among the many accounts of the Biermann affair, see Derek Fogg, "Exodus from a Promised Land: The Biermann Affair," in *The Writer and Society in the GDR*, ed. Ian Wallace (Fife, Scotland, 1984), 134–51. One of the most interesting reflections on it is by Biermann himself: *Wie man Verse macht und Lieder: Eine Poetik in acht Gängen* (Cologne, 1997), chap. 7.

97. Translation of an interview published in *La Stampa* on July 4, 1984, made for the Culture Division of the Party's Central Committee, ms. 32747.

98. The limits of this essay make it impossible for me to go into details, but I will list the dossiers in the papers of Hager's office that might interest other researchers: mss. 38788 (Volker Braun, Günther de Bruyn); 36834 (Volker Braun); 39000 (Christa Wolf); 38786 (Christa Wolf, Monika Maron); 39005 (Franz Fühmann); 38787 (Erwin Strittmatter); 38789 (Monika Maron, Heiner Müller); 36835 (Christoph Hein). In a discussion with Christel Berger, which was reported to Ursula Ragwitz and Kurt Hager in a memorandum dated Oct. 20, 1985, ms. 39000, Christa Wolf described the role she wanted to play in the GDR: she intended to devote herself to her writing far from Berlin in the town of Woserin, Mecklenburg, but she did not want to be cut off from the cultural and political life of the GDR. Despite the impossibility of debating substantive questions, she hoped to remain in the SED, as Erich Honecker had advised her to do, although she could understand if the Party wanted to expel her.

99. In a lecture given at Magdeburg on Nov. 14, 1992, Höpcke confirmed the widespread belief that Christa Wolf had persuaded the HV to insert the ellipsis dots: Höpcke, "Glanz und Elend der DDR-Kultur," p. 8 (typescript of a private copy sent to me by Höpcke, in a letter of July 14, 1994).

100. *Kassandra: Vier Vorlesungen: Eine Erzählung* (Berlin and Weimar, 1987; 1st ed., 1983), 110.

101. "Report on a conversation with Christa Wolf on 22-8-1983," a memorandum by Höpcke, presumably for Hager, in ms. 38786/2: "I asked her how it could be that in the third lecture on 'Kassandra' NATO and the Warsaw Pact were equated and unilateral disarmament envisaged (passages that we deleted from the GDR edition of the book). I could not follow her reasoning, and it was incomprehensible to me that she could have come to such ideas. Christa Wolf said that she was well aware of the views opposed to the opinions that she had consigned to writing. She had thought them through again and again. But in the end she had come to the conclusion that unilateral disarmament was the way out."

102. Among the many studies of Volker Braun and his best-known novel, *Hinze-Kunze-Roman*, see especially *Volker Braun in Perspective*, ed. Rolf Jucker (Amster-

dam and New York, 2004), and Kai Köhler, *Volker Brauns Hinze-Kunze-Texte: Von der Produktivität der Widersprüche* (Würzburg, 1996).

103. Braun to Sigrid Busch, Chefdramaturgin im Deutschen Nationaltheater Weimar, undated, copy included in a letter by Arno Hochmut to Hager's assistant, Erika Hinkel, May 7, 1969, ms. 36834/1.

104. Memorandum by the HV, Feb. 15, 1971, ms. 36834/1. See also Johannes Hornig, head of the science division of the Central Committee to Hager, Feb. 22, 1971, ms. 36834/1.

105. Hager to Ragwitz, Nov. 2, 1983, ms. 36834/1.

106. Memorandum on a meeting in the Culture Division of the Party's Central Committee on Jan. 7, 1976, in Ragwitz to Hager, Jan. 9, 1976, ms. 36834/2.

107. Ragwitz to Hager, "Report on a conversation with Comrade Volker Braun on 9/1/1976," ms. 36834/2. This report gave a remarkably full account of how relations between writers and the Party were understood at the level of the Central Committee. Ragwitz noted,

I asked him how he could reconcile his last two publications, "Gedächtnisprotokoll" and "Unvollendete Geschichte," with his position as a member of our Party, and said that this question had been put to us by many comrades of our Party who were upset and to some extent very aroused. This happened as much because of the attacks against the politics of the Party and state that the poem and story contain, as because of the reaction of the enemy. Volker Braun had provided [the enemy] with material for its anti-Communist propaganda, and at the same time he—V.B.—was being added to the ranks of the so-called dissidents.

I made it clear to B. that it now was unavoidable for him to make his true position clear. Therefore, it is necessary for him to speak out publicly in order to make his stance toward the Party believable and to repudiate unequivocally the speculation of the enemy. Naturally his conduct in his future publications must also be believable.

The style of my statements was calm, professional, but unbending.

V.B. then said that he was horrified by how the enemy had used him, that he had never wanted that, and that he wished to defend himself publicly. It thus became clear to me that he has a completely fanciful and confused apprehension of our reality and of the role of the writer. He expressed a great deal that was undigested or got up according to his special view. It is an important question, as I see it, that according to his conception, the critical function of literature should at the same time also be constructive. He claimed that the more critically a writer approached this society, the more constructive his contribution to its transformation would be. This, in his view, could happen only through the representation of cases, actually stories.

Here I attempted to make clear to him in great detail the difference between circumstances, cases that had definitely occurred, and the writer's view and evaluation—that is, his stance and responsibility in the process of making generalizations through literature.

108. Arno Hochmuth to Hager, Jan. 20, 1971, ms. 36834/1. The only two writers who defended Braun at meetings of the Authors Union on Jan. 12 and 20, 1971, were Stefan Heym and Christa Wolf. Braun was attacked in similar fashion at a meeting of the union four years later for "Gedächtnisprotokoll," a poem he published in the GDR review *Kürbiskern*. See the report of Konrad Nauman, party secretary of the Berlin Bezirksleitung, to Honecker, May 12, 1975, ms. 36834/2. In defending himself, Braun said he did not want to be associated with the position of Wolf Biermann: "That would be for him the worst thing that could happen to him, since he did not adopt that position."

109. "Zu Volker Brauns 'Che Guevara'—Ergebnisse einer Diskussion," unsigned memorandum to Hager, July 15, 1976, with an unsigned "Aktennotiz" carrying the same date, ms. 36834/1.

110. Memorandum about a meeting between Braun and Hager, July 5, 1977, ms. 36834/1. Hager told Braun to revise the text so that Guevara's role could not be understood as a criticism of the Party, and he noted, "Truth lies objectively in the representation of the Marxist-Leninist theory of revolution; that must also become clear through the characters and the course of the action."

111. The changes are described in two memoranda prepared by the Culture Division of the Party's Central Committee for Honecker, who initialed them. The first, entitled only "Information," was dated March 22, 1977; the second, "Zu Volker Brauns 'Guevara,' " was dated March 23, 1977. They appear together in ms. 36834/2. Braun sent Hager the text of a heavily revised version of the last scene along with an explanatory letter on April 29, 1977, ms. 36834/1. As far as I can determine, this text does not appear in any edition of Braun's writing.

112. Memorandum from the Culture Division of the Party's Central Committee, unsigned, dated Dec. 15, 1976, ms. 36834/1.

113. Report, unsigned and dated March 28, 1977, on a meeting between Hager and the Cuban ambassador, Nicolae Rodriguez, on March 25, 1977, ms. 36834/1.

114. Memorandum to Honecker from Paul Markowski, head of the International Relations Division of the Party's Central Committee, March 4, 1977. More details about the crisis can be found in a report by Erika Hinkel on a meeting in Hager's office on April 4, 1977, ms. 36834/1.

115. Memorandum "Zu Volker Brauns 'Guevara,' " March 23, 1977, ms. 36834/2, and the memorandum entitled "Information," March 22, 1977, ms. 36834/2.

116. Braun to Honecker, March 23, 1977, ms. 36834/2.

117. "Gespräche mit Volker Braun am 24/3/77," a report to Honecker by Hager, March 25, 1977, ms. 36834/2.

118. The most revealing of the many documents produced after the cancelation of the play is a "Notiz" about a meeting between Braun and Hager on March 31, 1977, drafted by Hinkel and dated April 5, 1977, ms. 36834/1. According to its account of their conversation, Hager stressed the necessity of defending the Cuban Revolution as a victory in the struggle against imperialism and as an event of enormous importance for public opinion throughout Latin America. Braun's portrayal of Castro undermined that cause. Moreover, his play seemed to endorse ultra-leftist attacks on "real socialism" and therefore was unacceptable in the context of the GDR. In reply, Braun defended "his right as an author to sketch the distance between the revolutionary ideal (endgame) and what is currently feasible [as represented by] a person." Hager rejected that argument by insisting that Braun's Guevara expressed "pseudo-revolutionary, irresponsible prattle" and that the play favored "ultra-left arguments (à la Biermann)." Braun said he was ready to rewrite the text yet again, but he would face a moral problem if the play were banned indefinitely: "He could not then (as an author whose work could not be performed) remain definitively employed by the Deutsches Theater and draw a monthly salary, but must withdraw from the public, unable any more to respond to its questions."

119. The most important documents connected with the prohibition of the play, aside from those already cited, are a letter from Braun to Hager, undated but after their meeting of March 31, 1977, which said that he now felt more optimistic about being able to continue with his work; a "Notiz" drafted by Erika Hinkel on a meeting that took place in Hager's office on April 4, 1977, and that involved members of the Deutsches Theater, members of the Culture Division of the Party's Central Committee, and officials in the Ministry of Culture; and memoranda from Hinkel to Hager dated June 1 and June 24, 1977, about phone calls from Braun concerning the future of the play. All are scattered through the run of documents about the play in ms. 36834/1.

120. The following account is based primarily on the archives of Hager's office and the Culture Division of the Party's Central Committee, especially mss. 34377, 36834/1, 36834/2, 38787, and 38788; but it owes a great deal to the superb edition of documents from the MDV, Ein "Oberkunze darf nicht vorkommen": Materialien zur Publikationsgeschichte und Zensur des Hinze-Kunze-Romans von Volker Braun, ed. York-Gothart Mix (Wiesbaden, 1993), cited henceforth as Oberkunze.

121. Köhler, Volker Brauns Hinze-Kunze-Texte, chaps. 2 and 3.

122. Hinze-Kunze-Roman (Leipzig, 1990; 1st ed., Halle, 1981), 58–61.

123. Ibid., 36–39.

124. Ibid., 119.

125. Holger J. Schubert, "Gutachten," July 12, 1982, in *Oberkunze*, 41. The other reader's report, by Harald Korall, July 22, 1982, follows on pp. 42–44.

126. Memorandum on *Hinze-Kunze-Roman*, in Hoffmann to Hager, Sept. 2, 1985, ms. 38788.

127. Hinnerk Einhorn, "Gutachten," Dec. 1982, in *Oberkunze*, 52.

128. Dieter Schlenstedt to Eberhard Günther, undated (Oct. 1983); Dieter Schlenstedt, "Arbeitsgutachten," Oct. 1983; and Hans Kaufmann, "Gutachten," Nov. 4, 1983, in *Oberkunze*, 62–80. Schlenstedt rewrote his report in the form of fictitious letters, which were published as the "Lesehilfe" at the end of the novel (in the 1985 ed., pp. 197–223) and which were ostensibly addressed to the publisher, to the reader, to Braun, and to a critic within the Authors Union.

129. Interview with Dieter Schlenstedt done after the collapse of the GDR, in *Oberkunze*, 229.

130. Helga Duty, "Verlagsgutachten," Jan. 13, 1984, in *Oberkunze*, 83.

131. Ibid., 84.

132. Eberhard Günther to Klaus Selbig, Jan. 13, 1984, in *Oberkunze*, 85–87.

133. Klaus Selbig to Klaus Höpcke, Jan. 28, 1984, in *Oberkunze*, 91. Selbig's letter showed a sophisticated understanding of Braun's text and of literature in general, which I believe was characteristic of the censors in the HV. For example, in the course of an acute exegesis of the manuscript, he quoted Michel Butor's interpretation of *Jacques le fataliste*.

134. Werner Neubert, "Gutachten," July 13, 1984, in *Oberkunze*, 93–96, quotation from p. 94.

135. Helga Duty, "Verlagsgutachten," Dec. 11, 1984, in *Oberkunze*, 100–104, quotation from p. 103. On these developments, see Selbig to Höpcke, July 13, 1984; Selbig to Braun, July 17, 1984; Günther to Höpcke, Dec. 11, 1984, and the memorandum produced by the HV, January 9, 1985, in *Oberkunze*, 97–114.

136. Höpcke, "Ein komischer Essay Volker Brauns," reprinted in *Oberkunze*, 117–25. In a rather strained argument, Höpcke claimed that Braun's social criticism should be put in the context of the recent successes of the GDR's planned economy and progressive administration: see, for example, p. 119.

137. Tiedke to Mittag, Aug. 21, 1985, ms. 34377. Tiedke sent an equally hostile letter to Hager on Sept. 9, 1985, ms. 38788.

138. The following account is based on the archives of Mittag's office, ms. 34377. The memoranda are unsigned and were clearly addressed to Mittag, who wrote his initials on each of them, indicating presumably that he had received and read them.

139. Memorandum, unsigned, Sept. 25, 1985, ms. 34377.

140. "Zu dem *Hinze-Kunze-Roman* von Volker Braun," unsigned memorandum, Sept. 3, 1985, ms. 34377.

141. Memorandum, unsigned, Sept. 25, 1985, ms. 34377.

142. The memorandum dated Sept. 25, 1985, ms. 34377, named those three authors and claimed that they belonged to a "solidarity front of those of the same persuasion [*Solidaritätsfront Gleichgesinnter*]."

143. "Zum 'Hinze-Kunze-Roman' von Volker Braun," memorandum from the MDV, undated (Aug. 1985), *Oberkunze*, 128–31.

144. Memorandum by Selbig, Aug. 28, 1985, included in a letter from Hoffmann to Hager, Sept. 2, 1985, ms. 38788.

145. "Zu dem 'Hinze-Kunze-Roman' von Volker Braun," unsigned memorandum, Sept. 3, 1985, initialed as received by Hager, ms. 38788. The memo stressed that Kunze was recognizable as a representative of the top members of the Party Apparat. Thus, for example, the indications of where Hinze parked the Tatra connected Kunze with the Ministry of the Interior and the Central Committee of the SED.

146. Hager to Ragwitz, Feb. 11, 1983, ms. 36834/1.

147. Hager to Ragwitz, July 7, 1982, ms. 36834/1. Hager noted that Braun's publications showed "that he had little comprehension of complicated economic and other problems. Also, they go beyond the limits of satire and humor."

148. Ragwitz reported to Hager about the measures taken to suppress the book in a memorandum of Sept. 9, 1985, ms. 38788. A more detailed report on the blocking of the sales was produced by H.-G. Hartwich, director of the division of book distribution of the HV, on Sept. 12, in *Oberkunze*, 131–32.

149. Memorandum by Ingrid Meyer from the division of book distribution of the HV, Sept. 27, 1985, and memorandum by Hinnerk Einhorn, Sept. 27, 1985, on the carefully managed reading by Braun the previous day, in *Oberkunze*, 140–43.

150. Ragwitz to Hager, Sept. 9, 1985, ms. 38788. In denouncing Braun, Ragwitz used language that typified her pronouncements on Party affairs: "For him the central leadership and planning, the leading role of the Party, of the state apparatus, clearly are decisive obstacles to the achievement of true democracy, of communism. His vague, utopian picture of communism, from which he criticizes the present, bars the way to a worldview that would give him access to the true dialectic of developed socialism."

151. Ibid. In another memorandum to Hager, dated Sept. 11, 1985, ms. 38788, his assistant, Erika Hinkel, confirmed Ragwitz's assertion that Höpcke had withdrawn *Hinze-Kunze-Roman* from the Plan for 1985 on the grounds that he hoped to win more concessions from Braun, and therefore he had issued the printing authorization on his own.

152. "Protokollnotiz" of meeting on Sept. 16, 1985, ms. 36834/1.

153. Hager to Honecker, Sept. 17, 1985, original copy initialed by Honecker as "E.H. 18.9.85," ms. 38788. I have found no record of further discussions of this affair

at the level of Honecker and the Politburo, although they almost certainly took place.

154. Hager to Honecker, Sept. 27, 1985, ms. 36828. Honecker underlined important passages and initialed this document in his usual manner. Another report—unsigned, dated Sept. 30 and filed in Hager's office (ms. 42277/1)—suggested that the meeting was not entirely hostile to Braun. It quoted him as saying that Hager's intervention had reassured him and had encouraged him to continue with his work.

155. Report dated Dec. 13, 1985, in Ragwitz to Hager, Dec. 17, 1985, ms. 38788. Several of the reviews commissioned to denigrate *Hinze-Kunze-Roman* in the East German press are reprinted in *Oberkunze*, 149–200.

156. Memoranda to Hager dated Sept. 13, Oct. 15, and Nov. 20, 1985, ms. 38788.

157. Ibid. and Hager to Günter Schabowski, Oct. 4, 1985, and Schabowski to Hager, Oct. 2, 1985, ms. 36834/1.

158. "Lizenzurkunde," Jan. 27, 1988, *Oberkunze*, 146.

159. Memorandum from Hilde Schmidt to Hager, Jan. 20, 1988, ms. 42321/2. The permission was granted quite casually, as Hager indicated in a note scribbled on the bottom of this memo. In a letter to Hager of July 14, 1987, Hoffmann had asked whether permission for the new edition could be granted, as the MDV had requested: *Zenzur in der DDR*, 161.

160. Some important documents concerning *Neue Herrlichkeit* were published in *Zenzur in der DDR*, 143–51.

161. Günter de Bruyn speech in X. *Schriftstellerkongress der Deutschen Demokratischen Republik: Plenum* (Berlin and Weimar, 1987), 128.

162. Christoph Hein, X. *Schriftstellerkongress der Deutschen Demokratischen Republik: Arbeitsgruppen*, 228.

163. Ibid., 233.

164. Minutes of a meeting of the executive committee of the Authors Union, June 24, 1987, ms. 42277/1.

165. Memorandum on a meeting between Hager and Höpcke on Feb. 18, 1988, ms. 42325.

166. Memorandum on a meeting between Hager and Höpcke on Nov. 14, 1988, ms. 42325.

167. Memorandum on a meeting of the executive committee of the Authors Union with Höpcke on June 28, 1989, ms. 42277/1.

168. Braun to Hager, July 17, 1987, ms. 42321/2. Further details in a memorandum to Hager by Hilde Schmidt dated March 31, 1987, about a phone conversation between Braun and Höpcke, and a memorandum on a telephone conversation between Hager and Braun on July 17, 1987, both in ms. 42321/2. See also the documents published in *Zenzur in der DDR*, 161–65.

169. Braun to Hager, March 28, 1987, ms. 42321/2. Braun characterized the refusal as a "thoughtless, arbitrary act [*gedankenlosen Willkürakt*]." The *Reisekader* problem became clear in a letter from Hoffmann to Hager of March 27, 1987, ibid.

170. Hager to Schabowski, Feb. 4, 1988, and Braun to Hager, Feb. 8, 1988, ms. 42321/2.

171. Braun to Hager, Jan. 22, 1971, ms. 36834/1. The use of *Du* was not automatic among fellow members of the Communist Party: see Janka, *Schwierigkeiten*, 18.

172. Rainer Kerndl to Hager, undated but noted as received on Jan. 7, 1988, ms. 42313. For a similar example of assertiveness by an author, in this case Peter Hacks, who protested about demands that he modify the text of an essay he had written for *Sinn und Form*, see the memorandum from Hilde Schmidt to Hager dated Oct. 4, 1988, ms. 42322.

173. Schneider to Hager, Jan. 15, 1988, ms. 42313.

174. Ragwitz to Hager, March 6, 1989, with a memorandum about the meeting, ms. 42322/2.

175. Remark by Höpcke at a seminar in the Wissenschaftskolleg zu Berlin on July 6, 1994, according to notes I took at the seminar. Höpcke said that the informer, Ulrich Franz, provided him with information about what Ragwitz and the others in Kultur said about him behind his back. He also said that they had their own confidential sources of information about authors and books. Therefore, his sessions with Kultur took place in an atmosphere of mutual suspicion, and they were difficult but courteous and correct. Ragwitz always maintained a quiet tone in their meetings and should not be described as a "witch" (*Hexe*). The only person at the top of the Party hierarchy for whom Höpcke expressed strong criticism was Günter Mittag, who, he said, was brutish in his treatment of others and would have been happy to ruin Höpcke's career, had the judicial procedures protecting nomenklatura not stood in the way. Of course, Höpcke, like many other prominent figures from the GDR, may have been trying to defend himself against accusations of abuse of power. Although he received a good deal of criticism after the collapse of the regime, he held his ground in answering his critics. See Wolfgang Kohrt, "Als ob die Seele eine Mauer hat: Klaus Höpcke, einst stellvertretender DDR-Kulturminister: Eine deutsche Karriere," *Süddeutsche Zeitung*, Nov. 27–28, 1993, p. 11, and Höpcke's account of his administration, "Glanz und Elend der DDR-Kultur," the text of a lecture that he gave at a colloquium in Magdeburg on Nov. 14, 1992, and that he sent to me in a letter of July 14, 1994.

176. Ragwitz to Hager, March 3, 1989; Ragwitz to Hager, March 6, 1989; and Höpcke to Honecker, March 3, 1989, ms. 42322/2.

177. Höpcke to Hager, July 20, 1989, ms. 42313.

178. Hager to Honecker, April 1, 1987, ms. 42313. Honecker wrote "agreed" [*einverstanden*] across the memorandum in which Hager recommended forbidding the work.

179. Hager to Honecker, May 13, 1987, and Höpcke to Hager, May 14, 1987, ms 42313. The HV had granted the printing authorization on the basis of a recommendation from the publisher and two readers' reports, but one of the censors, Gerda Barz, admitted that she had failed to read the text, owing to an overload of work two days before she took a vacation. After the book was published, the Institute for Marxism-Leninism protested to Hager about its false account of history and the book was repressed: report by Gerda Barz, May 14, 1987, ibid.

180. Höpcke to Hager, July 20, 1989, along with a memorandum from the HV dated July 17, 1989, ms. 42313.

181. Höpcke to Hager, Dec. 16, 1988, and E. Strnad to Hager, March 4, 1989, ms. 42313.

CONCLUSION

1. The best-known case is probably that of William Prynne, who had his ears cut off following his condemnation for seditious libel in 1634. See Annabel Patterson, *Censorship and Interpretation: The Conditions of Writing and Reading in Early Modern England* (Madison, Wisc., 1984), 52–127. Horrendous as it seems today, Prynne's case involved legal proceedings that tilted the arguments in his favor and that did not seem outrageous to his contemporaries, whose views were shaped by Tudor-Stuart statecraft. See Mark Kishlansky, "A Whipper Whipped: The Sedition of William Prynne," *Historical Journal* 56, no. 3 (Sept. 2013), 603–27.

2. For surveys of reader-response criticism, see *The Reader in the Text: Essays on Audience and Interpretation*, ed. Susan R. Suleiman and Inge Crosman (Princeton, 1980), and *Reader-Response Criticism: From Formalism to Post-Structuralism*, ed. Jane P. Tompkins (Baltimnore, 1980).

3. Leo Strauss, *Persecution and the Art of Writing* (Glencoe, Ill., 1952). Strauss explicitly rejected the kind of "historicism" that I am advocating in this book.

4. In the 1870s, M. Kempson, an official in the Northwestern Provinces (roughly Uttar Pradesh and Uttaranchal today), recommended manuscripts for publishing subsidies and prizes, such as a thousand rupees and a watch, despite his general view of "native" literature as "little else than patchwork clearings in the jungle." Robert Darnton, "Book Production in British India, 1850–1900," *Book History* 5 (2002): 247.

5. Nicholas Cronk, "Voltaire and the Uses of Censorship: The Example of the *Lettres philosophiques*," in *An American Voltaire: Essays in Memory of J. Patrick Lee*, ed. E. Joe Johnson and Byron R. Wells (Newcastle-upon-Tyne, 2009).

6. In this respect, I would invoke the testimony of J. M. Coetzee, whose understanding of censorship was informed by the experience of writing under it in South Africa. See his *Giving Offense: Essays on Censorship* (Chicago, 1996),

especially pp. ix–x, 9, 18–19, and 185–203. Some recent studies combine insights derived from poststructuralist theories with rigorous empirical research. See, for example, Peter McDonald, *The Literature Police: Apaertheid Censorship and Its Cultural Consequences* (Oxford, 2009); Deborah Shuger, *Censorship and Cultural Sensibility: The Regulation of Language in Tudor-Stuart England* (Philadelphia, 2006); and Jonathan Bolton, *Worlds of Dissent: Charter 77, The Plastic People of the Universe, and Czech Culture under Communism* (Cambridge, Mass., 2012).

7. Aleksandr Nikitenko, *The Diary of a Russian Censor* (Amherst, 1975). One of Nikitenko's main themes was his commitment to literature and collaboration with gifted writers. His account should be contrasted with the scholarly survey of the subject by I. P. Foote, "Counter-Censorship: Authors v. Censors in Nineteenth-Century Russia," *Oxford Slavonic Papers*, n.s., 27 (1994): 62–105. *The Black Book of Polish Censorship* (New York, 1984) is less revealing, although it contains examples of terms and subjects that were taboo to the censors in Poland during the 1970s and 1980s.

8. Aleksandr Solzhenitsyn, *The Oak and the Calf: Sketches of Literary Life in the Soviet Union* (New York, 1980; first published in 1975), 29.

9. Ibid., 10.

10. This account is based on Dusan Hamsik, *Writers against Rulers* (London, 1971), which includes the text of Kundera's speech. Quotations are from pp. 176 and 174–75.

11. Ibid., 90.

12. Ibid., 93.

13. Ibid., 86.

14. Ibid., 173.

15. Norman Manea, *On Clowns: The Dictator and the Artist* (New York, 1992), ix.

16. Ibid., 87.

17. Ibid., 89.

18. Ibid., 88.

19. Danilo Kis, *Homo Poeticus* (New York, 1992), 91–92.

20. Czeslaw Milosz, *The Captive Mind* (New York, 1953), 14.

21. Ibid., xii.

22. Ibid., x.

23. See Coetzee, *Giving Offense: Essays on Censorship*, and McDonald, *The Literature Police*.

24. See Thomas Lahusen, *How Life Writes the Book* (Ithaca, 1997), a remarkable study of the production and diffusion of *Far from Moscow*, by Vasilii Azhaev, an epic novel about the construction of a pipeline in the Soviet Far East. Although condemned to the gulag himself for counterrevolutionary activity, Azhaev became a devout convert to Stalinism and worked closely with the censors, who directed him to cut 300 pages and to rewrite 200 pages of his 1,000-page

manuscript. The book was a huge success among Soviet readers. Celebrated as a classic of socialist realism, it received the Stalin Prize in 1949.

25. As an example of debate among anthropologists about the problems of understanding the point of view of "natives", see Gananath Obeyesekere, *The Apotheosis of Captain Cook: European Mythmaking in the Pacific* (Princeton, 1997), and Marshall Sahlins, *How "Natives" Think: About Captain Cook, for Example* (Chicago, 1995).

26. Stanley Fish, *There's No Such Thing as Free Speech, and It's a Good Thing, Too* (New York, 1994), 110.

ILLUSTRATION CREDITS

Page 25: Title page, *Nouveau voyage aux isles de l'Amérique*, 1722. Private copy.

Pages 26–27: Approbations and Privilege, *Nouveau voyage aux isles de l'Amérique*, 1722. Private copy.

Page 39: *billet de censure*, 1751. Bibliothèque nationale de France.

Page 42: "Feuille des jugements," 1786. Bibliothèque nationale de France.

Page 97: The British Library. Title page of *Nil Durpan*, copyright © The British Library Board, 11779.c.94 title page.

Pages 108–109: The British Library. Pages 10–11 of the *Bengal Library Catalog of Books, for the Second Quarter ending 30th June 1879*, copyright © The British Library Board, ORW 1986.b.149/3 (June 30, 1879), pages 10 and 11.

Page 149: "The Control Mechanism for Literature in the GDR." Private copy.

Page 152: "Themenplan 1990." Private copy.

Page 155: "Themenplaneinschätzung 1989." Private copy.

Pages 200–201: Page 110, East German edition of Christa Wolf's *Kassandra*. Private copy.

INDEX

Page numbers beginning with 247 refer to notes.